AIOL

AIOL

A Chanson de Geste

FIRST ENGLISH TRANSLATION
BY
Sandra C. Malicote &
A. Richard Hartman

Italica Press
New York
2014

Copyright © 2014 by Sandra C. Malicote &
A. Richard Hartman

Italica Press Medieval & Renaissance Texts

ITALICA PRESS, INC.
595 Main Street, Suite 605
New York, New York 10044

All rights reserved. No part of this publication may be reproduced, stored in a retrieval system, or transmitted, in any form or by any means, electronic, mechanical, photocopying, recording, or otherwise, without prior permission of Italica Press. For permission to reproduce selected portions for courses, please contact the Press at inquiries@italicapress.com.

Library of Congress Cataloging-in-Publication Data

Aiol : a chanson de geste / first English translation by Sandra C. Malicote & A. Richard Hartman.
   pages cm
Includes bibliographical references.
   ISBN 978-1-59910-286-3 (hardcover : alk. paper) -- ISBN 978-1-59910-287-0 (pbk. : alk. paper) -- ISBN 978-1-59910-288-7 (e-book)
1. Chansons de geste--Translations into English. I. Malicote, Sandra, translator. II. Hartman, A. Richard, 1939- translator.
PQ1419.A4E5 2014
841'.1--dc23

2014005470

COVER ILLUSTRATION: Fol. 114r from the unique manuscript of *Aiol*, BNF fr 25516: This is how Aiol came to Orleans / and how the king of France and his people mocked him.

For a Complete List of
Medieval and Renaissance Texts
Visit our Web Site at
www.ItalicaPress.com

ABOUT THE EDITORS

Sandra Malicote (Ph.D. Indiana University) is the author of *Image and Imagination: Picturing the Old French Epic* (2009). Her articles on the Old French *chanson de geste* have appeared in *Romania, Romanic Review, Olifant,* and *(Kentucky) Romance Quarterly.* Professor (ret.) of French at the University of North Carolina at Asheville, she was a *lectrice d'anglais* at the Université de Lille III and formerly chaired UNCA's Humanities Program and its Interdisciplinary Studies Program. Her articles on French literature and civilization have appeared in *The French Review* and in *Contemporary French Civilization*. With A. Richard Hartman, she edited and translated the *chanson de geste, Elye of Saint Gilles* (Italica Press, 2011).

Richard Hartman received a B.S. degree from the U.S. Military Academy, a Licence ès lettres from the Université de Nantes, a Maîtrise de lettres modernes from the Université de Bordeaux, and completed a year of course work at the Universidad de Navarra. He holds a Ph.D. in French literature from the University of Colorado. He has published articles on the Old French epic in scholarly journals, such as *Marche Romane, Olifant* and *Revista Hispánica Moderna*. An independent scholar, he currently divides his time between Stillwater, Oklahoma and Steamboat Springs, Colorado.

CONTENTS

ABOUT THE EDITORS	V
INTRODUCTION	IX
The *Geste de Saint Gilles*	IX
Aiol	X
The Christian and Muslim Epic Worlds	XI
Structure and Composition	XI
Notes on the Translation	XII
AIOL	
Part One	1
Part Two	118
Part Three	136
Part Four	202
APPENDIX	281
ILLUSTRATIONS	283
NOTES	289
SELECTED BIBLIOGRAPHY	295

For Kee Jung †

INTRODUCTION

The *Geste de Saint Gilles*

Around eighty Old French epics are known in written form from the precious thirteenth-century manuscripts, which were carefully preserved and passed down by the aristocratic families who had commissioned them and financed their preparation. These poems, often called genealogical epics and sometimes closely related to contemporaneous ancestral romances, served a number of purposes, from entertainment at important courtly occasions, such as marriages and investitures, to edification and instruction in the vernacular for the courtly world. Excerpts of these "songs of deeds" or *chansons de geste* were sung after masses on Sundays for the amusement and instruction of the ordinary people, sometimes to the displeasure of disapproving clerics, such as the author of the *Poème moral*, in the first attested reference to *Aiol*, who lamented that people didn't even wait until the Mass had ended before dashing into the street to catch the latest rendition of Aiol's sufferings.

Taken together, two of these epics, *Elye of Saint Gilles* and *Aiol*, have become known as the *geste de Saint Gilles*, because they relate events in the lives of Julien of Saint Gilles, a literary epic hero first found in *Le Couronnement de Louis*, and Julien's progeny, including his son Elye and Elye's son, Aiol. The two poems are preserved in only one manuscript at the French National Library, the richly decorated and ornamented BNF fr 25516, first identified in the 1405 inventory of Margaret of Flanders, duchess of Valois. The *geste* forms the centerpiece of the manuscript, preceded by the romance epic *Beuves de Hanstone* and concluded by the epic *Robert le Diable*. The codex contains a total of fifty miniatures, some painted with gold, seventeen of which decorate the *geste*.

It has been proposed that this *geste* was presented at the Parisian court of King Philip Augustus upon the occasion of the lavish, festive wedding in 1212 of Jeanne of Constantinople, countess of Flanders, and Ferrand of Portugal. Jeanne was the daughter of Count Baldwin of Flanders and Hainaut, who had, during the Fourth Crusade, been elected emperor of the Latin Empire at Constantinople, thus uniting the western and eastern empires of Christendom, and who had perished in 1205. Ferrand was the son of King Sancho I of Portugal, who had successfully led the Reconquest of his country from the Arabs. The marriage itself had been arranged through the finances and political machinations of "Queen Mathilda," Sancho's sister and the widow of the famous Count Philip of Flanders for whom Chrétien de Troyes had composed *Perceval* or *Le Conte du Graal*. The *geste de Saint Gilles* is thought to narrate in fiction the renowned historical exploits of both Jeanne's and Ferrand's ancestors, including the founding of the kingdom of

# AIOL

Jerusalem during the First Crusade (told in *Elye*), the Reconquest of Spain and the Fourth Crusade. The latter two stories are related in *Aiol*, a polyvalent name, one of whose meanings is, in fact, "ancestor."

AIOL

Aiol was well-known to important literary figures in the early thirteenth century; both northern *trouvères*, such as Rutebeuf, and southern *troubadours*, such as Raimbaut IV of Orange, alluded to it, as did chroniclers such as Albéric de Trois-Fontaines. In addition, besides its attestation at Jeanne's court, contemporaneous Flemish and Middle Dutch translations clearly based on the extant poem were produced at neighboring courts during the early thirteenth century. Later, in the fourteenth and fifteenth centuries, there existed both Italian and Spanish versions of *Aiol*.

The Picardian version of this poem was edited simultaneously in the late nineteenth century by rival German and French editors. Their bitter polemics surrounded both editions, complete with detailed philological and historical disputes. These researchers, along with other scholars of both the nineteenth and twentieth centuries, routinely criticized the poem's form and content as representing a rather pale rewrite and watering-down of what was originally supposed to be a much earlier traditional epic into a meaningless series of random "adventure stories." One critic even concluded that the poem had been "badly tampered with" by a rewriter and now consisted only in a "continuation," which had degenerated into a "second- or third-rate" romance because of its "digressions." Such a judgment naturally resulted from attempts to read and make sense of the poem as though it were a nineteenth-century popular novel.

However, scholars who took the time to study this poem in its thirteenth-century courtly and manuscript context, and who insisted upon a rigorous textual analysis of the unique manuscript, in place of interpreting a hypothetical oral poem imagined to be the "original" text, discovered to their amazement and utter delight, a well-ordered, integrated literary work, rich in rhetorical and prosodic development and erudite in its sophisticated intellectual treatment of the *disputatio* (the medieval university's dialectical argumentation), beautifully textured in word and image and richly deserving of its original thirteenth-century fame. In short, far from a third-rate hack job, the poem showed itself to be worthy of renewed close literary study.

The tale itself records the exploits of the young knight, Aiol, who reclaims by word and deed his father's and mother's unjustly stolen heritage; he gains the love of a Saracen princess who converts when she is convinced by his warrior's prowess of the truth of the Christian God. He aids the French king Louis in ending a debilitating war lead by rebellious vassals and similarly helps Emperor Grasien, the king of Venice, end his own war against an enemy to

✤ Introduction ✤

the East (an allusion to the Fourth Crusade). Aiol ultimately brings justice to the kingdom of France. But the poem is far more than the tale itself.

The Christian and Muslim Epic Worlds

Aiol, like many other crusading and romance epics, artfully recreates both the Christian culture of the West and the Islamic (or "Saracen") culture of the Levant. Literary topoi abound, such as the demoniac figuration of "Mahomet" or "Mohammed," who is venerated in the guise of a hollowed-out statue or "idol," from which a peasant, hidden inside by the devious Arabs, discourses with prospective converts. Mohammed is joined by the Greek god Apollo and the Roman deity Jupiter, along with the vague traditional "Tervagant." In addition, the poem alludes to the Prophet Mohammed, who is acknowledged as a historical religious leader initially chosen by God, although the poem quickly reverts to the traditional fictional portrayal of the Prophet's "pride" and "downfall." The "mahomerie" or place of worship corresponding to the Christian church, is equated with the "synagogue"; these are common literary allusions found, for example, in the *Chanson de Roland* and throughout Old French poetry.

These literary allusions and fictive representations do not suggest an ignorance on the part of the medieval poets, who wrote for courts that knew well and first-hand the Arab world. Pre-conversion Mirabel's "Mohammed, how great you are!" supplies an extremely authentic *Allahu Akbar!* Nor do they particularly indicate a "hatred" of the Islamic world in general, and especially in medieval Spain. There had long been fruitful (as well as military) interaction between the "two worlds," and Islamic scholars were respected in intellectual circles in the twelfth and thirteenth centuries; translators in centers such as Toledo and at the court of Henry II during the Anglo-Norman Empire, briskly adapted works of Arabic science and medicine for the edification and amelioration of medieval Europe. Poets writing in medieval French created richly textured literary metaphors or fictions about both the Christian and Muslim world, and they were themselves well aware that even though they were treating historically-based materials, they were additionally fabricating fictions and fictive truths, tropes and figures as literary art.

Structure and Composition

Study of illumination, rubrication and ornamentation has rewarded us with the realization that *Aiol* is structured or organized into four main parts, each opened by a miniature functioning as rhetorical synecdoche, which sums up the subject of the division, in combination with a three-line decorated initial. The poem's first section recounts the young knight's preparation and early testing (1–4684), while the second major division relates his official winning

of "companions," that is to say an appointed company of fellow-knights, and their embassy to Saracen-held Pamplona on behalf of the king of France (4685–5359). The knightly quest both for a bride and for the metaphoric "right way" home, dominates the third part (5360–7988), and the final part is a systematic amplification of the topoi of the first three (7989–10990).

Miniatures function in the poem as visual equivalents of rhetorical amplification and are systematically and logically related to one another. In addition to the pictures, two-line decorated initials with pen-flourishing distinguish, within the four major divisions, twenty-seven episodes. Each of them develops with variation an ethical consideration about the Aristotelian "privative contraries" of justice and injustice, applied to courtly life and governance. Each of the four parts formally develops aspects of dialectical argumentation (the *disputatio*) in the Boethian mode, examining ethical questions and subtle psychological variants on delicate questions of feudal loyalty and the very nature of justice itself. The potentially dry Scholastic development of these Aristotelian and Boethian topics of "privative contraries" are fascinatingly explored in the every day context of human relationships: king and knight, lord and vassal, husband and wife, father and son. The sociopolitical institutions of the monarchy, social class, marriage and the family are explored and developed in relation to these topics in a poetic enterprise that vivifies what might otherwise have become a sterile philosophical debate. Dialectical argumentation structures the entire work into a richly instructive, psychologically compelling and socially pleasing and constructive tool of edification and poem alike.

Notes on the Translation

Our translation is based on our own edition of *Aiol*. In preparing our edition and translation, we routinely compared the only extant manuscript version in BNF fr 25516 to the critical edition of W. Foerster (F) and to that of J. Normand and G. Raynaud (NR). These nineteenth-century French and German editors of the poem routinely emended to regularize the orthography, grammar and syntax of the manuscript, which they believed to be copied by a Picardian scribe from a Francien original. The great scholar of Old Picard, Charles Théodore Gossen, however, clearly noted that Picard was by its very nature hybridic, and that doublets and multiple variants existed side by side and contemporaneously within literary texts and cartularies alike. Recognition of this hybridity precludes regularization of form in our edition.

As with our edition of *Elye of Saint Gilles,* we have chosen simplicity and directness in editorial approach; we avoid regularization and emend in the case of scribal error, such as an omitted nasal bar or an obvious omission or repetition of a letter or of a word. In the translation, we standardize the orthographies of the proper names for clarity for the reader. We've used

❧ Introduction ❧

modern punctuation, while attempting to incorporate the most recent research on punctuation as a guide to oral presentation of medieval narrative.

Our translation intends to be faithful to the spirit and meaning of the Old French poem; we originally translated into decasyllabic and dodecasyllabic verses, as the poem was written. However, for the modern reader of English, such rhythmic repetition becomes stultifying, so we opted for free verse. At times, we emulate the poet's rhetorical figures, repetitions or echoes, and we shift, as the poet did, from the past to the historical present to give a sense of what the auditory reception and dramatic effect of the poem was like. To avoid confusion, we clarified the vague pronouns so characteristic of all Old French narrative. Cultural and literary observations are noted by asterisks with notes following the text. We have provided a sample of our edition of the Old French text in an Appendix. The full edition with facing English translation has also been published by Italica Press in 2014. We've aspired to create a lively, interesting and engaging translation that nonetheless allows the reader to savor the rich intellectual and artistic context of the original.

AIOL

A Chanson de Geste

Here begins the accurate account of Aiol and Mirabel, his wife, as you will hear from this book

PART ONE

I.

Now hear me my lords, may God be your friend,
The king of holy glory who was hung upon the cross
Who established heaven and earth,
And Adam and Eve formed and blessed.
Would it please you to hear a song of noble events?   5
Cease your chatter and gather around me.
These new minstrels have no shame,
Because of the fables they tell, all truth has been forgotten,
Authentic history has been rejected and abandoned.
I will relate to you an account, which is indeed well done.   10
As witnesses, I could call forth many a well-born noble,
Many a duke, many a count and many a powerful marquis.*
Is there a responsible minstrel who doesn't know this tale?
Then before the high-born he should not appear!
These troubadours think they know much who know very little.   15
But I will relate to you an account, which I have learned very well.
There was once in sweet France a good king, Louis*;
He was the son of Charlemagne, who conquered so many kingdoms,
Who stripped away the crown from so many powerful kings.
He had a sister, never so beautiful a woman had been seen,   20
Her name was Avisse, a noble, high-born personage,
There was no lady so beautiful in sixty countries.
It pleased the Lord God, who never lied,
That Charlemagne died and was buried in Aix-la-Chapelle.
Louis inherited his lands and his countries.   25
The enemies of France began to wage war against him;
Louis had no idea to whom to turn for help,
Nor did he know in which castles to take refuge
Up until the day, which you will be able to hear,
When he gave his sister in marriage to a well-born count.   30
His name was Elye; he was brave and bold,*
Never a better knight had donned a hauberk.
When he had wedded the sister of Louis,
His rightful lord who held him in esteem,
Elye took up arms against the enemies of France.   35
When he captured them, he took no ransom,

🕮 Aiol 🕮

He never demanded goods or payment.
When it came to capturing and killing, all were equal,
The more high-born the man, the greater justice he received.
Never did Elye spare the great or the small.   40
Before a year was out and had passed away,
He had so thoroughly secured the land for the king
That there was no man left who was waging war against him.
Louis, Charlemagne's son, rewarded Elye badly:
He took away his lands and those he should have held   45
And drove Elye from France into exile and hardship,
Through the counsel of Makaire, who deserves God's wrath,
A malicious flatterer, a rogue from bad lineage.
The duke fled into the pine forests of Bordeaux;
Then came seven years when he never drank wine.   50
Moses, a hermit, sought him out;
Beside his chapel he built a dwelling.
The lady was pregnant when she left France.
When she came to the hermitage, she gave birth to a son,
As God willed it and as was his pleasure.   55
Never was a more beautiful child of mother born.
The hermit raised him above the sacred font and made him a Christian
By giving him baptism in his tiny monastery.
There was no man or woman or servant beside him
From whom he could choose a name to give to the child.   60
But now listen closely to what happened:
There were so many wild creatures in that dense forest,
Snakes, serpents and huge pythons.
Beside the child Moses spotted a great python,
A wild beast, of which you've heard,   65
Which everywhere all fear, great and small.
And because of this creature that the holy man spied,
He called the child *Aiol*, this we find in written records.*
Later, Aiol became a courageous and daring knight
And won back for his father his lands, free and clear,   70
And served the lord God of glory with a willing heart.
It came to pass that after his death he was placed in a reliquary.
He still lies in Provins, as it is written.

2.

My lords, now listen to me, may God do you great good,
The glorious One, our heavenly Father,   75
Who has all heaven and earth in his keeping.

2

❧ A Chanson de Geste ❧

Hear a good song of marvelous, knightly deeds.
Many of you have heard it said far and wide
That Elye remained in that forest for fourteen years,
Heartbroken, suffering, poor and so sickly 80
He could not get up at Christmas or at Easter,
On the day of Pentecost or on the highest feast days.
Never could he put on a shirt or hosiery.
His high-born wife very tenderly looked after him.
Moses, the hermit, sought him out. 85
Beside his monastery he built a dwelling:
In one section was the duke, and his wife in another,
Aiol in the third, Moses in the fourth,
Elye's warhorse, Marchegai, was in another,
His hauberk was in the fifth area, in the sixth his shield. 90
His lance was so long that it couldn't fit in the dwelling,
But remained outside in the wind and storms.
When Elye first arrived at the hermitage,
It pained him that his lance could not be sheltered;
Taking his sharp sword with its slicing steel blade, 95
The nobleman cut off three feet plus a palm's width,
Enough that it could enter the dwelling.
When he had cut off and removed that great mass,
You could not find in France a lance that came within a yard
   of its length.
The duke often wept, cried out and sighed through his tears, 100
Longed for sweet France, his castles and his lands:
"You did wrong, Louis, dear brother-in-law, Charles' son,
When you forced me from France and became close to Makaire.
Never a day will go by when I won't hate you!
Alas! Dear son Aiol, I don't know what to do with you: 105
If you stay in these woods you will never be well-informed;
You'll become completely dull, childish and uncivilized.
There's no one here to teach you about horses and arms.
But may it please God, our heavenly Father,
That you'd to go to France, to Paris or to Chartres. 110
If you had my horse and all my arms,
Then you'd be helped by God, our heavenly Father."
"Sire," said Aiol, "I don't know what to do
When I see you so distraught, anguished and sickly.
If I dared to ask your permission, I'd gladly go there. 115
Look at my lady, how she's weeping bitter tears.
Entreat her, dear sire, not to be so sad.

3

⚜ Aiol ⚜

For the love of God, our heavenly Father,
If you give me your leave, I'll take up your arms,
I'll ride off to France to try to win back your lands." 120
"Dear son," replied Elye, "May God do you great good.
In time, you'll manage to recover my lands."

3.
"Dear sister, sweet friend," said Elye,
"We are destitute and poor, with nothing to live on.
We would have been dead long ago without the hermit. 125
If Aiol were to go to Orleans, that fortified city,
To mighty King Louis, who is our lord,
If there were a pitched battle
And God gave him the opportunity to perform knightly deeds,
He'd make himself loved by the king and the queen." 130
"My lord," replied the lady, "Why are you saying this?
My child's so young, he has no life experience.
The French will make him the object of ridicule.
If I lose my child, I will be heartbroken.
He's my reason for living, my pride and joy." 135

4.
"Dear sister, sweet friend," said the noble,
"Don't discourage the youth, or argue with him,
But rather let's request that, by his goodness,
He go to sweet France to speak to the king.
If he enters a battle or participates in a joust, 140
God will very quickly come to his support,
So that he will be among the best loved at court."
"Sire," replied the lady, "God have mercy.
My child's so young, he's at such a tender age,
He doesn't yet know how to look for lodging, 145
Nor does he know how to speak to a nobleman.
The French are proud and overbearing,
They'll want to slander and insult him.
He couldn't endure or tolerate it.
He'd react hysterically, for he knows so little. 150
The French would quickly drive him mad.
I would be despondent and heartbroken.
I would never be happy again in all my life.
I have nothing to give him to take with him."
When Aiol heard this, the young noble burst out laughing, 155

❦ A Chanson de Geste ❦

"Be quiet," he said, "my lady, speak no more of this.
Woe to him who gives up, because of poverty,
On my going to France to speak to the king.
If you don't have wealth, God has plenty,
He'll supply me from his abundance in great quantities." 160
When Elye heard this, he broke out laughing:
"Now you'll depart, dear son, with God's blessing,
May Jesus let you perform, through his goodness,
So that the king favors you best of his court.
Don't play, dear son, chess or backgammon; 165
He who knows the most about these games is considered a fool,
For if one person likes them, another hates them,
Then begins a cruel war without quarter.
Be careful not to love someone else's wife,
For this is a sin that God surely hates, 170
And if she loves you, leave her alone.
Make sure you don't get drunk,
And be aware that drunkenness is a serious vice.
If you encounter an honorable man, do serve him,
If you are seated on a bench, do get up. 175
Honor both great and small.
Resist making fun of any poor man,
Because you might lose before winning."
"I'll do it, dear father," replied the young noble.

5.

"Now you'll go off to France, dear son Aiol, 180
And you'll bear my arms and my armor,
And you'll lead Marchegai along with you.
When you come, dear son, to the king's court,
You'll find many dukes and counts,
Bishops, archbishops and lesser nobles. 185
You'll be destitute and needy,
Dressed in rags and wretched,
But there will be none nobler than you,
For you are the emperor's nephew,
I'm sure of this, it's certain that you're his sister's son. 190
Steel your heart against all ordeals.
You will win so many battles and conflicts
And end so many wars in the eyes of all.
When the king learns of this, he will recognize your worth."
"I'll do it, dear sire," said Aiol. 195

❧ Aiol ❧

6.

"Dear son," said Elye, "listen to me.
I'll instruct you now as is my duty,
And give you counsel in good faith.
You're leaving for France to serve the king.
There's a lady in Orleans who, if she's still alive,   200
Would help you out if she met you.
She's your mother's sister, so it would be her duty.
Conceal your identity from everyone
Until you've engaged in battles and great tournaments,
And ended wars in the sight of all the French.   205
The king will have to recognize your great worth."

7.

"Now you're leaving for France" said Elye.
"I commend you to God's care, Mary's son,
Who established heaven and earth.
When you arrive in France, that powerful land,   210
Watch out for Makaire, may God curse him.
Don't become friendly with him at all,
For he's vicious, backstabbing and full of envy.
Through his treachery, he drove me from France.
Find long-established, reputable lodging,   215
Eat heartily with good grace.
Don't drink too much strong, aged wine,
For that's not thought wise, no matter what they tell us,
Rather they're besotted before the hour of compline."

8.

"Now you're going off to France with God's leave,   220
You'll be leading Marchegai, my good warhorse.
By the faith you owe your handsome head,
There's not a better horse in any kingdom.
But he's been poorly nourished and groomed.
The horse is very thin and weak,   225
And he's lost all four of the shoes from his hooves.
Make sure the horse has enough to eat.
Hay and oats should not be lacking in his diet.
Dear son, not a whole month will have passed
Before he's defeated all of France's horses,   230
When he's given free rein in a race over a league's length.
You won't need to use your spurs even three times.

⚜ A Chanson de Geste ⚜

Take care not to sell or pawn him;
He'll soon look a lot better than all the rest.
My lance is very crooked, my shield is old,   235
My hauberk hasn't been burnished in a long while,
And my helm hasn't been polished or shined up.
For this first departure you'll be poor,
Since you won't be leading either a foot soldier or a squire.
You'll have three sous' worth of coins on you.   240
Have your innkeeper exchange them right away,
And you'll have five sous' worth or more of Cologne currency.
Your host will be a majordomo and administrator.
You'll be as magnanimous and generous
As if you possessed a hundred marks.   245
Son, when this money runs out, God in heaven,
The King of holy glory, the righteous one,
Will send you what you need."
When Aiol heard this, he became very happy
That he had heard his father's instructions.   250
He completely absorbed all of these words.
He sealed them in his heart, and
Oh God, later he would have great need of them!

9.

Lords, you know that it's the truth:
The wild bird in the dense forest   255
Preens itself, as you well know.
So Aiol in the woods had prepared himself for knighthood.
His father's counsel he had learned and absorbed.
There was no young knight in France who was better educated,
Or could better engage a gentleman in conversation.   260
Of horses and arms he was well-informed,
I'll tell you how this happened, if you'll allow me.
It's because his father had had him mount up often
There in an open clearing in the forest,
And gallop the good horse and wheel it about.   265
Elye had taught him appropriate speech.
Aiol wisely absorbed this well.
About the trajectory of the stars and all their movements,
About the moon's waxing and waning,
Of all this he had completely mastered all there was to know.   270
Avisse the duchess had taught him.
There was not a better-informed woman in ten cities.

❧ Aiol ❧

Moses the hermit had instructed him,
Had schooled him in writing and grammar.
Aiol knew how read and write very well   275
And knew how to speak Latin and French,
The language of the land where he was headed.
He called out lovingly to his father:
"Sire, for the love of God, hear me out;
You're sending me to France to win back your lands.   280
To Louis, the strong king, I'll be going there to speak.
I've not learned to bear arms,
When I've not yet seen men jousting,
Charging towards other knights who're armed.
Sire, for the love of God, teach me about it,   285
Through words and verbally, if you know how,
If I'm in a battle and have entered upon a field of strife,
And a knight is rushing at me to do me harm,
How could I best defeat him?"
"Dear son," said Elye, "you're very courageous,   290
Courteous, noble, wise and thoughtful.
Certainly it's smart of you to ask this.
You shouldn't be reproached by anyone for doing it,
And I'll tell you the truth about it:
Actively spur your warhorse on its flanks   295
And lower your lance and brandish it.
Approach him as fast as your horse can gallop.
Deal him a great blow on his shield,
So that you strike down both him and his horse.
As you wheel around, constantly pull on the reins.   300
Shout: 'Monjoie, Charlemagne!' at the top of your lungs.
Often and repeatedly, deal great blows,
Which will cause you to be feared and dreaded.
This is what your father did whom you see before you."
"Sire," said Aiol, "it's true.   305
I recognize that what you've said is true.
I pledge you my complete loyalty.
I'll never commit a cowardly act in my life,
Or even consider a criminal betrayal.
Never will my family be the subject of blame   310
That there's been lying or fraud."
"By God," said Elye, "you are truly noble.
I'm sure now that I'll have my lands back
Thanks to my child Aiol, whom I've sired."

⚜ A Chanson de Geste ⚜

"You'll certainly have them," said Aiol, "you'll get them back.   315
Of this you can be completely assured.
If God leads me safely to France,
So I can speak to King Louis,
Before you see a whole year pass by,
I want to deed and hand all of them over to you."   320
When Elye heard this, the nobleman became happy.

10.

"Now you're going off to France, Aiol, noble son.
I entrust you to the keeping of almighty God
Who made sea and sky and earth and wind.
May he safeguard you from death and suffering.   325
Dear son, act intelligently and with clear senses.
And remember my instruction well.
May God of holy glory be your shield!
As far as you know, in all your life,
Never keep company with evil men.   330
You'd soon be shamed, in my view.
I have a nephew in France, who's your relative,
The son of my sister, Lady Hersent.*
His name is Gilbert, a handsome young man
Who's waging war against the king who reigns over France.   335
He's doing all this for me, for whom he's grieving
That Louis took my lands and my fiefs.
Dear son, go to him first of all,
For if he got to know you at all,
I'm sure he wouldn't fail you."   340
"My lord," Aiol replied, "this would come to nothing.
Rather I'll go to my uncle who reigns over France.
From him I'll hold my lands and my fiefs.
I won't ever seek out anyone else
Until I've heard what agreement I get from him,   345
Because he's the most powerful of my relatives."
When Elye heard this, he became very joyful:
"Dear son, I'm really astounded that you've come up with this.
Where do you get this memory and this good sense?"
"Alas!" said Avisse, the noble lady,   350
"It certainly is a wonder that my heart doesn't break,
This heart that's now beating here in my breast,
When now my child's going off in such poverty,
Without costly arms and equipment.

❦ AIOL ❦

He'll never enter into any of our people's lands 355
Without being vilely ridiculed."
"My lady," said Elye, "this is foolish talk!
You're wrong in feeling so sad;
I'm sure that you'll be happy again.
Last night I had a pleasant dream 360
That brought gladness to my heart:
Your noble son, Aiol, was riding along,
And the woods, the copses, the great forests
Were coming towards him bowing and stooping;
Bears, lions and leopards, wild boars, serpents 365
Lay down before him upon the wide road.
With their tongues they were licking his feet.
Aiol took them with outstretched hands
And plunged them into a vast, wide water.
Before my eyes all the birds of France 370
Came to him walking on foot,
For none at all had wings.
Aiol gave them back their feathers right away
And quickly made them glad and joyful.
Then came a strong and powerful eagle 375
Who began to reign over the other birds.
He was accompanied by two white goshawks.
Right away they set off for Spain,
Straight to Pamplona, the great city.
The city walls before them 380
Approached them, bowing down before them.
There the brave Aiol conquered an image —
No man had ever seen such a beautiful one in his lifetime —
Which he brought back to France along the great road.
Priests, monks, canons and clerical teachers 385
Came swiftly to the Church of the Holy Cross.
They baptized the image right away.
It did seem to me that the image was pregnant.
I saw two white doves emerge from the image,
Then I awoke from my dream and don't know what happened afterwards." 390
"Sire," said Moses, the learned cleric,
"This means that something good's going to happen to you.
I've been a hermit for thirty-six years
And have a good understanding of astronomy.
I'll explain your dream's meaning to you. 395
I'm sure I can do it successfully.

⚜ A Chanson de Geste ⚜

Where Aiol, your brave son, was going,
The woods and the copses, the great forests,
Which were coming to him, bowing down,
This will be a great and vast kingdom   400
That will become subject to Aiol's rule.
He'll have a crown upon his head.
The bears, lions, wild boars and serpents
Who went before him along the great road
And were plunged by your son in the vast water,   405
These will be Saracens, Turks and Persians
Whom he caused to seek God the almighty
And have themselves truly baptized.
All the small and great birds of France,
Who were rushing on foot towards him   410
Because they had no wings at all,
Aiol immediately gave them wings,
And right away made them glad and joyful,
These will be knights and good foot soldiers
Of that land of France   415
Who have lost their lands and fiefs.
Through Aiol they will get them back.
Here is the meaning of the white goshawks
Who will accompany Aiol to Spain:
They'll go straight to Spain   420
Right down to Pamplona, the great city.
The image that you saw, brave, valiant duke,
Will be a very beautiful maiden.
Aiol, your brave son, will have her as a wife.
She will be pregnant with two children   425
Who on Spain will totally impose their will.
If this dream is true and does not lie,
The two children will be kings;
Each one will wear a crown upon his head."
"Oh, God," exclaimed Elye, "almighty Father,   430
Lady, St. Mary, will I live long enough
That I'll experience such joy from my child?
I wouldn't try to live any longer!"
"Sire," replied Moses, the learned cleric,
"Don't be so amazed.   435
In my opinion, you're still a young man.
You're not yet even thirty-six years old.
You'll be able to see all this and even further into the future."

⚜ Aiol ⚜

11.

"Sire," said Moses the holy hermit,
"I've explained to you what the dream has prophesied   440
And the meaning of everything it contains.
Your son's certain to become a king."
Noble Avisse then kissed Aiol, her son,
His eyes, his mouth and his chest.
Breaking out in sobs, she began to speak to him: 445
"Now you're going off to France, my son, noble lord,
May God, Mary's Son bless and keep you,
He who established heaven and earth.
May he keep you from committing any vile act."

12.

"My godson," said the hermit, "I'll take my leave.   450
I gladly baptized you and did you good.
I gave you the name *Aiol*, that's what I called you,
For the love of the python I found beside you.
Now I'll let you see how much I loved you:
When I was young, I carried a document on me.   455
There was never anything better and never will be.
It truly contains the names of Jesus Christ."
"Sire," said Aiol, "I know this very well,
For I've looked at it many times.
May the Lord God continue to protect you when it's mine."   460
"My godson," said the hermit, "I'll give it to you."

13.

Moses took the document and gave it to him;
He sealed it upon his right shoulder.*
Aiol, Elye's son, studied it;
Before he had folded it, he looked at it.   465
Then he began to speak in an appropriate manner:
"Oh, God!" said the young man, "What a document we have here!
Makaire of Lausanne will pay dearly because of it.
If even one of his blows reaches me, he'll lose his head.
He'll return my fiefs and my lands."   470

14.

"My godson," said the hermit, "you have the document.
There was never a better one, and never will be.
As long as you have it on you, don't be afraid of anything.

⚜ A Chanson de Geste ⚜

Fire won't burn you nor water drown you."*
"Sire," said Aiol, "it will be well taken care of." 475
He addressed his father lovingly:
"You're sending me off to France to win back your lands,
To meet and deal with mighty King Louis.
You know well that no youth or squire
May bear arms, unless he's been dubbed. 480
Outfit and equip me, sire, for the love of God.
When I appear before the king who reigns over France,
Let me not be mistaken for a squire."
When Elye heard this, he became very glad.
"Dear son, you're so intelligent and well educated. 485
I'll gladly provide you with arms."
He quickly had him outfitted and equipped.
On his torso they put a doubled hauberk,
And Avisse laced the helm on his head.
Then Elye lovingly told him 490
That he wanted to gird on the steel blade
And to dub him so that he'd be a knight.

15.

"Now you're going off to France my son," said the mother,
"To serve King Louis, our emperor.
May Jesus let you perform military service in such a way 495
That your body and soul will remain safe from harm.
In the name of God, don't ever forget your dear father
Who'll be back here, very ill, in this land.
He won't see his brother or his relatives."
"Lady," said Aiol, "may God the Savior, 500
Who made heaven and earth and the vast sea,
Protect you and me and my dear father.
Your brother committed a grave sin
When he exiled you from France.
But in that land, if I can enter 505
A pitched battle or a joust,
I'll strike such great blows with my sword and my fists
That within a year, my sweet mother,
I'm convinced I'll have won back so much of your land
That once again you'll be hailed as a great lady. 510
I'll leave right now, because dawn has broken."
He approached the bed where his father was lying.
Speaking the ritual words, Elye girded on him his sword

⚜ Aiol ⚜

Which was so long, broad and sharp.
Moses the hermit had brought it, 515
And had kept it throughout fifteen long years;
He had often burnished it and dried it off
So that it was neither soiled nor rusted.
Elye strapped it on his side,
But the strap was very worn and broken. 520
Elye raised his palm high above him,
And dealt his son a dubbing blow.
"Dear son," said the duke, "may God the Savior
Give you long-lasting esteem and knightly qualities.
I'm delighted you have very good arms. 525
The chain mail you're wearing is so tightly woven
That you'll never be wounded by a blow.
The helm that's protecting your head
Has saved me from death in great melees.
It was never even dented by a sword's blow. 530
The sword you've girded on is so well tempered
That there's none better in seven lands.
If God gives you possessions and high position,
For his sake, do not forget your mother,
Who'll remain here, lost and alone." 535
The hermit went back immediately
And entered his sacred chapel.
Taking recourse to God's weapons,
He sang Mass for the young knight Aiol.
Completely armed, Aiol heard Mass. 540
He mounted Marchegai when it had ended
And hung from his neck his broad shield,
Then took up his huge lance, which was hardened and old.
His father and mother he placed in God's keeping.
At the moment of departure there was such great sorrow 545
For the young man that the lady fainted three times.*
Aiol set off right away,
Crossed fields and woodlands,
Hills, mountains and valleys.
Now he'll go to win back his father's lands 550
Of which his mother was unjustly deprived.
He'll never rest until she's been reestablished
And he's brought her back to France.
But before this happens, he'll have greatly desired it
And will have paid dearly for it. 555

🜲 A Chanson de Geste 🜲

16.

Now Aiol sets off; he's taken leave.
He immediately plunged into a great, vast forest.
For five full leagues around them there was no farm,
Nor town nor any refuge where he could find lodging,
Except for the hermitage he'd just left. 560
He appealed to the Lord God, the true one of heaven:
"Lord God, Father, Giver of true and just laws,
Who reigns over the seas and mountains,
Preserve me from death and harm.
I've left my sick father in the woods; 565
He's taught and shown me little of battles.
What if I flee if a man attacks me,
As when one comes up and they don't know each other?
I've heard a lot about knights
When they're armed, on their warhorses. 570
They spur on their rapid steeds.
Each one attacks the other as best he can.
Right away, they deal each other great blows
And the one who doesn't fall has done the best.
If they break their lances, they become angry. 575
They throw their broken lance stubs down at their feet,
Then draw their steel-bladed swords.
Wondrous blows they strike to their heads.
Lord God, holy Father, I don't know anything.
I've never seen knights joust, 580
Nor seen a war started or begun!"
So he spurred Marchegai, his good warhorse,
And Marchegai leaped forward fourteen feet for him.
"Oh God!" said Aiol, "how dearly I love him!
There's not a day of my life that I'd want to exchange him!" 585

17.

Then Aiol set off, the noble youth,
Down the path through the woods, feeling very uneasy.
He called upon the God of paradise:
"Glorious One," he said, "who made me,
And reigns over heaven and earth, 590
Protect me from death and danger.
I've never seen one knight strike another,
Nor seen any battle begin or continue on.
May it please God, who made the world,

❧ Aiol ❦

That I should enter into Louis' France.   595
If I'd personally been able to watch knights jousting,
By observing them, I might have learned something."
Oh God, he might do just that, that's my own view!
If it hadn't been for the prayer offered up back there by Avisse,
His courageous, noble mother,   600
And that Elye, his father, prayed too,
To Jesus of holy glory, who never lied,
Aiol would have been quickly captured or killed.
On the road coming out of the forest,
There were four knights, all Saracens.   605
They'd been ravaging the land; much they had conquered.
They were loaded with booty: gray squirrel furs,
Silver, coins and fine, pure gold.
They'd left King Mibrien's army
And come from Pamplona, the great city;   610
They had scoured the fields and thickets.
At high noon they had dismounted
To rest and cool themselves.
They lay down in the shade of a spreading pine tree.
Their squires were playing at jousting on their ponies.   615
They'd hung their lords' shields around their necks
To be able to have fun on the hillside.
One of them charged towards another, tried to strike him,
Hitting him squarely, his lance knocked him to the ground
And the other squire sprang to his feet and remounted his pony.   620
Aiol, who'd just come out of the woods, watched them.
He burst out laughing at the sight of them
And swore to the Lord God who never lied,
If they were expecting a blow, he'd surely give them one.
He spurred Marchegai, his mount.   625
The horse felt them and quivered;
The golden spurs caused him to tremble all over,
For it had been a long time since he'd felt them,
Except for the first practice runs he'd made in the woods.
Out of the woods Aiol came onto the hillside.   630
Galloping all the way, he rushes towards them.
The squires stared at him because they'd spotted him.
One of them rushes swiftly towards the other.
The Saracen goes to strike a blow on the gray shield,
But it was so stout and strong that he couldn't harm Aiol.   635
There wasn't a better shield in any country.

A Chanson de Geste

Then he smashed his lance to splinters and conquered no more.
Aiol behaved like a bold and noble knight.
He steadied himself on his horse and didn't shy away.
He looked at the coward, struck him right away   640
And pierced the paint and varnish on the squire's shield.
A great blow Aiol dealt him in the center of his chest.
The iron of his spear he plunged into his chest;
With the length of his lance he struck him down dead.
Aiol was still so childishly inexperienced   645
He didn't think he'd done the Saracen harm and said to him:
"Young squire, get back up on your pony right away.
Tomorrow, if you're back here, you'll do better."
"Craven," said another squire, "you've killed him!"
"So help me God," said Aiol, "I couldn't help it.   650
I just thought I was playing as you two were.
But since I've killed him, watch out for yourself.
I'll be able to strike another such a blow,
Or it might turn out to be an even greater one.
Lord God, what good luck!" said Aiol.   655
"This is the first man that I've ever struck
And I really do think I've killed him.
May God grant that he was a Saracen.
I don't want to strike blows against Christians."
"Idiot," said another squire, "he certainly was.   660
But you'll pay for it, by Apolin!"
When Aiol heard this, he became very happy.

18.

So here was Aiol, the young knight, in the meadow
And the three squires are all very angry
That their companion was lying dead in a ditch.   665
One of them came towards Aiol, full of rage.
He brandished his iron-sculpted sword hilt
And went to strike the old, smoky shield.
It was so stout and strong that it wasn't pierced.
Aiol was a stalwart and wise knight.   670
He steadied himself on his steed and wasn't unhorsed.
If God will help him, he'll stay safe.
He eyed the evil Saracen and struck back.
To the center of his chest he gave such a blow
That he forced right through his body   675
The good lance with the sharpened steel tip

🙥 Aiol 🙥

And struck the Saracen down dead in the meadow.
When the two squires saw him, they became angry.
They rapidly turned away and began to flee.
They came to the Saracens and began to shout: 680
"By Mohammed,* lords, save yourselves!
There's a young man crossing this meadow,
Who's wounded and killed our companion.
Judging by his weapons, he seems to be a demon!"
The four pagans heard this and became angry. 685
They sprang to their feet,
Came to their horses, mounted up,
Took up their shields with golden bands
And seized their iron-tipped lances.
They galloped towards the young knight, in full charge. 690
God protected Aiol through his goodness
So he was not captured, wounded or killed.
If he can't defend himself through God's bounty
He'll be quickly wounded and killed,
Because he hadn't brought relatives or cousins with him. 695

19.

Now young Aiol was out in the middle of the meadow
And the four pagans were near the forest.
They had mounted on the horses from their region
But they only had two gold-banded shields,
And they had two thick, long, steel-tipped lances. 700
The others had all remained on the field
With the squires who were out on the meadow.
The pagans rode out without any hesitation.
Swiftly towards the young knight, they let their steeds run.
One of the pagans shouted to him: "Traitor, robber, 705
Whore's son, son of a bitch, draw your sword!
Hand it over to me now. And it's clear
You've killed my squire. He was my brother."
Aiol swore to God the Savior:
"If you're not any tougher than the others were, 710
You'll pay for what you've undertaken."
Right away, he spurred on Marchegai.
The pagan quickly whirled around towards him.
Great blows they're going to exchange on their broad shields.
The Turk shatters his lance with its new iron tip, 715
But the old, dried and brittle one Aiol's holding

18

⚜ A Chanson de Geste ⚜

Pierced and broke through the Turk's shield,
Ripped through the hauberk he was wearing,
And it passed all the way through his body.
The lance's iron tip was all bloodied   720
After having struck him dead in the middle of the field.
With a loud voice, he shouts: "May God save my father!
All his old arms have protected me very well.
Whore's son, pagan, now you'll get what you deserve.
Your new lance is worse than the dried, brittle one.   725
If I were given a cartload of new ones,
I wouldn't give up mine, I like it so much."
Then Aiol picked his thick lance back up
And raised it high aloft, up towards heaven.
"Lord God," he said, "Lord and Father,   730
Protect me today, true Savior."
He charged to strike the other knight who was waiting for him,
And broke through the center of his shield.
The Saracen, who'd begun to fear him, swung around.
From Aiol his lance escaped straightaway   735
And stayed stuck in the hole in the pagan's shield.
The pagan fled across the field,
Dragging the old, dried and brittle lance.
Aiol reached down and drew his sword,
And went to deal the Turk a great blow,   740
Which severed his head from his body.
The fourth Saracen swiftly fled,
And when noble Aiol saw this he didn't like it.
He cut him off and attacked the Saracen
Who was dragging the old, dry and brittle lance.   745
Aiol rapidly closed from behind
And shouted to him: "Friend, good brother,
Give me my lance right away, if you please,
I don't want any of your new-planed ones,
Because mine is stiffer and garnished with more iron.   750
I'll give you four sous from my region,
Those that my father entrusted to me the other day."
The pagan, who was fleeing in disarray, heard him.
He looked down at the lance he was dragging
And with a twist of his hand, he threw it down.   755
Spurring his mount, he fled across the meadow.
And Aiol quickly recovered his lance.
He raised it above him, high towards heaven.

🟎 Aiol 🟎

"Lord God," he said, "sire, glorious Father,
Now I've had a good look at a serious joust.   760
Ah, if you only knew, Elye, father,
That I've gone through such a great battle.
Oh God! Avisse, my mother, would be so happy!
I don't know who they are or where they're from.
May God, the true Savior, confound me   765
If I ever carry off any of their booty!
I'm not a merchant, meant for money.
Instead, I'll set off to win back my father's lands,
From which my mother was wrongly exiled."
He set out along the great, paved roadway   770
And crossed mountains and valleys
Until it was drawing close to vespers.
Aiol prayed to God, the true Savior,
That he give him good lodging.
He found a hostel in a clearing in the forest.   775
Holy monks from his home region lived there.
For the love of God they gave him good lodging
And bread and wine for God's sake.
They stabled Marchegai, his warhorse.
They led him to the center of the house   780
And gave him hay and oats.
Oh God! They acted nobly, it's a proven fact.
In that region, there were six robbers.
They often attacked the monks at daybreak.
Before midnight, they broke into the house   785
And attacked the monks inside.
They tore open their chests and their coffers,
Threw out all the books and the linens,
And all the other possessions they found.
The thieves loaded it all on Marchegai;   790
They didn't find Aiol who was sleeping elsewhere.

20.

The robbers have attacked the holy monks,
And tied and bound the servants.
The trunks and the coffers, they've torn open.
They've thrown the books and the linen out of them.   795
Everything has been secured on Marchegai.
Aiol was in separate room.
The young man was asleep there and knew nothing.

❧ A Chanson de Geste ❧

The thieves hadn't found him at all.
My lords, this isn't a lie, it's the truth.   800
Anyone God wants to help, he's found.
Aiol awoke and saw the bright light
Because the robbers had lit a fire.
They'd tied and bound the servants.
Aiol saw the monks who'd been attacked,   805
He saw the chests and the coffers all ripped open,
And then he saw his horse being led off.
Now don't bother to ask if he was angry.
He prayed to the Lord God of majesty:
"Lady St. Mary, help me now.   810
If they lead off my horse, I'll have taken a bad turn.
I'll never seek to enter into sweet France
Nor give my father his lands back."
He jumped out of bed and sprang to his feet.
His weapons were close by and he armed himself.   815
He donned his hauberk, laced on his helm,
Girded his sword at his side
And tightened his shield across his chest.
He leaped out of the room into the light.
In a loud voice he shouted to them   820
And spoke to them boldly: "Stop, my lords!
Why have you attacked these monks
And tied and bound these servants?
Give me back this horse, if you please.
I'm certain you don't have any right to it.   825
My father raised it and gave it to me.
I'd suffer a great loss, if you took it from me."
And the leader of the thieves replied: "Come over here.
You'll be shorn and tonsured right away.
We'll give you a monk's shaved crown before we leave,   830
And you can stay with these monks.
You'll be singing matins and compline."
When Aiol heard this, he was beside himself
At hearing that he'd not be shown mercy.
Trusting in God, he proudly defied them.   835
Then he drew his sword that hung at his side
And went to strike the thieves' leader, who'd just spoken.
High on his head the sword struck
And made his head fly off from his body.
Then Aiol turned to strike another, cut him   840

❧ AIOL ❧

And with great fierceness, shouted "Monjoie!
You're not holding up very well, robber, whore's son,
This is Aiol the young knight whom you've found,
Who was raised in the woods, who doesn't know anything,
But he'll want to learn about all of this,   845
About how knights should confront each other
And in a pitched battle bear their arms.
You're all captured and killed if you wait around.
Before this sword you'll have no safety.
Instead, you'll all be dead and finished off.   850
Because my father told me this as I left him:
That there wasn't a better sword in ten cities,
And I've found that everything he told me is true."

21.

Aiol had killed two of the robbers,
He shouted to the other four: "Surrender!   855
Or it will be my pleasure to hang and burn you."
The robbers answered him: "Foul god of lies!
You've slain and killed our companions.
You'll pay for it dearly before daybreak."
The robbers had huge clubs; they attacked Aiol with them.   860
Aiol raised his shield to cover his face,
Swung at one of the robbers whom he hit,
And whose head he severed from his body.
Then he shouted "Monjoie" with great enthusiasm,
"Whore's son, robber, you've been vanquished."   865

22.

Aiol has slain three of the robbers.
He strikes the fourth one with great fury,
From his body he sends the robber's head flying.
The remaining two thieves turn and flee.
Aiol pursued them furiously;   870
He captured one of them and killed the other.
He returned along the road to the abbey,
Then he considerately untied the monks.
Loudly he called out: "Take this one thief
And hang him from the branch of an oak tree,   875
For that's the way robbers should be dealt with!"
And the monks did it quickly, without delay.
This was when noble Aiol began to render justice.

⚜ A Chanson de Geste ⚜

Afterwards, he continued to do so throughout his life.
From now on you'll be able to hear the truth   880
About how he won back his father's fiefs for him,
From which Elye was exiled by a treasonous act.
Aiol spent the night there until daybreak.
He took leave of the monks, armed himself,
Mounted his horse and rode off,   885
Taking the main road.

23.

Now Aiol rides off, his lance held high,
And crosses regions and plains,
Great ravines and valleys.
He came to Poitiers in five days.   890
Now it was on a Thursday, at vespers,
Aiol entered the town, riding down the main street.
His lance was twisted, dry and brittle;
His shield was old, the buckle flat,
Its strap was broken and retied,   895
The hairs of his neckpiece of hide were all ripped and torn.
His warhorse saw the poor condition of his arms;
He wrinkled up his nose and his mouth gaped.
Aiol gripped the reins tightly
And held his head high,   900
As though he were a hunted stag
Pursued by hounds through the woods,
So knights and townspeople now stared at him.
Ladies and maidens climbed up the towers' stairs
And said to one another: "Look, my friend,   905
Well, I declare! Who *is* this robber?
He must have stolen the arms he's carrying!
But he's got a noble expression and a handsome face,
And does seem to be the son of a noble woman."

24.

Now Aiol rode along, very much chagrined,   910
When everyone, high and low, is mocking him.
Suddenly, a drunkard came running out
Of a tavern, intoxicated from all the wine he'd consumed.
He'd been playing at dice and had lost everything.
He ran up to Aiol and grabbed his halter,   915
He tugged the bridle with great force.

⚜ Aiol ⚜

"Master," said the drunkard, "so you've come!
You've waited so long up until this happy hour.
My companions really want you, they've lost everything.
This horse is very thin and pitiful;   920
He'll be payment for the wine we've drunk,
Along with this stiff lance and this buckled shield.
Who gave you this harness of beaten gold?
Its reins are broken, but they were good."
He seized Aiol's warhorse by his bridle, and pulled him to a stop.   925
Marchegai looked at the drunkard and didn't recognize him.
He raised his right hoof and struck a him such a blow
In the middle of his caved-in torso, below the belt,
That his entire hoof disappeared into his body.
Struck down dead, the drunk lay stretched out beside the horse.   930
"Rogue," said Aiol, "so did he strike you, then?
Why are you lying there? So get up!
I'll redeem my pledge by five sous or more."
The townspeople were laughing about what they'd just seen.
They said to one another: "Get back down in the wine cellar!   935
He definitely came out of the tavern too soon.
It seems like it's one of King Arthur's horses:
It can't stand for a man to touch it.
Oh, God! This shield was made to be praised.
It resembles the arms belonging to Lord Esau   940
Who lived a hundred years or more."
When Aiol heard this, he was chagrined.
He prayed intensely to King Jesus.

25.

Now Aiol rode on through the marketplace.
He didn't care if the low-life has been killed,   945
Because he had mocked and insulted him greatly.
Many townspeople continued to follow him on foot,
Servants, merchants and squires,
And ladies, maidens and their maids.
Never had such a source of merriment entered Poitiers.   950
And they said to one another: "Cousin, look here!
Once again, we've won everything back,
Because a knight has come to us
Who seems to be from Lord Audengier's family."*
The townspeople are cruel and full of evil intentions.   955
They heaped abuse and harsh blame upon Aiol:

⚜ A Chanson de Geste ⚜

"Tell us, my lord, where are you leading that horse?
Congratulations to the person who taught you to ride:
One day, you'll avenge Fouré!
In this affair of our monks,* take pity: 960
It's not your affair anyway, so let it be!
They will pray for you from their psalters
When they sing in their monastery,
For it's a serious sin to rob an ordained man.
Make a practice run for us across this marketplace. 965
Our city's dogs have made bets
That they'll be feeding on this horse's flesh.
Go find lodging with Pieron, the shoemaker.
Give him five sous' worth of our money,
He'll teach you how to cut leather. 970
You'll live well from this trade.
There's no shame in earning your living."
When Aiol heard this, he became angry.
Calmly and courteously he answered them:
"My lords," said the young knight, "just go away. 975
May God pardon all your sins.
Return to your homes and leave me in peace.
I don't consider myself to be a churl at all.
I won't deny that I'm a foreigner from another land.
No matter who thinks I'm contemptible, I know I'm worthy." 980
Some of them who felt pity for him turned away.

26.

My lords, you know well that it's true
That no man under heaven of mother born,
No matter how young, strong and hardened he might be,
If he found himself exiled in a foreign land, 985
Being poorly clothed and destitute,
He would be insulted and greatly mocked,
And would be considered as despicable.
That's the way it was in Poitiers for noble Aiol
Who was pursued by everyone throughout the town. 990
"Baron, knight, sire, speak to us now!
Were these arms made in your kingdom?
Was Audengier your father, who was so noble?
And Raiberghe* of the bright countenance your mother?
Those are the arms he always used to carry! 995
Come on, stay with us this summer.

❦ AIOL ❦

We'll make fine sport of you this Pentecost.
Your horse will be cleaned up and watered,
And we'll play with him throughout the town."
When Aiol heard this he became very angry.　　　　　　　1000
He heard himself harshly insulted and cruelly mocked
And all this anger and callousness, as well you know,
Can enflame even the staunchest man.
It occurred to him and he began to want
To draw from its scabbard his sword with its engraved blade,　　1005
And to rush at them swiftly,
When he remembered his father's advice
And the counsel he'd received in the dense forest.
This caused him to calm his emotions.
He answered them politely and humbly:　　　　　　　　1010
"My lords, may God bless you; let me be.
You're doing a base act by mocking me,
And evilness and sin and great wrong-doing.
In all my life, I've done you no harm.
If I'm a poor man, God has riches in great quantity,　　　　1015
The majestic King of holy glory,
Who reigns over heaven and earth,
And will give me generously from his abundance.
When God wills it, I'll have plenty."
Some who felt pity for him turned away　　　　　　　　1020
Because they heard him speak quietly and courteously.
Then a vagrant came up who was completely inebriated.
In a wine cellar, he'd been getting extremely drunk
And had pawned all his garments and lost them.
He seized Aiol's mount by the bridle and pulled hard,　　　　1025
Which caused Marchegai to back up four paces.
"Baron," said the churl, "what do you say?
Tonight you'll be lodging at my place!
You'll have one of our girls in bed with you,
The best-looking one — you'll be able to choose —　　　　1030
Or the ugliest, if you like that better.
We'll take your hauberk to be pawned for food.
For your helm, we'll get enough for lots of wine.
We'll have plenty of fish from your mailed hose."
Quickly the drunkard stepped in front of the horse　　　　1035
And lifted the bridle from his head.
Bridle in hand, he turned to go back to the tavern.
When Marchegai felt that he'd been freed

A Chanson de Geste

From the bridle that had been taken from his mouth,
Never was such a horse to be found.   1040
I've heard the master* say he was a fay horse.
He galloped off after the lout,
He laid back his ears and seized him
Above the scruff of his neck, grabbed him there.
He raised him up four feet above the ground.   1045
He shook his head, then let him go.
The drunk fell to the ground and passed out
From the loss of blood, spurting from his nostrils.
Aiol then expertly turned the drunk over
And trampled him under his horse's hooves,   1050
So that three of his ribs were broken.
The young knight leaned down from his horse
And took the bridle from the drunk's fist.
He put it back on his horse's head.
"Baron," said Aiol, "come on, get up!   1055
If you want some of what's mine, you'll have it!
I certainly didn't come here to quarrel with you."
This incident was the subject of jokes throughout the town.
Merchants, young nobles and knights
Said to one another: "For God's sake, look!   1060
Such a horse hasn't ever been found!
It could be true that he's fay."

27.

Now Aiol rides on, angry and sad,
Because everyone, all through the town, is ridiculing him,
Merchants, young nobles and young ladies.   1065
"Baron, knight, noble lord, now speak to us!
Were these arms specially made for you?
We've never seen the likes of them in all our days!"
Aiol answered them very courteously:
"My lords, may God bless you, leave me in peace.   1070
A noble man who ridicules another foolishly
Ought to lose his lands and liberty.
People should insult robbers who do harm
And those who are guilty of heresy."
Some townspeople turned away, chastened.   1075
They went over to the drunkard and shouted at him
That he should have himself taken to his girls.
The lout left lamenting, breathing heartfelt sighs;

❧ Aiol ❧

He can say no more and asks for a priest.
And young boys and ribald men all yell at him: 1080
"You grabbed the bridle; now that's got you nothing!"
Now there appeared a rich and influential burgher:
His name was Gautier of St.-Denis.*
For five years, he'd been Duke Elye's steward.*
The memory of his rightful lord caused him to stare at Aiol 1085
Who seemed to him to resemble Elye more than any man alive.
So he'll speak out now, very frankly:

28.

"My lords," said the burgher, "let him alone.
Each one of you should consider this well:
There's not one man in this kingdom, 1090
No matter how strong a young knight he might be,
If he were exiled in another land,
If he were shabbily dressed with little clothing,
If he heard himself insulted and ridiculed,
Wouldn't already be much more ashamed and hurt, 1095
Indignant, suffering and offended.
You can see that he's young, not yet knighted.
He hasn't yet learned to bear arms well,
He hasn't wounded or killed anyone else.
He hasn't robbed anyone or stolen anything, 1100
And yet you've insulted and slurred him.
You ought to take him in
And, for God's sake, give him shelter and lodge him."
The good man then addressed Aiol in a friendly manner:
"Young, well-born noble, I'll tell you what; 1105
If you want a place to stay, don't hide it from me.
I'll take you in as a charitable act,
For the love of my lord whom you resemble,
The high-born duke Elye, who was so noble.
He was driven out of France by force 1110
Through the advice of treasonous Makaire.
You look like him more than any man alive.
Because of his friendship, you'll have a place to stay.
If your horse weren't so scrawny,
It would look like Marchegai more than any other. 1115
Because of the love of that warhorse that I've just mentioned,
This horse will have oats in abundance."
And Aiol responded prudently:

❦ A Chanson de Geste ❦

"My lord, may God who gave us life reward you!"
The good man took him to his hostel, 1120
And that night Aiol was lodged very well.
Marchegai, too, he had stabled well.
He had all his four hooves shod.

29.

Aiol, Elye's son, was lodged.
His host who took him in was named Gautier. 1125
For five full years, he was Elye's steward;
In many ways he was very well off.
He led Aiol to his upper chamber,
In friendship, he had Aiol sit beside his wife,
Before a fireplace of costly marble 1130
Next to an ample and glowing coal fire.
His host spoke to him in a friendly manner:
"Where are you from, from what country, dear friend?"
"Sire, I'm from Gascony," Aiol replied.
"My father was a great man, you can be sure. 1135
He was heaped with wealth,
But as the result of a great war, he's now exiled
And currently lies weakened by illness.
When I left him, he was so lacking in possessions
That they weren't worth even four pennies, 1140
No more than the four sous that he gave me.
He has entrusted me with these arms and this warhorse.
He's sending me to France to succeed and triumph,
To mighty King Louis, to come before him."
"My friend, may God through his mercy give you good counsel. 1145
Before you attain this, you'll experience great suffering."
Then they called for water and are going to eat.
Considering they are in the Lenten season, they are well off:
They have plenty of fish, bread and aged wine.

30.

When they had eaten copiously, 1150
His host spoke to Aiol in friendly tones:
"Young, well-born nobleman, speak to me.
You must travel to France, as you've told me,
To mighty King Louis, in order to succeed and triumph.
The arms you're carrying are certainly ugly, 1155
And your shield is old and tarnished by smoke.

29

❧ Aiol ❧

Your horse is emaciated and scrawny.
The French are proud, overbearing,
And have the habit of offensive speech.
They'll want to insult and abuse you."   1160
"Sire," said Aiol, who was so noble,
"I'll have to endure much suffering,
And I'll be hearing all their words,
Ignoring both the good and the bad,
Until it pleases Jesus of majesty   1165
That my wealth should increase."
"My friend," said his host, "you've spoken well.
If you can accomplish all that, you'll triumph.
You'll be seeing damaged and ruined roads,
Which will be swarming with robbers.   1170
If they steal your horse, what will you do?
And all the armor you're wearing?
You'll never get to sweet France!"
"My lord," said Aiol, "enough of this.
Whoever wants to conquer them and take them from me   1175
Won't take possession of them right away,
But will pay dearly before wearing them."
"My friend," said his host, "now listen well.
There's a lion right out of antiquity
Who's escaped from the king's zoo.   1180
It was sent to him from Rome as a gesture of friendship.
It ate and devoured its keeper.
Now it's roaming in the depths of the forest.
There's scarcely a man who dares enter there alone.
It's wounded and killed a hundred men.   1185
My brother, you'll be taking the road to the left.
The other road, to the right, don't take it,
Because if you meet up with the lion, you'll have no chance.
Neither you nor your horse will survive.
You'll both be eaten and devoured."   1190
"Good sire," said Aiol, "enough of this talk.
I'm not going to be stopped by any lion
If God protects the sword I've got at my side.
I want to go straight down my road.
Anyone God wants to defend is well protected.   1195
I'd really like to get some sleep, if it's all right with you."
When the burgher heard this, he got up
And had Aiol's bed made up as a friendly gesture,

❧ A Chanson de Geste ❧

And Aiol, who was very tired, went to bed.
The burgher went to lie down at his wife's side. 1200
He entered his marbled bedroom.
When he was in bed, he said to her:
"Sweet sister, dear friend, listen to me.
Oh, God! This young man's in pitiful shape!
See how fair, well-born and handsome he is! 1205
If he were well-dressed and equipped,
There wouldn't be a fairer youth in ten cities.
But he's so poor and destitute.
In more than thirteen spots his skin shows through,
Which is as white as flowers in the fields. 1210
Sunday will be Easter, as you well know,
When everyone should be wearing their best.
He should be wearing white breeches.
If for the love of God we can set our minds to it,
That he could have all new clothes when he gets up, 1215
If he were dressed in a coat with a tunic,
This would amount to great alms and charity.
We could soon be rewarded for it."
This idea caused the burgher's wife to become angry,
And she snapped back cruelly. 1220
"My lord," said the lady, "enough of this talk.
Where the devil is all this do-gooding coming from?
You've amassed your great wealth
And conquered it through all your business dealings,
And I, as a frugal wife, have been able to hold on to it. 1225
This is some ne'er-do-well tramp
Who's not had anything in his entire life
That's worth a new, lined mantle.
I think he's stolen the armor
That he's brought here with him. 1230
And he's robbed this scrawny horse."
This outburst left the burgher with a heavy heart,
But he didn't want to quarrel with his wife.
He had no desire to argue or dispute.
He doesn't make an issue of it until the next morning, 1235
When Aiol had gotten dressed and outfitted
With his poor, wretched clothing.
It is torn, tattered and ill-fitting.
His host looked at him and was filled with pity.
If he had taken his wife's advice, 1240

❦ Aiol ❦

He would not have given him new clothes and equipment.
However, he disregarded her advice.
He went over to his chest and unlocked it.
He pulled out a white shirt and breeches
Of delicate, flowered linen.   1245
He went over to give them to Aiol, Elye's son.
Aiol thanked him in the name of God of holy glory.
Soon he will be rewarded,
As you will be able to listen to and hear
Before this song has ended.   1250
Then Aiol went to church to pray to God,
Because he's not forgetting God's service,
Since his father had explicitly required it of him.
Then he returned to his lodging,
And the worthy man was prudent and wise.   1255
Before Aiol set off, he had him eat dinner.
Then Aiol picked up his equipment, armed himself,
Came to Marchegai and mounted him.
He took leave of his host and turned to ride off.
The burgher was prudent and judicious;   1260
He mounted a good palfrey
And brought Aiol his shield and lance.
He's had him leave behind the town's mocking
And gladly rides along with him for three leagues.
Then his host addressed Aiol graciously: 1265
"Worthy, well-born young man, you're leaving now.
May your entire person be commended to the Lord God of glory,
Your person, your prowess and your integrity.
You're setting out so alone and destitute
And wearing threadbare, tattered clothes, almost naked.   1270
It's certainly caused me to have a heavy heart.
Now accept this gold ring through charity,
If you're in need or impoverished,
You can pawn it at your lodging."
"My lord," said Aiol, "you show yourself to be truly noble   1275
When for your rightful lord you honor me so.
May God bless the soul of the person
Who taught you such generosity.
I now firmly pledge you my loyalty,
So that if Jesus lets me find a nobleman   1280
Who'll accept me willingly into his service,
This honor will be repaid you."

32

🏵 A Chanson de Geste 🏵

He tenderly kisses him at their parting.
He commends him to God of holy glory.
Then Aiol sets off; his host stays behind.   1285
"Oh, God!" said the young man, "Thanks to your goodness,
At the first house I've entered,
Things have worked out well for me!
Oh, Elye! Father! If you only knew,
And Avisse, my mother, in the dense forest!   1290
It's true that I wouldn't be so happy
If I were given all a city's gold."
He set off down the main road
And rode until mid-afternoon
Without encountering a single man born of woman   1295
Or a hermit with whom he could speak.
He rode up a high hill
And then went down into a low valley.
He saw a field before him.
Beyond a hedge, in a clearing in the forest,   1300
He saw the lion coming out,
Which his host had mentioned the past evening.
That same day it had killed a huge wild boar,
And it had gorged itself on it.
It had come to drink at a watering spot it knew well.   1305
When it spotted Aiol, it whirled around
And turned towards him, its jaws gaping like a devil's maw,
Because it wanted to strangle and eat him.
You'll never see a fiercer beast.
Aiol saw him charging and was frightened.   1310
He prudently got down off his horse
And tied him to the branch of an oak tree,
Because he was afraid his mount would be mauled.
Then he drew his sword from its sheath at his side
And strode towards the lion.   1315
With its jaws gaping like a devil's maw,
It rushed crazily toward the young man
To eat and devour him.
It attacked him, smashing its two forepaws
Against the top of the old, smoky shield,   1320
Punching through it with its claws.
Then it pulled the shield toward itself
And came close to pulling Aiol down,
But he struck with his lettered blade.

He dealt the lion such a blow 1325
That he hacked off all its paws.
The wounded lion let out a howl,
But Aiol wisely renewed his attack,
So that the lion's chest was all slashed,
And it was struck down dead. 1330
Never had any mortal man ever done so much.
It had strangled and eaten hundreds.

31.

Aiol has battled heavy and hard.
A fine adventure has come his way. 1335
He kept the lion's paw
And hung from it from his saddle horn.
He'll never abandon it, and it will be seen
And recognized by many people.
It will prove to be a great help to him.
Without delay, he mounts Marchegai 1340
And rides through the dark forest.
Marchegai trots proudly along,
And they come to Châteauroux straightaway.
He rides down the town's main street.
He found there a large crowd of townsfolk 1345
Who, it happened, were all making fun of him,
Until they recognized the great paw
Of the wild beast who was hard to kill,
And who was exacting such a heavy toll on the region.
Then they stopped their scoffing. 1350

32.

Now Aiol the noble youth rides on,
Through Châteauroux he came at ease.
There he found many fools and many scoundrels.
All of them were jeering at him contentiously,
Until they spotted the paw of the great lion, 1355
Who had been destroying the countryside.
Because of this, no one had dared to enter the forest.
This is why there was no scoffing at the noble man.
Politely they called to him in their dialect:
"Where do you come from? From what region, noble young man? 1360
Where did you get that lion's paw?"
"My lords, I found it at the foot of that mountain.

⚜ A Chanson de Geste ⚜

That's where it ferociously tried to eat me
When the Lord God kept me safe
With this sword I'm carrying at my side.   1365
I cut off its paw by St. Simon.*
I left it dead on the sand."
When the townspeople heard this, they were filled with joy.
That day he had the blessings of many folk.
Then there appeared a knight whose name was Raoul,   1370
A local nobleman, with the rank of vavassor.
He asked Aiol for the paw of the great lion,
And he lodged him in his house.
That night he provided Aiol with wine and fish.
Aiol was seated beside the coal fire.   1375
When they had eaten copiously
And Marchegai had had his feed —
Hay and oats in abundance —
His host addressed Aiol and began to speak:
"Where do you come from, handsome young man?   1380
Where do you come from, from what region? Where are you headed?"
"Noble lord, to sweet France," answered Aiol.
"To mighty King Louis, Charles' son.
If he'll give me some of what's his, I'll stay on."
And the host replied, who was a worthy man: 1385
"My friend, by his true name may God protect you,
Because in Louis' court there's a malicious scoundrel,
Makaire of Lausanne they call him.
There's no one, in any country, more treacherous.
It's sad to say that he's duke of Lausanne.   1390
He knows so well how to flatter the king.*
To his dishonor, he drives away worthy men."

33.
"My friend," said his host, "Listen to me.
You've told me you've got to go to France
To mighty King Louis, to seek to conquer.   1395
If you accept my advice, you'll go elsewhere.
Ride straight towards the Hague Castle,
You'll then turn towards Pontieu, there ahead.
There you'll find Rainier and Aimer
And Gilemer the Scot, who are all noble,   1400
And the lord of Bourges, with the bright countenance.
They're waging a fierce war against the king,

⚜ Aiol ⚜

Because he disinherited their uncle,
Elye the noble duke, who was so worthy."
When Aiol, the young knight, heard this, 1405
Who had carefully listened and paid attention,
He bent over, very low
When he heard his relatives mentioned.
He muttered between clenched teeth — so none would hear —
That he'd never seek out cousins or relatives 1410
Until he has spoken to Louis.
Then he'll want to inquire and query
And hear the truth from the king's own lips
Concerning why he disinherited his father.
That night, he stayed there until daybreak. 1415
Aiol took up his arms again, armed himself,
Went to Marchegai and mounted up.
He took leave of his host and set off.
He entered the main road,
All day long he spurred his mount. 1420
He looked out across a field
And saw in the shade of a tall spreading tree,
Two monks engaged in deep mourning,
Having been stripped of all their clothing.
Aiol stopped to inquire: 1425
"My lords, for the love of God, what's happened to you?"
The monks replied: "Here's what happened.
Look over at those robbers in the middle of this field.
They've just stripped us of everything we have.
They've left us with neither a habit nor cotton robe, 1430
Neither cloak nor boot, it's plain to see.
Lord, for God's sake, take that other road.
If they encounter you, you'll have no defense.
Neither you or your horse would survive.
They'd quickly rob you of everything you have." 1435
And Aiol replied, "Enough of this talk.
May it never please the Lord God of majesty
That my path should be altered because of them.
Rather I'll get you back your clothes if you want."
"My lord," said the master, "don't make fun of us." 1440
Because they sincerely believed it to be true
That Aiol was the robbers' crony who's deceiving them.
Aiol spurred his horse on its flanks,
He stopped in front of the robbers.

⚜ A Chanson de Geste ⚜

Fiercely he yelled at them, "My lords, don't move! 1445
Why have you robbed those monks?
Give them back their habits and their cloaks!
You have their cotton robes and boots!"
The robber's leader replied, "Come over here!
Give me that hauberk and that helm right away. 1450
And the shield and the sword that you're carrying.
One of my companions wants to wear them."
"My lord," said Aiol, "all right, come take them.
I'll abandon them all to you.
If I can't defend them, they'll be yours. 1455
By God's goodness I'll defend them!"
He spurred Marchegai by his flanks
And charges to strike the leader he'd just heard.
Straight through his body he thrust the iron lance head,
Killing him and striking him down dead. 1460
Then he drew the sword from his side
And struck another robber, who rushed at him,
And severed his head from his body.
The third robber escaped from him, fleeing into the dense forest.
He took flight, filled with fear. 1465
Aiol didn't want to pursue him because he didn't know
Anything about the region or the kingdom,
And the noble youth did not want to stray from his route.

34.
Aiol did not want to veer away from his route.
He didn't know the region or the kingdom. 1470
He returned the monks' things to them without delay.
He gladly took their clothes back to them.
They got dressed and put on their shoes.
Full of happiness, they put on their capes.
"Sire," said the master, "for the sake of God in heaven, 1475
Come stay the night with us."
And Aiol replied, "With pleasure,
If it's along the route that leads straight to Orleans,
Because I don't want to deviate at all from this path."
"Listen, by my faith, sire, it's a happy coincidence for you. 1480
Your route passes right in front of our door."
They came to the monastery at vespers, at nightfall,
And had a blacksmith called without delay.
They have Marchegai shod and cared for;

❧ Aiol ❧

He gets his feed without fail.　　　　　　　　　　　　　1485
In the morning, Aiol took communion at Mass
Together with the monks, as a gesture of friendship.
He stayed with them all day, which was a holy day
On which he didn't want to ride or travel.
Monday he set off on his warhorse.　　　　　　　　　　1490
Upon departing, he takes leave of the monks.

35.
Now Aiol rides off, his lance held high,
And crosses hills and valleys.
Now you'll be able to hear what destiny
Jesus for the young man that day decreed.　　　　　　　1495
Makaire of Lausanne had a brother,
He was known as Rustan in his region.
He's going to seek arms from the emperor.
Two valiant knights were travelling with him.
When they spotted Aiol, they began to scoff at him:　　1500
"So now you're coming to great and vast France.
We'll have you play the fool in our region.
Our emperor, Makaire of Lausanne,
My dear brother, will have great merriment.
My friend, we were sired by the same father.　　　　　1505
And were carried by the same mother."
"Oh, God!" said Aiol, "What a destiny!
Since Makaire of Lausanne is your brother,
Your father's soul should be cursed,
Because he entirely disinherited my noble mother.　　　1510
I now challenge you in the name of God, my father!"
He instantly spurred his horse
And brandishing his old, smoky lance,
Charges to strike Rustan. As the two meet,
Aiol thrust his lance straight through his body　　　　　1515
Striking him down dead in the middle of the field.
Then he reached down with his hand and drew his sword.
From its scabbard he drew it out bright and shining.
Then he charged the two squires
And slew them both down dead amid the field.　　　　 1520
"Oh, God," exclaimed Aiol. "What an adventure!
Lady St. Mary, honored Virgin,
Now I've truly found a serious joust!
Oh, if you only knew, father Elye!

⚜ A Chanson de Geste ⚜

I've closed out one part of your war. 1525
I don't know if Makaire has any other brothers,
But this one won't lay any more land to waste."
He set off on his route, wide and paved,
And left their horses, in the middle of the field.

36.

Now Aiol rides off down his road, 1530
Leaving Makaire's brother behind.
He rode all day up until midday.
At an opening in the forest near the road,
In the shade of a big, leafy laurel tree,
A pilgrim was lying on the grass. 1535
He was returning from Jerusalem, from serving God.
He had a pilgrim's staff, palm branch and pouch,
A good, ambling donkey at his disposition
And a valiant squire to serve him.
He was dressed in the manner of a well-born man 1540
And had a white beard and snow-white hair.
He certainly seemed to be a nobleman, a duke or marquis,
Who possessed a castle or a city.
Upon Aiol's arrival, he got to his feet when he saw him.
First of all, the pilgrim greeted him: 1545
"My lord, may the Lord God, who never lied, bless and keep you."
"And may God bless you," said Aiol.
"Where are you coming from, from what region, fair, good friend?"
"My lord, from Jerusalem, from serving God.
I was at the Sepulcher, where he arose from the dead, 1550
And on the Mount of Calvary, where he suffered death.
In the holy River Jordan, thanks to God,
I bathed there this year, on the third day of April.*
In St. Abraham's garden I took this palm."
"Where are you returning to, noble pilgrim?" 1555
"My lord, my route runs right through the middle of France."
"Tell me some news, my dear, fair friend.
Have you heard anything about the war?"
"Yes, so help me God, I have," replied the pilgrim.
"In the city of Orleans I saw Louis, 1560
The emperor of France, who was sad and sorrowful.
The inhabitants and family of Berry have begun to wage war
 against him,
And they won't let him come out through the gates of Orleans."

❧ Aiol ❧

"Have you heard if he'll take on mercenaries?"
"Yes," said the pilgrim, "if any would come to him."   1565
"Sire," asked Aiol, "would he accept my service?"
The pilgrim directly looked at him.
He saw that he was poor, almost naked and pale.
His clothes were tattered and he was ill-clothed,
His huge lance was twisted, his shield tarnished,   1570
His stirrups were damaged and ill-fitting,
And he was seated on a scrawny horse.
The pilgrim leaned on his staff and smiled at this sight.
"My lord, I don't know what to say, so help me God.
Around the king, I saw so many furs,   1575
Expensive finery and high-priced horses,
That I don't believe the king would retain you."
When Aiol heard this he became angry and sorrowful,
But he was worthy, well brought-up and prudent.
He breathed a heart-felt sigh   1580
And his eyes welled up with poignant tears.
"Sire," said the young man, "what you've said isn't true.
The heart is not located in furs,
Nor in rich finery, nor in expensive clothing,
But it has been placed in a man's chest by God,*   1585
Who, if it pleases him, can help me."
When the pilgrim heard this, he took pity on him,
Because he had replied so intelligently,
And regretted that he had ridiculed him.

37.

The pilgrim was well-born and noble.   1590
He looked at Aiol and felt pity for him.
He saw that he was penniless, destitute and poorly clothed.
He regretted that he had scoffed at him,
Because Aiol had responded so thoughtfully;
He remembered his excellent up-bringing   1595
And showed himself to be good and noble.
He reached down into the pouch he was carrying
And pulled out an alms-purse he had placed there.
He took out a gold Byzantine coin he had placed there,
Came over to Aiol and gave it to him.   1600
He addressed him politely and courteously:
"Well-born young nobleman, sire, listen to me.
For the love of Him that formed you,

❧ A Chanson de Geste ❧

Who preserved me from the sea's great peril,
And who brought me straight to safe harbor,   1605
Take this gold bezant. You'll appreciate it,
For you could end up in a spot where you'll need it."
Aiol took the bezant and hugged him:
"Sire, may God, who created everything, reward you.
May you be repaid through Jesus Christ.   1610
God will accomplish it eventually, when he sees fit."
And later Aiol did have furs and good horses,
As you will be able to hear as it will be told to you.

38.

Aiol called to the pilgrim and addressed him:
"Sire, noble pilgrim, what's your name?   1615
So if I ever encounter you again, I'll know you."
"Rainier, Gerard's son they call me.
I'm a duke in Gascony, I have a house there.
I have two sons, knights of great renown.
And you, noble young knight, what is your name?"   1620
"They call me, dear sir, the youth Aiol.
If you ever come back to France, speak to me,
And I'll serve you with great affection."
He recommended the pilgrim to God, the glorious one.

39.

Aiol, Elye's son, wants to take leave   1625
Of the valiant knight who had acted so admirably.
Before he left him, Aiol addressed him once again:
"For the love of God, my dear sire, give me some advice.
You'll be rewarded for it and I certainly need it.
Who is waging war against the king who reigns over France?   1630
Do you know of a duke or prince who hires knights?
The count of Bourges has no love for him.
If I were to go, dear lord, to the city of Orleans,
Would I be retained by the king who reigns over France?
I'd have great need of earning a living."   1635
The pilgrim heard him and bowed his head:
"My lord, I don't know what to say, so help me God.
I stayed in Orleans for eight whole days.
There I saw the king who reigns over France,
And he must have had around him more than a thousand knights, 1640
All of whom were dressed in furs

❧ Aiol ❧

And had very fine weapons and good, swift horses.
I'll tell you something I want you to know:
There's none so noble from here to Montpellier,
That if he came into their midst in the city of Orleans,   1645
Equipped with all his arms on a swift steed,
That he wouldn't be scoffed at and ridiculed by some.
I know that he could well be lacking in soldiers for hire.
Don't be annoyed that I've told you this,
Because your weapons are so ugly and your warhorse   1650
And your equipment are of so little value,
And your hose are completely threadbare.
I still have a castle that's dear to me.
It's called Beaufort and is located in the Marche.
And I have four sons — two are knights.   1655
If I had you there, by all the saints in heaven,
I'd have you admirably outfitted.
But it's no use. We're too far away.
May the Lord God bless and keep you, the glorious one of heaven.
May the King of kings have pity on you.   1660
I've never seen such a poor knight."
This caused Aiol, Elye's son, to sigh
When he heard his poverty described.

40.

Aiol, Elye's son, breathed a heartfelt sigh
And said to the pilgrim: "May God accompany you!   1665
You've described very well my dire poverty,
And your words have left me with a heavy heart."
The pilgrim replied: "My lord, don't be too hasty;
I want to talk to you a little while."
He called his squire: "My friend, come here.   1670
Bring me that chest and open it up."
And the squire replied: "Sire, as you command."
He quickly ran to bring the chest.
The pilgrim rapidly unlocked it with a silver key.
He pulled out a pair of hose, you'll never see better,   1675
You'll never hear of a finer scarlet*;
A handsome pair of spurs, made of fine, engraved gold;
The pilgrim had brought them back from overseas.
He'd bought them in front of the Temple of the Dome.
He weighed out for them a mark of sterling silver.   1680
He had intended to use them for his eldest son's dubbing.

⚜ A Chanson de Geste ⚜

Now you can truly say that he exemplified genuine nobility,
When the equipment he had bought
For his very own son, he consented to give away!
When he met the stranger, he offered them to him.   1685
Pleasantly and courteously he began to address Aiol:
"My lord, take these hose, through charity.
And these expensive spurs, you'll never see better,
By the great faith that I must bear towards you.
A man wearing such fine hose is never thought undressed."   1690
When Aiol heard this, he was filled with joy:
"Sire, may he bless and keep you, who was hung on the cross.
May God allow me to repay your kindness someday."
Oh! God will make it happen so that this destiny is not altered!
He sat down under the tree and pulled on the hose.   1695
Oh, God! How well they fit him, those golden spurs!
He went to Marchegai and mounted by the stirrups.
He commended the pilgrim to God and started off on his route.
Barons, back then, in the time I'm describing
There were very few people on earth,   1700
Neither the castles nor the cities were as populated
As they are now. Don't doubt me on this.
Instead, there were ancient forests, vast dense woods,
Which have since been cut down and laid to waste.
No man would take a wife until past the age of thirty,   1705
And the betrothed maid was also more mature.
When the time came for them to wed,
They were both very modest — this you can believe.
They thought the eyes of all were upon them
Because there was trust and loyalty in the world then.   1710
But, since then have been rising greed, debauchery,
Evil and filth, and goodness declining.
One family member can't trust another,
Nor can the child trust his father, so much evil has arisen.
They now have two twelve-year old children wed.   1715
Beware of the heirs that those two might produce!
Because of this, the world's been reduced to nothing
And has diminished, as you'll be able to hear.*
Aiol, Elye's son, was deeply depressed
Because he had ridden and journeyed all day.   1720
He saw evening coming on and vespers approaching.
He prayed to God to give him good lodging.
He rode on, feeling very insecure.

43

❧ Aiol ❧

In front of him, in the forest, he heard people shouting,
And looked to his right and saw a castle wall before him   1725
And a deep moat and a high gate tower.
A forest ranger* lived there, who was well housed.
His name was Thierry, and he was worthy and brave.
He was responsible for all the forest around him.
Aiol saw the house and was very reassured.   1730
He pulled on his reins and headed in that direction.
He didn't stop until he had arrived at the house.
He found the forest ranger in front of a burning fire.
Aiol greeted him politely, as you will hear:
"May the Lord God bless and keep you, sire," said Aiol the brave. 1735
The forest ranger sprang to his feet when he saw Aiol all armed:
"My lord, may he protect you who brought you here.
Are you armed because you're afraid of someone
As you travel through these ancient forests equipped as you are?
It's been quite a while since I've seen a man outfitted like that." 1740
"I'm a knight. You'll never see one poorer.
I haven't been dubbed for a month yet,
And I don't have any squire, you can be sure of it.
I need to carry my arms myself, as you can see.
I don't have a chest or coffer to store them,   1745
Nor any other clothes I need to store.
And I don't want to leave them in a castle or in a city,
Because I'll soon have need of them, if I'm challenged.
The king of France is waging war, so I've heard.
Tomorrow morning, I'm leaving for the city of Orleans   1750
To see if I can enter into his service.
Tonight, if you please, I'd like to request lodging,
For the love of heaven, if it's acceptable to you.
I'm a poor man. You'd be doing an act of true charity."
"Sire," Thierry replied, "I'd be delighted and happy to.   1755
No nobleman has ever been refused lodging in my home,
And never will be, in all my days."
Aiol dismounted and had Thierry remove his armor.
His equipment was placed under a table.
His horse was stabled in one part of the great room   1760
And was provided with plenty of hay and oats.
Then Thierry got busy and rapidly had their dinner prepared.
They sat down to dinner without further delay.
They had venison and wild boar in abundance.
When they had eaten and drunk copiously,   1765

⚜ A Chanson de Geste ⚜

Thierry looked at Aiol and began to address him:
"Well-born young knight, my lord, listen to me:
You want to go to France to seek to enter the royal service,
Because the king is fighting a major war, they've told us.
You're poorly outfitted and equipped   1770
Since your arms are ugly and your horse is scrawny.
The French are proud and so overbearing,
I'm afraid they'll want to ridicule and scoff at you,
And you won't be able to stand it or put up with it.
They'll have quickly injured or killed you.   1775
If you'd like to, my lord, stay on with us.
Through these woods we'd roam at our pleasure,
And you'd take deer, stags and wild boar;
I'd teach you all about bow-hunting.
I'd give you my daughter, a noble, honorable person.   1780
Know that there's none more beautiful in this entire kingdom."
"My lord," said Aiol, "I've never heard of such a thing!
I have a strong suspicion that you're making fun of me.
In no region do I have a castle or a city,
Nor house, nor fortress, tower or stronghold,   1785
Nor so many possessions, you can be sure of it,
That if pawned, would only be worth ten deniers,
Except just these pitiable arms that you see here
And this tired, worn-out horse you've lodged.
The marriage you've envisioned would be too impoverished."   1790
"My lord," said the maiden, "you're protesting too much.
If you don't have possessions, God will provide in abundance.
But if you wish, my lord, to stay on with us,
Every day I'd serve you, whatever you'd desire."
"Fair maiden," said Aiol, "five hundred thanks from heaven,   1795
By the faith I owe God. You've spoken virtuously,
But may it please Jesus, who was hung on the cross,
That I not have a wife and be married
Until with my arms I've conquered another honor,
Because all of my descendants would incur reproach."   1800
When the maiden heard him, she almost lost her mind.
She entered her chamber and began to grieve to herself:
"Unlucky, miserable girl, you've been badly treated
By the most handsome knight who was ever born.
I'd be cured right away if he deigned to love me.   1805
Cursed be the hour when he entered this house,
For I'll never have another so noble in all my days."

Thierry dropped the matter and went to rest.
He saw very well that Aiol wasn't interested.
He had a good bed prepared for Aiol where he'll rest,   1810
And Aiol slept until the following day at daybreak.
When the noble saw the dawn, he arose early.
He leaped to his feet, crossed himself,
Took up his equipment and outfitted himself.
Thierry had his horse brought to him.   1815
Aiol, Elye's son, mounted using the stirrups.
Blessing his host, he set out on his route.

41.

Now Aiol sets out, riding along his route
And crosses through lands and wild ravines.
He rode through the day until high noon   1820
And found three robbers, may God condemn them,
Who kept watch over the roads and the paths.
No one could pass by, neither pilgrim nor palmer,
Merchant or burgher, who wasn't condemned to death.
If he has a beautiful wife, she's shamed and humiliated.   1825
"My lords," said the master robber, "I see a knight coming,
Carrying weapons and wearing armor, trotting along on a nag.
In all my days, I've never seen anyone so well-outfitted!
I'll give that good horse to my host Gautier.
He'll take his ashes to the town and to the market."   1830
The other robbers replied: "You've spoken very well,
Because you promised him one a full month ago."
"He'll have it," said the master thief, "without fail."
Now here comes Aiol who greets them courteously,
For God of holy glory who lives in heaven above.   1835
"Upon my head!" said the master robber, "This is no use to you.
I couldn't care less about you or your greeting.
With you, I'll go off into that great, dense woods.
I'll give you such an offering, which you wouldn't need,
And when I get finished with you, you'll be a knight no more."   1840
He seized Marchegai by his solid gold rein,
Because he wanted to lead him deep into the dense forest
To strip, shame and dishonor him.
When Aiol saw this, it made him angry.
He couldn't use his lance since he's gotten too close.   1845
Aiol let his lance fall down to the ground
And drew from his side his naked blade*

✤ A Chanson de Geste ✤

And struck the robber on the top of his head.
Down into the brain he gashed and split it.
Aiol twisted his blow and struck him down.　　　　　1850
The remaining two robbers turned and fled: they're terrified
By the great blow they've seen from the strong, steel sword.
They wouldn't stay around for all the gold on earth,
But Aiol chases them down, caught the middle one,
And dealt him such a blow with his steel sword　　　1855
That he cut off his head from on top of his shoulders.
The third robber escaped him and plunged into the forest,
Which is thick and dense — and that's a pity and a real sin!
Aiol had no intention of pursuing him any farther.
Rather, he returned and picked up his lance.　　　　1860
The robbers were very well-dressed,
But Aiol would be damned before he'd claim a single garment.
Rather he swore to the Lord God, the righteous Father,
That he wouldn't wear a robber's clothes
Or anyone else's if he couldn't earn them honorably.　1865
Soon he'd come to a place where he'd be recognized,
And he could well be shamed and dishonored.
He strikes out through the wilds, plunges into the woods;
He doesn't stop until he's reached the castle of Blois.
That night, Aiol was lodged at vespers　　　　　　　1870
With a rich burgher whose name was Gautier
Who gave him food and drink in abundance,
And hay and oats for Marchegai, his warhorse.
Aiol offered him the four sous' worth of deniers
That his father had entrusted to him when he left.　　1875
But the burgher refused to accept or even touch them.
He provided food as an act of pure charity.
That night Aiol slept there until daybreak,
Then he took up his arms and mounted his steed.
He took leave and rapidly set off.　　　　　　　　　1880
He left Blois. He didn't want to delay.
He began to ride along the Loire River.
Before nightfall he came to Orleans.
There he found the king who reigns over France
And, because of his arms, became the object of much
　　scorn and ridicule.　　　　　　　　　　　　　1885

⚜ Aiol ⚜

42.

Now Aiol is riding along the Loire River.
From Poitiers to Orleans he's come in five days.
It was on a Wednesday before Easter
When Aiol entered the streets of Orleans all alone.
But in this situation he reacted well, as a high-born noble.　　　1890
He rode up to the Church of the Holy Cross to worship there.
In front of the church there stood a hitching stone.
In it was sunk a gold ring, great and round,
Which had been sealed in the stone by the ancestors.
Noble Aiol attached his warhorse to it　　　1895
And laid his lance and his shield against it.
Then he entered the Church of the Holy Cross.
He knelt in front of the main altar.
He prayed to the Lord God, invoking his Holy Names:
"Glorious Lord Father," said Aiol,　　　1900
"Who for so long was in the body of the Virgin
And came to earth for our sakes,
From her you were born — we know this for certain —
In Bethlehem on a stone floor.
Just as this was true, we sincerely believe　　　1905
That you are King and Lord of all the world,
Then bring swift help to my father,
Whom I left sick, needy,
Suffering and dressed in rags,
Who is with the hermit deep in the forest.　　　1910
Holy Blessed Lady, I pray this of you."

43.

Now Aiol, the young knight, was in the church;
He knelt down before the main altar.
He prays to the Lord God, the true one of heaven:
"Lord God," he said, "my righteous Father,　　　1915
Who rules the land and the sea
And reigns over heaven and earth,
Protect me from death and from all trials
And give me adventures through your mercy,
So I may yet help my father　　　1920
And see my mother again, who is in need of it.
Lady St. Mary, help me with this."
When Aiol had finished his sincere prayer to Jesus,
He took four deniers from his purse.

⚜ A Chanson de Geste ⚜

The knight placed them on the altar 1925
Very willingly, as a holy offering.
Now the four sous are all depleted
That Elye, his father, had entrusted to him.
Aiol still has three sous and eight deniers
And a pure gold bezant, 1930
Which he had been given through love of God, by the good pilgrim
Whom he encountered on the road to Poitiers.
Since then, the pilgrim has received praise and repayment:
He has furs and good warhorses.
Aiol raised his hand and crossed himself: 1935
"Blessed Holy Cross, I'll take leave of you.
I'm going to look for lodging, of which I'm in need.
Now I pray you that you help me intercede with God."
In great humility he left the church
And found his horse tied up 1940
Where he had attached it to the hitching stone.
He had no squire or servant with him,
So he picked up his sword and shield himself.
He searched through all the streets of Orleans.
He found there many servants, knights, 1945
Ladies and maidens from their high solars.
Aiol didn't speak to them nor did he search them out,
Nor did he ask for lodging, about which he knew nothing;
He wasn't used to this kind of search.
His lance was very twisted, his shield old, 1950
His helm was not shiny, but rusted;
Its laces were slack and broken;
It tipped to one side, almost falling over.
And Marchegai trots along, holding his head high.
Intense is the ridicule heaped upon this knight 1955
By the ladies and maidens at the upper windows
And the rich burghers and the butchers.
One began to comment to the other:
"Let's be assured, joyful and glad;
Not one of us need be dismayed any longer. 1960
Now we've won everything back.
Here comes one of those soldiers for hire,
Hardened in battle, bold and fierce.
He'll serve the king who reigns over France
And will win back his lands and his kingdom. 1965
He'll find a way to bring this war to a close.

❧ Aiol ❧

He's been raised and educated by a powerful man,
Who sent him here to provide outstanding service.
He'll certainly conquer with his lance.
He has an excellent appearance with his arms, his warhorse   1970
And his fine, costly equipment.
In no land is there such a knight.
If he now meets the inhabitants of Berry in battle,
They'll all be dead, captured or hacked to pieces.
In my opinion, he wouldn't yield one foot   1975
If his enemies totaled fifteen thousand."

44.
"By my faith, sir," another spoke up,
"Such crazy talk's an outrage.
This knight is not the one for such foolishness.
It doesn't seem, judging by his horse and his arms,   1980
He'd have such bravery in his heart
To allow him to liberate France by his noble deeds.
And his lance is so twisted, he's holding it low.
The shield hanging from his neck is bothering him."
Isabelle, the countess who was so prudent and judicious,   1985
Was seated at a high window, on a tan cushion.
She spotted the young knight Aiol who rode by below her,
And who was her sister's son, of her own lineage.
In her heart, she took great pity on him.
Lusiane,* her daughter, noticed this reaction.   1990
She was courteous, worthy and wise as well.
She came running up to her mother and spoke to her.

45.
Lusiane was a very well-born maiden,
Courteous, well-mannered and comely.
She was the niece of the king of St.-Denis.   1995
She addressed her mother and began to speak to her:
"By my faith, my lady," said the maiden,
"This man, who's riding by down there, isn't rich.
Since this morning he's been going around this city.
He's passed by the old city wall five times.   2000
Knights and burghers continued to jeer at him.
It seems to me this is childish and despicable," said Lusiane.
"I think he's looking for lodging for he has nowhere to stay."
And Isabelle replied: "Go on down to him, my daughter.

⚜ A Chanson de Geste ⚜

By the faith that you owe St. Mary, 2005
If he looks poor to you, don't ridicule him in the least,
Because that would be a contemptible sin.
If he wants lodging, bring him here with kindness
For the love of Jesus Christ, the son of Mary,
And for the soul of my father who raised me." 2010
"My lady," said Lusiane, "I won't fail."
Through the throng of townspeople, she made her way.
To anyone who might have seen the young woman,
With her fair skin and smiling face,
The idea of cowardliness would never have occurred. 2015
She'd put on a rich fabric under her ermine;
Her skirts were indigo, blue and green.
She had hose of gold cloth, embroidered shoes.
She took Aiol's rein, gently guiding him towards her:
"Speak to me a moment, young knight, my lord. 2020
Today you've ridden around town a lot:
Three times you've passed in front of the old city wall.
Knights and burghers have been jeering at you.
This seems to me to be arrogant and absurd.
If you want lodging, be frank about it! 2025
Tonight we'll give you good lodging
Because of our friendship with God, the son of Mary;
I'm not doing it for any other reward."

46.

Lusiane was of very great repute.
She looked at the young man Aiol, who was very handsome, 2030
But he was poor, needy and dressed in rags.
Thus poverty produces anguish in a man.
She called to him lovingly:
"Well-born young man, where are you from?
Where are you going? To what land? What are you looking for? 2035
If you want lodging, tell us!
Tonight we will gladly take you in."
"For the love of God, the glorious one,
Thank you so much, lady," said Aiol.
"We aren't looking for any other kind of reward." 2040
Then she took him by the rein and started back.
That day, the French look on with astonishment,
Ladies, maidens and young boys.
They didn't stop until they'd reached the courtyard.

❦ Aiol ❦

There Aiol dismounted at the big mounting block.　　　2045
She held his stirrup lovingly.
"My friend, take off your helm. Give it to me
And go up into that tower.
Don't worry about your horse down here,
Because he'll receive the best possible care.　　　2050
My lady is a widow without a lord,
But she'll make sure you receive the best of care,
Until God gives you a better servant."
"Many thanks, my lady," said Aiol.

47.

Aiol climbed up to the solar.　　　2055
The fair Lusiane with the light step
Turns his warhorse over to a stable hand
Who curried him and rubbed him down well,
Dried him off, watered and cared for him.
He leads him into the stable for his lodging.　　　2060
He took off the bridle he had on his head
And attached him with a deerskin halter.
He's given hay and oats to eat.
Then Lusiane returns quickly to the knight.
She places an ivory footstool at his feet.　　　2065
She removed both his spurs;
Then she wiped them off and polished them.
She attaches them firmly to his sword's belt.
The knight can take them from it,
When he's ready to mount his warhorse.　　　2070
He didn't have a servant to help him.
"Oh, God," said Aiol, "what a squire!
I was in dire need of this service."
If Isabelle had known that he was her nephew,
Her services would have been even more wide-ranging.　　　2075

48.

Isabelle was very attractive; her daughter even more so.
At first sight, Aiol had made a good impression on her,
But he is poor, dressed in rags and so very quiet:
Thus poverty makes many a man reserved and insecure.
"My friend," said Isabelle, "where are you from?　　　2080
Where are you going and to what land? Who's escorting you?
As far as I can see, you're not leading a squire."

❧ A Chanson de Geste ❧

"My lady," said Aiol, "the person of Jesus,
Truly, I don't have any other defense but him.
If anyone wants to harm me, I have him as a safeguard."   2085

49.

"By my faith, my lady, I'm from Gascony,
From the fertile borderlands of King Yon.*
My father's lying ill in his house.
They call him Gautier of Pont Elie.*
At the Rogation Days' Feast,* it will be seven years   2090
Since he's been able to put on his spurs.
He's lacking in possessions and protection.
So he's given me his arms and his equipment,
And he's sent me off to France completely destitute.
We've looked for lodging so long that we've found it.   2095
From the Lord God of glory who made the world
And on the Holy Cross accepted the Passion,
May you receive merit and reward."
"For God's sake," exclaimed Isabelle. "Well, think of that!"
She turned to Lusiane the fair and said to her: 2100
"By the faith that you owe St. Simon,
Go get us some perch, eels, salmon
And spices, claret and venison.
This young knight seems to me to be from an excellent family.
For his sake, let's get on with the feast."   2105
So the young woman ran through the house,
With the sleeves of her blouse pushed up.
Whoever might see her moving so rapidly,
She would seem to him a praiseworthy woman.

50.

Anyone who saw the prudent maiden   2110
Would be reminded of a well-born woman.
She called the head steward to her
And charged him to prepare the dinner.
Venison and wild boar meat
They had, and wine and spices in abundance.   2115

51.

That night, Aiol was well lodged
Because they had prepared food in abundance,
And they had good stewards, good servants,

53

❧ Aiol ❧

Cooks, majordomos and bottle bearers.
My lords, he who the Lord God wants to help,   2120
The true one of holy glory, through his mercy,
No one will be able to harm him, ever.

52.

Isabelle took her daughter by her right hand,
Led her into her chamber, and began to speak to her:
"My daughter, this young man seems to be of proud lineage.   2125
The Lord God of glory, the heavenly King,
Who made the sea and the world, birds and beasts,
May he grant that he find what he's seeking.
For God's sake, my daughter, I'm asking you to serve him well.
Let him not be lacking anything that's on earth."   2130
"My lady, as you wish," said the maiden.

53.

Lusiane the fair served him gladly;
She does all that she can to serve him willingly.
The maiden who is so wise and brave,
From the solar comes down all the steps   2135
And comes to Marchegai to look after him.
She combs his mane and rubs down his flanks.
She's brought a stable hand with her
And has him check his hooves to see if they're well shod.
They found that indeed they were still well nailed.   2140
Then the beauty, with the shapely figure, turned away
And leaves the horse well lodged.
She has him given hay and oats in abundance.

54.

The noble young woman turns away
And leaves the horse clean and well provided for.   2145
She enters a chamber of dark gray marble.
There she gladly made up Aiol's bed.
She put on gold cloth covers
And the sheets are silk, not linen.
The bed coverlet is of marten fur, wide and thick.   2150
The pillow was made of an oriental cloth.
She called to Aiol and said to him:
"Young knight, come in here to sleep now."
She takes him by his wrist and leads him to the bed.

⚜ A Chanson de Geste ⚜

Garin holds the candle and serves the wine. 2155
They both drank some of it at their ease.
Then she had him undressed, his hose taken off.
And when he went to bed she pulled the covers over him.
She gently massaged him to help him fall asleep.
He rolled over, looked at her and let out a sigh. 2160
He had never seen a well-born man served,
Because he had been raised in the forest
And hadn't learned the pleasure of young women.
He prayed to the Lord God, who never lied
That he show his good mercy to his father 2165
Whom he had left sick and ailing,
Both him and his mother, in the dense forest.
But beautiful Lusiane served him well,
Behaving as if he were her prisoner.

55.

Gently the maiden strokes him. 2170
She put her hand on his cheek.
Now hear exactly what she said to him:
"Come on, turn towards me, handsome young man.
If you want to kiss me, or any other game,
I really feel like serving you gladly. 2175
So help me God of heaven, I'm a virgin.
I've never had a male friend in any land,
But the thought comes to me that I want to be yours,
If it's to your liking that I should serve you."
"Fair maiden," said Aiol, "the heavenly King 2180
Who made wind, sea, heaven and earth,
May he reward you for all the good that you're doing me.
Now go off to bed — it's high time for it —
There in your chamber with your maidens
Until tomorrow, when dawn appears. 2185
Then you'll find out what I think about you.
By tomorrow at vespers, we'll be well-acquainted."
The young woman had no desire to rest.

56.

The young woman turned away, full of anguish,
And left Aiol in his chamber. 2190
As soon as she possibly could, she enters hers.
She lay down in a bed. She's highly agitated,

❦ AIOL ❦

But for all of France, she can't sleep
Because she's set so much of her hope and her heart on it.
For a long while, she bemoans her fate, then begins to reflect upon it.   2195
"What bad luck!" said the maiden,
"That I want to love him, and he's got no idea!
Oh, God! Please advise me with your true power.
I'll make a very fine offering to St. Denis:
Fourteen silver marks, accurately weighed out."   2200

57.

The maiden went away with a heavy heart.
She enters her chamber and shuts the door,
But she could not rest or sleep at all.
All night long she thinks out loud:
"Noble young knight, you're so high-born and noble.   2205
I've never seen a man of your age
Who didn't want a woman to turn his way.
You'd make a good monk if you wanted to be one.
So go and take the cloth! What are you waiting for!
I'll just have to live with only the thought of your love,   2210
When I just can't stop loving you.
In my heart I've fallen so much in love with you
That it will be extremely hard for me to forget you."
And Aiol slept until it was bright daylight,
Because he did not want to love this woman or any other.   2215
The noble knight was thinking of something else:
He would win back his father's lands before
He would want to enter into friendship with a woman.
He knows for certain and as a true fact
That he could quickly forget his father,   2220
Because a woman's love changes everything
And turns a man's thoughts all astray.

58.

All night Aiol lay in bed until daybreak.
When the young knight saw the dawn, he was overjoyed.
Quickly he put on his shoes when he was dressed   2225
And went to the Church of the Holy Cross to hear Mass.
He followed the procession up until noon
Because Elye, his father, had told him
He should constantly make an effort to serve God.
Anyone God wants to help will never be shamed.   2230

⚜ A Chanson de Geste ⚜

When Mass had been said, he returned to his lodging.
The meal was all prepared when he arrived;
Aiol and his good hostess sat down at the dinner table.
The majordomo served them wine attentively.
When they had eaten copiously, in a pleasant atmosphere, 2235
Aiol took the deniers from his purse.
He turned to his hostess and said to her,
"My lady," said Aiol, "I'd like to give you my sincere thanks
For all the good that you've done for me, since I've arrived here.
May God, who never lied, reward you. 2240
Please accept these four sous, which I have here.
I think that four deniers are lacking
That I gave as an offering at Holy Cross as thanks to God.
If my bill is more, I'm completely prepared
To promise to pay you and to settle my debt. 2245
I've still got a coat of mail and a nag
And a steel helm, which hasn't been polished,
And the one who gave it to me didn't despise it.
He wouldn't have pawned it for its weight in gold.
In many a battle, it's protected him from death. 2250
And I have a steel blade, I won't lie,
I don't think there's a better one in this region.
I've got a gold bezant. Here it is,
A pilgrim gave it to me for God's love.
And I have a large, solid gold ring 2255
My host gave me when I took leave of him.
He's a burgher in Poitiers, may God help him."
Isabelle replied: "You're very well-bred.
Put away your deniers, my good, kind friend.
With God, who never lied, as my witness, 2260
I wouldn't accept a single one of them before April.
I'm not one of this town's merchant women;
I've not yet sold any bread or wine.
On the contrary, I'm a high-born woman, sister to Louis,
The emperor of France, of St.-Denis, 2265
Who reigns over all this land."
When Aiol heard this, he became very happy.
Now he knows for certain that this is his aunt, a close relative,
Because Elye, his father, had told him,
And he said, between his teeth, so no one could hear him: 2270
"Lord God, sire, father, gratitude and thanks
For this, at your pleasure might I render,

❦ Aiol ❦

Because from this grave sin you've protected me:
That Lusiane came close to causing me shame.
Yesterday evening she wanted to go to bed with me; 2275
She's my first cousin. I know it for certain.
Anyone God wants to help will never be shamed."

59.
"My friend," said Isabelle, "you're a fine youth.
Put away your deniers, don't mention this again.
Just barely two months ago, 2280
If you had come to seek conquest,
You wouldn't have been able to go any farther,
Because the people of Berry have seized all our lands.
They pillage and plunder us with great furor.
I'm not one of this town's merchant women. 2285
Rather, I'm the sister of Louis, who this kingdom
And all these lands has to rule over.
Duke Miles of Aiglent,* who was so noble,
And held ten castles and three cities,
Through his goodness, asked my father for my hand in marriage. 2290
My father couldn't have found a better match for me.
He gladly and willingly gave me away.
He had no other heir than this daughter you see before you.
Fourteen peers killed him through high treason.
One of them was Makaire the arch felon. 2295
He's the proven author of many a treason.
Since that time he's beguiled the French
And twisted laws and judgments in his favor.
Of all our nobles, he's swindled everyone.
Elye, my brother-in-law, who was so noble, 2300
Makaire's disinherited through treason.
Now he holds all of Elye's castles and cities.
My sister has been exiled because of it, this I know well.
It's made my heart anguished, grieved and sorrowful."
When Aiol heard this, he lowered his head. 2305
If the youth had wanted to pursue the matter further,
At that moment they would have gotten acquainted through their love.

60.
"My friend," said Isabelle, "I am truly saddened
Because of a sister of mine whom I know has been exiled.
Both she and her lord are in another land; 2310

⚜ A Chanson de Geste ⚜

Makaire of Lausanne seized their lands.
But the king of this city has a special affection for me,
Because he is my brother and my lord.
May the Lord God of glory, Mary's son,
Who reigns over heaven and earth, 2315
If it pleases him, return to Elye his lost fiefs
And condemn Makaire, the evil traitor,
Who unlawfully and sinfully seized their lands."
When Aiol heard this, the high-born noble youth,
He bowed his head low down towards the floor 2320
And muttered between clenched teeth, so no one at all could hear him:
"By the faith that I owe St. Mary,
You won't see Palm Sunday come to pass,
If I encounter Makaire, the evil traitor.
With my sharp sword of burnished steel 2325
I intend to show him such boldness that
He will be left lying lifeless in a pool of blood."

61.

"My lord," said Isabelle, the noble woman,
"Well-born young knight, is it your intent,
Do you want to speak soon 2330
To mighty King Louis, who reigns over France?"
"My lady," said Aiol, "I don't know how to go about it,
Nor do I dare undertake this so rashly.
A young knight who's a youth of my few years
Shouldn't go to court so precipitously 2335
If he doesn't have fine arms and equipment.
Immediately everyone would begin to scoff at him,
But may it now please almighty God
That a battle or tournament might come to the city gates,
I would be the first to ride out. 2340
My heart and all my senses would be devastated
If I were cowardly, evil or slow to act."
"My friend," said Isabelle, "this happens all the time,
Because the people of Berry come here to us frequently
And Saracens, too, treat us harshly. 2345
They're taking Pamplona from us surely."

62.

It was after Easter, in the summer months,
That it occurred to the count of Bourges

❦ Aiol ❦

To order all of his liegemen to come to him.
There were seven score of them in total, all dubbed knights.   2350
The people of Berry had entered France by night
Into the Suberie Valley, below Val Cler.*
There they established a secret observation post.
Four of those knights left that position
And brought the battle to the city   2355
Where Aiol will be able to put himself to the test
And make a convincing demonstration of his knightly prowess.

63.

Of the four robbers who went to the city,
It seems to me I'm sure I know their names.
They are Nivar, Aliaume, Foucart and Sanson.   2360
They had shining weapons and banners,
Good, swift and strong Gascon warhorses.
They came to Orleans, crossed the bridge,
Pounded violently on the city gate
And loudly bellowed their war cry: 2365
"So where are you, Louis, Charles' son?
Come on out here so we can see you!
We challenge your right to the lands Charles conquered.
You wear your crown wrongfully, that's what we say!
We'll never cease waging this war   2370
Until we've killed or captured you!"
When the king heard this, it caused him anguish.
The French ran to get their arms and equipment.
Aiol, Elye's son, heard the call to arms.
The idea of war filled him with joy. It was a good thing for him,   2375
Because he intended to exalt his name, if he could.

64.

The call to arms rang out: the noise was deafening.
As one, the French ran to get their arms,
And Louis of France imposed his prohibition:
No one would leave the city, neither knights or foot soldiers,   2380
Until the time that he commanded it.
Aiol was at his lodging, angry and sad
That he had no friend or relative
To whom he'd dare reveal his plans.
Instead, to Jesus he sent up a heartfelt prayer: 2385
"Oh, glorious Father, almighty Lord,

A Chanson de Geste

Who protected St. Lazarus from death,
Whose holy body was resurrected,
You made the sun, the moon and the howling wind.
If all this is true, and I believe it to be so,   2390
Please do this much for me today:
Let me defeat knights all alone upon the field of combat.
Let me leave them dead, captured or pleading for mercy.
May Louis find this out and all the French,
So they won't go around ridiculing me tomorrow.   2395
Alas, how they mock me, those cruel French!
If some good comes to me in the coming days,
My father would think better of his child."
When Aiol had finished his sincere prayer to Jesus,
He came up to Marchegai, his warhorse.   2400
The knight put on the saddle and the bridle,
Then donned his stout and trusty hauberk,
Then laced on his dull, unburnished helm,
And girded Elye's sword on his side.
In all the kingdom of France there was no sharper blade.   2405
Lusiane the fair came to stand before him.
She addressed him courteously.
That young woman was worthy, wise and attractive.
In her heart she loved him deeply,
More than any other man alive on earth,   2410
But he had absolutely no thoughts for her.
On the contrary, his heart was heavy for his father
Whom he had left ill, in great need,
Lacking possessions and in want
In the vast hermitage at Mongaiant   2415
And for Avisse, his mother, the worthy woman,
Whose lands had been seized through treachery
By Makaire of Lausanne, the foul traitor.
"My friend," said the worthy maiden,
"Put your arms back down, let things be for now,   2420
Because King Louis has decreed a ban:
Neither knights nor foot soldiers will leave the city,
Nor any man alive on this earth,
Until the time when he commands it.
Your arms are very old and look bad,   2425
They're not handsome, brilliant or shining.
Those knights are scoffing and full of taunts.
If you were to ride out onto the plain

❦ AIOL ❦

And became the prisoner of those traitors,
They could quickly kill you. 2430
No man alive would venture out to rescue you.
On the contrary, in my opinion, there'd be such a din
That you couldn't even hear God thundering."*
"Fair maiden, don't speak to me like that," said Aiol.
"Those people do taunt and ridicule me a lot, 2435
But little do they know of my heart and my mind,
Because if Jesus gives me his command
That I can ride out on my warhorse,
Cross the great bridge over the Loire
And find combat out there on the plain, 2440
I wouldn't refuse for any man alive
To ride out there to strike immediately,
Knock down a knight from his warhorse
And have him dead, prisoner or pleading for mercy,
So that Louis should know it and all the French. 2445
May it not please the Lord God, the almighty king,
Who was born of the Virgin in Bethlehem,
That I should remain inside here all my days."
With a heavy heart the maiden heard
That he would do nothing at all for her. 2450

65.

"My friend," said Lusiane, "noble young knight,
Put down your arms and that hauberk.
Today no knight will leave this stronghold.
The king has decreed a ban by St. Michael."
"Now that's fine with me," Aiol answered. 2455
"If any knight goes out, I'll go after him.
I don't have fine equipment or a fur cloak,
Nor do I carry a painted lance or a banner.
Those old men and young nobles ridicule me.
If I don't strike powerful blows in this battle, 2460
I'll have a shameful return to this castle."

66.

"My lord, noble young knight," said the young woman,
"Lay down those arms that you've taken up.
Today, no knight will go out of this city:
The king has decreed a ban for himself as well. 2465
Look out at these streets, how crowded they are,

🜲 A Chanson de Geste 🜲

And those huge, tall towers that are so ancient.
There are so many rich knights and ladies.
If now you were to ride out wearing your armor,
The French — who have hearts full of evil — 2470
When they spot a poor man, jeer at him.
There's nothing they won't say, for God's sake.
You're not outfitted according to their custom.
You don't have a cape of fur or ermine.
There'd be such an uproar throughout this city! 2475
I'd rather be dead and buried
Than have them cause you harm or shame.
From my point of view, I'm feeling really depressed."

67.

Her words did not deter noble Aiol at all.
Rather he came to Marchegai and mounted up. 2480
"My lady," he said, "quickly, hand me that shield.
I'm riding out into those streets to have some fun.
In my opinion, if a knight rides out of the city,
I'd want to follow him right away.
If it came to a battle or a joust, 2485
I'd rather be dead than remain here."
"My friend," said Lusiane, "you're truly courageous.
I'll just have to be content with the memory of your love.
Since I can't do any more to stop you, I'll let you go.
May you be placed under the protection of God of holy glory: 2490
Your person, your prowess and your nobility.
May he protect you from death through his goodness.
Don't be killed, captured or injured.
May he bring you back safe and sound to the city,
So that I might again speak to you. 2495
I love you more than any man born of woman."
She hands him the shield, and he took it from her.
By its straps he immediately pulled it tight against his body.
And she gave him his sharp sword.
"Beautiful maiden," said Aiol, the noble young man, 2500
"Jesus of holy glory, of majesty,
Who reigns over heaven and earth,
May he reward you for your courteous service,
And may he give me adventure through his goodness,
That it will be quickly repaid." 2505
Out through the middle of the street, away he rode.

⚜ AIOL ⚜

A hundred knights looked at him, the young and the bearded,
Ladies, maidens and young noblemen.
They were watching the battle for their amusement.
It was a beautiful sight to see.   2510
Then here came Aiol, so poorly equipped.
After that, no one spoke of the combat any more,
And they said to one another: "Let it be.
Oh, God! Where's he been hidden?
Where in the devil has he been for so long?   2515
Right now, he'd like to be in the battle;
He'd have already killed or wounded five opponents!
Today he'll avenge Fouré's death."
When Aiol heard this, he became angry.
He turned down a street   2520
And rode by a tavern.
A large rabble had gathered there.
That morning they had fought with each other and made up.
Their clothes were all in tatters and badly damaged.
The tavern keeper led them back inside and took the dice.   2525
He brought out his largest board for chess and dice.
He spoke to his companions:
"My lords," said the tavern keeper, "now listen to me.
Into this cup I've carefully poured out
Some of the finest wine in this tavern.   2530
Whoever doesn't want to begin drinking wine with us,
Let him leave my wine cellar and leave us in peace.
As for the disputes and the fighting that you've indulged in,
I can't stand arguments or quarrelling.
My friends, I want to have complete peace in my establishment."   2535
And they all answered as he wished,
Right away they sat back down to the dice game.
At that moment, here's Aiol who's passing by
In front of the wine cellar, completely armed.
The tavern keeper saw him and spoke.   2540
He said to his companions, "My lords, look out there!
I see a knight straight out of a fairy tale!
Now I'll give him a piece of my mind."
All excited, the tavern keeper rushed out in front of Aiol
And boldly said to him, "My lord, listen to me: 2545
Inside they sell good wine and drink!
Two soldiers just now played a drinking game.
One of them lost heavily and has ruined himself.

⚜ A Chanson de Geste ⚜

He says I've played with loaded dice.
Now I'm considered an honest man in this town, 2550
So I wouldn't want to be blamed in the least.
My lord, brave knight, sire, look at these dice.
One of them is small, another squared
And the third is big. Good for playing.
Hold them in your hand and look at them. 2555
My lord, if they're good dice, let me know,
And we'll conform to your just judgment,
Because we've bet and wagered on what you'll say."
Aiol replied: "Forget about it.
Never in my life have I seen anyone gamble. 2560
Ask your companions back there.
Whatever they'll say, agree to it,
Because I can't arrive at a valid judgment,
Since I've never learned anything about dice games."
"My Lord," said the scoundrel, "you're not going anywhere!" 2565
He grabbed Marchegai's bridle and pulled on it.
He backed up to right in front of the wine cellar.
Marchegai looked at him and let him go backwards
Then with his right hoof, which was large and angular,
He struck the middle of his chest. 2570
Such a marvelous blow he gave him
That it shattered three of his ribs.
His heart almost exploded.
It made him fly through the air into his tavern.
The tavern keeper certainly had miscounted the steps! 2575
The drunkard couldn't stand any more and passed out.
When he finally sat up and could speak,
He wished a hundred thousand devils on Aiol.
Aiol and his horse couldn't do anything else.
Aiol, Elye's son, kept on riding 2580
Until he entered Orleans' main marketplace.
Burghers and vendors began to mock him intensely.
They threw the lungs of their cows at him.*
"Look at that, brother Pierre," said Eldré.
"Oh, God! This knight has delayed too long. 2585
If he'd have joined the battle out there,
He wouldn't call for a truce before Christmas!
Oh, if only Hagenon, the lush, were here,
And Hersent, his broad-bellied wife —
She knows how to insult and slander anyone. 2590

⚜ Aiol ⚜

She never sees any man pass by here
That she doesn't know some joke to make about him.
If she had her large, steel knife,
She'd have already cut the tail off his nag.
This would make him more docile to lead."   2595
Aiol responded: "Leave me in peace.
You've revealed your own baseness, because you're ridiculing me
Wrongly, through great sinfulness and maliciousness.
I never did you any wrong in all my days.
When the Lord God wants it, I'll have plenty.   2600
From his bounty, he'll provide for me in abundance."
Some of the townspeople left him, taking pity on him,
Because they had heard him speak so nobly.

68.

"My lord," Houdré spoke up, "It's insane
That you've taken up your arms this morning,   2605
And you want to kill our Christian people.
Fouré is your relative, whatever they say!
Through his rashness he died outside of Paris.
You'll avenge him after compline.
With your steel sword you'll leave him in a blood-bath.   2610
Yesterday evening you spent a lot of time riding around this city.
You think you'll drive our folk mad.
Those arms you're carrying are all rotten.
It's true that Saracens have poisoned them.
A person who's wounded by them has no chance of surviving."   2615
When Aiol heard him, he became very angry.

69.

Now Aiol rides on, angry and sorrowful
Because he'd heard himself taunted and insulted.
Servants and squires continued to mock him,
Even Louis, who reigns over France,   2620
Who was in his great and vast palace,
In the morning got up from his breakfast table,
Saw the young noble Aiol in the marketplace
And the townspeople who had scoffed at him so much.
The king summoned his knights to him.   2625
In a loud voice he cried out: "Barons, look out there!
Here comes a knight who's all equipped,
Who'll want to be there for the first blows,

❧ A Chanson de Geste ❧

Who'll free my lands and my kingdom.
He'll want to bring my war to an end. 2630
He's been raised and taught by a powerful man
Who's sent him here to render great knightly services.
He'll conquer them with his lance."
When Aiol heard the king, he became angry.
He spoke to an old, white-haired burgher 2635
Who stood before him in the marketplace:
"My friend," said Aiol, "may goodness descend upon your head.
Who are those people who are ridiculing me from that solar?"
"My lord, that's the king who reigns over France,
And he's mocked and insulted you." 2640
When Aiol heard this he became very angry
And muttered between clenched teeth, so no one could hear:
"Oh, God! That's my uncle, I'm his nephew!
He shouldn't be scoffing at me at all."
If the emperor had known that Aiol was his nephew, 2645
He wouldn't have ridiculed or insulted him,
But rather he would have been splendidly equipped.
By insulting him, the king is not behaving correctly,
But very soon Aiol will indeed be avenged
When he'll strike Louis down from his warhorse 2650
With knights and foot soldiers looking on.

70.

Now Aiol rides on, angry and sorrowful
Because of the people who keep ridiculing him.
The marketplace was crowded with all kinds of people,
And different people are following him along. 2655
They keep on mocking Aiol, Elye's son.
Suddenly there appeared big-bellied Hersent,
Who was a bad-mouthed bitch,
Wife of a butcher in the important town of Orleans.
Before that, they were born in Burgundy. 2660
When they first came to Orleans,
In my opinion, they didn't have on them
Five sous in worldly possessions.
On the contrary, they were wretched vagabonds,
Suffering, starving and begging for bread. 2665
But through their frugality they achieved so much
They managed to save twenty sous' worth of deniers.
They went about lending for pawned items and at a usurious rate,*

⚜ Aiol ⚜

Until more than five years had passed.
These devils had been multiplying   2670
Those twenty sous worth of deniers that they were loaning out —
Such great wealth they were amassing —
That two-thirds of Orleans owed them money.
Ovens, mills and castles they went about buying,
And kept on impoverishing all noblemen.   2675
When once they had amassed vast possessions,
They began to deny other people their rights.
Soon they were seized by an overweening pride.
They didn't let any living man survive.
Hersent was treacherous and evil-tongued,   2680
Mean, cruel and slandering.
They went around ridiculing the city's burghers.
What she said about them caused general hilarity.
When they saw her coming, they began to shout:
"Make way for Lady Hersent!*   2685
Open a path for her to the knight, if that's her wish!
She'll tell him off in her own special jargon!"
Hersent hurried up to Aiol.
Standing in front of his horse, she seized his bridle.
She had a protruding paunch and a large rear end.   2690
...........................ugly,*
She said to Aiol in a toadying tone,
"My lord, knight, sire, now do this much for me!
From now on be a member of my household.
I'll make you a most enticing offer: 2695
It will be a long sausage, large and drooping.
We'll attach it to your lance with the sharp iron head,
So that everyone will know, big and small,
That you're part of my household from now on.
And you can go around inspiring fear because of me,   2700
Because I'm a butcher's wife, that's for sure,
But I've not sold meat for a good fifteen years.
Nevertheless I've always had that surname."
Aiol replied to her in like manner:
"My lady," said the young noble, "let me be.   2705
You've certainly ridiculed me, and I'm suffering because of it.
But one thing does give me consolation:
That you have that repulsive body
Hideous, ugly and stinking.
And don't ask me to enter into your service —   2710

68

❧ A Chanson de Geste ❧

By almighty God, those flies really love you! —
Because, in my opinion, you're their mother.
I'm sure they're finding dung around you,
Because they're following you around in great swarms."
This caused the low-life lady to have a heavy heart,   2715
But she couldn't think of anything at all to reply.
She fled away through the great throng.
The townspeople were jeering at her,
And a number of them were yelling at her:
"You've met your match, Lady Hersent!   2720
We've never ever seen any man alive
Who's dared to answer you back barb for barb!"
Then the traitor, Hagenon appeared on the scene.
He was the lord of the evil-speaking Hersent.
When he spotted Aiol, he spoke up right away: 2725
"My lord, you're not too intelligent,
Because you're going around upsetting people like that.
If I had my best sharp knife on me,
You'd pay for it right away,
Because I'd make you pay for lashing out!   2730
You're insulting the most refined butcher's wife
To be found in all of France, which is so vast and wide."
This caused such a roar of laughter to echo throughout
    the marketplace
That you wouldn't have been able to hear God thundering.

71.

When Aiol left Hersent the tripe monger,   2735
He turned to ride down along the river
Passing beside a stone house.
He heard the noisy cackling of women who were there
And who spotted him beside the house's wall.
One of them shouted to the others, "Dear companions,   2740
Raiborghe, Holduit and Geniève,
Look over there at that knight who's in a daze!
He's taken up his arms, he really looks the part!
Through his great knightly prowess, we'll get all our goats back!"
Raiborghe shouts to him in a loud voice: 2745
"Listen to me, you noble warrior.
Inside there a man is lying dead on his bedding.
You can render him an excellent charitable service.
Lend us your shield. We'll make a bier out of it.

❦ Aiol ❦

When we've carried him to St. Peter's Church, 2750
There we'll bury him on his bedding."
When Aiol, the noble warrior, heard this,
He responded to them calmly and forcibly:
"Whores, witches, enough. It's peace I want.
May Jesus, the righteous one, damn you." 2755
Then Aiol rode off along the river.
He prayed to the Lord God and then to St. Peter.

72.

Now Aiol rides away, suffering and miserable
Because of all the jeering and insults he'd heard.
But he was a worthy and noble knight. 2760
It did not matter to him in the least all they had said.
He accepts it, enduring it and suffering,
Because Elye, his father, had told him,
Had cautioned him and taught him well,
That the man is shamed who quarrels the most. 2765
A hundred young boys pursue him, big and small,
And throw at him old shoes, brown gravel,
Lungs, carrion and dung as well.
"Children," said Aiol, "get out of here!
It's doing you no good to taunt a man who's in trouble. 2770
I know full well that I'm a beggar
And in this land I don't have a relative or a friend.
Go on home with my thanks.
May Jesus, who never lied, pardon you.
I've got my own pride, no matter who thinks I'm vile. 2775
Oh, my dear sire and father, you told me
An exile from afar should hide himself."
Some of the boys turned away who took pity on him,
Because he had responded to them so nobly.

73.

Aiol came to the gate towards Berry, 2780
And he'd done to the other as he'd wanted to be done to him,
Because he was neither drunk nor reckless!
He found the gatekeeper who was supposed to serve him.
He was sitting on a block of marble.
This low-life was cruel, false and unruly. 2785
He jumped to his feet and came before Aiol.
He held out a corner of his cloak,

❧ A Chanson de Geste ❧

Folded it in his right fist and said to Aiol:
"My lord, now take my pledge, I surrender to you.
You'll do me justice, just as you please."   2790
When Aiol heard this he was heartsick,
Since he knows and hears that he's being ridiculed.
He felt like drawing his sword and he was going to strike
   the gatekeeper,
When he remembered the wisdom and good advice
That Elye, his father, had given him   2795
In the Mongaiant forest, upon setting out:
"The man who quarrels the most is the most shamed."
He thrust back into its sheath the burnished blade.
"My friend," said Aiol, "so help me God,
I know for a fact that you're just kidding with me,   2800
And I want you to be able to say anything you please,
But open that gate and let me go out
So I can join the battle I see out there.
If I win a palfrey or a good nag,
Give me your right hand, I'll give you my pledge   2805
That I'll give you that much when I return.
The agreement will be made as you wish,
I'm not a rich knight."
And the gatekeeper replied: "Listen to me.
By the faith I owe you, my fine friend,   2810
Today you're not going to leave this city.
Put your nag back in the stable:
He's eaten few oats in this month of April.
You'd behave like a devil out there.
They're armed and well equipped.   2815
You couldn't inflict an Angevin coin's worth of damage."
When Aiol heard this, he was heartsick.

74.

Now noble Aiol sits astride his warhorse,
Upon Marchegai who's dear to him.
He spoke to the gatekeeper in a friendly tone: 2820
"By your head, open that gate for me!
I'm going to enter the fray, to take part.
Give me your right hand, I'll give you my pledge.
If I win a palfrey or a good warhorse,
I'll give you your share when I return."   2825
"Those devils would fix it so you wouldn't win anything."

⚜ Aiol ⚜

When Aiol heard this, he became angry.
He muttered between clenched teeth, so no one would hear:
"God," he said, "Father who reigns over everything,
This reprobate has ridiculed me so much today,   2830
If I strike this low-life with my steel blade,
Immediately he'd have his head cut off,
But I still wouldn't be truly avenged
Of all those who've jeered at me today.
And I see before me this scruffy townsman.   2835
It makes me look better to put up with all his harangues
And all his worthless words,
Than to embark on an action
For which I would be blamed and dishonored."
Right then, the evil gatekeeper called out to him again: 2840
"Listen," he said, "my good, fine friend.
Because I can see that you're disheartened.
I want to teach you a very fine trade,
Because you obviously don't know a thing about being a knight!
Pawn that lance for four deniers.   2845
It will be good for cleaning fishing nets.
My wife has asked me for one,
And I'd gladly give them to you for it.
Your shield's worth twelve deniers.
You'll need it in town, if a fire breaks out.   2850
As for your helm, it's worth at the most three sous.
For your coat of mail, it will bring easily ten sous.
This will buy you four bushels of oats,
And you can give them all to your nag to eat.
He'll be big, strong and fattened up.   2855
He'd make a good horse for a cart driver
Who would transport wool to this marketplace.
We'd gladly buy some.
Or you can carry coal on your packhorse.
You really seem like a man who's meant for that trade."   2860
When Aiol heard this, it made him angry.
A burgher was watching him from an upper window.
His name was Kikernart, the baker.
He who was and will be, that glorious God,
May he send bad things his way,   2865
Because he was treacherous and evil-tongued!
He was a relative of Makaire, the betrayer.
Very early in the morning he had eaten

A Chanson de Geste

And drunk strong wine, which had gone to his head.
It made him undertake very foolish acts, 2870
And he had mocked the young noble Aiol.
He was leaning out of his main window.
He began to shout loudly at the gatekeeper:
"Say there! Go on! Let him go out right away!
Open the gate for him to ride on out, 2875
Because he's going to avenge us of our enemies.
If he's killed, it will bring him great honor.
You'll have four deniers from my purse
And a good gallon of my best wine.
Louis will grant all of this. 2880
You won't be beaten or insulted."
Now listen to the traitor, the coward.
Although he thought he was speaking evil, he was telling the truth.
When the gatekeeper heard him, he was overjoyed:
"My lord, knight, sire," said the gatekeeper. 2885
"Now I'll willingly open the gate for you,
Because that burgher has given me permission to do it.
I'll have four deniers from his purse
And a full gallon of his best wine.
Louis will grant all of this. 2890
I won't be beaten or insulted.
Now I'll willingly open the gate for you,
Since through your friendship I've won these things.
Give me some of your warhorse's tail.
I'll make a leash for a greyhound out of it. 2895
My landlord just recently asked me for one."
"Gladly," said Aiol, "just come over and pull it out."
The low-life approached the steed —
The coward, the scoundrel, may woe come to him!
He didn't even try to pull out the tail, 2900
Quite the contrary, he intended to knock Aiol off his warhorse.
He thought he could make the youth fall down to the ground,
So that the laughter would break out again.
Marchegai didn't recognize him. He raised his hoof.
He dealt the wretch a marvelous blow, 2905
Striking him down below his jaw
And breaking three of his ribs.
He landed upside down in a dung heap.
"Coward," said Aiol, "did he hurt you?"
"Yes," replied the scoundrel, "and he's maimed me too. 2910

⚜ Aiol ⚜

You didn't warn me about his kicking.
May your horse go to the devil today!
He ate oats last night and is in a lot better shape."
And Aiol answered him: "I do think so."
He swore to the Lord God, the true one of heaven: 2915
"If you don't open the gate for me willingly,
You'll lose your head to this steel blade.
No man on earth will be able to protect you,
Since I see that my requests do me no good."
He drew it a half a foot out of its sheath: 2920
When the wretch saw the gleam of the blade,
With what strength he had left, he got back up
And came rapidly to the gate.
When he had pulled the iron bolt towards himself,
With the gate's crossbar he struck Aiol with such a blow   2925
That it almost made him fall over backwards,
But the knight didn't even feel it
Because the noble was gladly galloping out.
The wretch went to his lodging and went to bed
And didn't get up for months. Aiol didn't care!   2930
Aiol galloped out on his warhorse.
Now may God protect him, the true one of heaven,
So that he's not killed, captured or shamed,
And may God punish all those
Who mocked and insulted him so much.   2935
"Oh, God," said Aiol, "show me your mercy.
Today they've ridiculed and insulted me so much.
It would be of great use to my father
If I performed such deeds against knights
For which I would be honored and esteemed.   2940
So now I wouldn't renounce for any man on earth
Going to strike the very first one
Of the four robbers without delay.
If I can't bring them to justice by my arms,
Then I'll just let happen to me whatever comes along.   2945
I'll fight with no man forever more,
Because I haven't been taught or learned how.
Lady, St. Mary!" he said, "help me.
From now on, I want to be your knight."

☙ A Chanson de Geste ☙

75.

The robbers hastily all returned*	2950
Straight to their rear lookout post.	
They carried their lances straight upwards	
And the wind whipped their pennants.	
They're taunting Louis, Charles' son,	
And shouted loudly on the bridge.	2955
None of the knights dared come out,	
None went to enter into combat with the scoundrels.	
But before the sun would set,	
They would be singing a different tune.	
The boldest of those in the fight	2960
Wouldn't want to be there for Rheims or for Soissons,	
Or for all of King Charles' kingdom,	
Because Aiol mounted up, the well-born man,	
Upon Marchegai, with his spurs on.	
He galloped swiftly out through the gate	2965
And has soon ridden across the bridge over the Loire.	
He is taking no peer or companion with him.	
He calls upon the Lord God by his holy name.	
Between clenched teeth, he begins a prayer:	
"Oh! Glorious sire," said the noble man,	2970
"Who became incarnate in the Virgin,	
And was born of her, it's known by all.	
There rose in the sky a shining star,	
The three kings observed it from their kingdoms.	
Then each one left his home.	2975
All three of them you assembled without error.	
They came to Herod, the evil king.	
He asked them where they were going and what they were seeking.	
They hid nothing from him, but told him all:	
The prophet had been born and they were searching for him,	2980
Who would be King and Lord of all the world.	
Herod was sorely grieved in his evil heart,	
Since he wanted no lord but himself:	
He definitely believed himself to be king of the whole world.	
He treacherously hid his true intent from them:	2985
'Go search him out, my lords,	
Then return here to me right away.	
I'll go to adore him; I'll be his liegeman.'	
The three kings replied that's what they'd do,	
However, they were ignorant of the deceit	2990

❧ Aiol ❧

And of the evil intent of this wretched man
Who wanted to kill them through treachery.
The father of the world guided them knowingly.
They searched for the King until they'd found him.
Three offerings they brought through a covenant: 2995
Gold, myrrh and frankincense. They brought these because
By these three offerings we know you!
We give you gold because you are the King of this earth;
Frankincense since we recognize your priestly state.
You understood the mind of these three nobles, 3000
Because no one can hide himself from you.
You received them all without disdain.
For their gifts they'll have a gracious reward.
Expertly you guided them, Father of the world.
You protected them from Herod, the evil king, 3005
Who intended to kill them treacherously.
And when this evil man saw that they had gone
And had made a mockery of the idea of coming back to him,
He felt great anger and sorrow in his cruel heart.
He had all the children in his kingdom sought out — 3010
Every one of them, near and far —
And chose the boys from them
Up to two and a half. No older ones were chosen.
Then he had them decapitated. They were innocent!
If this is actually true, as we believe, 3015
That you are the King and Lord of the whole world,
Keep me safe today from death and capture
And put combats on my path by your holy name,
That I may help my father, who needs it,
And my gracious mother, deep in the forest. 3020
All these worthless people have mocked me so much today
And have made jokes about my coat of arms.
If I don't fight these four who are leaving,
I'll have no self-respect, no pride at all."

76.

When Aiol rode out from the streets of Orleans, 3025
He hadn't gone far before he saw
The four robbers up on his right.
And when Aiol spotted them, he recognized them right away.
Because he was neither a coward nor an empty-headed fool,
He got down on the ground off his horse 3030

⚜ A Chanson de Geste ⚜

And cinched up his saddle girth tightly and energetically.
A hundred knights were watching, young and gray-haired,
Ladies and maidens, who are looking down from the city walls.
They said to one another: "Now I've seen him!
The battle has been put off. You won't see any more of it.　　3035
That young knight is drunk; he's had too much.
My lord, come on back, while you still can!
Let them leave, don't disturb them!
Killing someone is a great and hideous sin.
No better knight than you has ever been seen.　　3040
You'll get your payment as soon as you're back inside.
At this coming Pentecost you'll be clothed
In an ermine and thick bear skin cloak.
These are the two choices: you won't belong any longer
To those who are lacking in possessions, you can be sure of it!"　　3045
When Aiol heard this, it caused him pain.
He devoutly prayed to King Jesus:
"Oh! Glorious Lord, who reigns above
And who came down to earth for us,
You were placed and stretched out upon the cross,　　3050
And were struck by the lance into your side,
Which made blood and water flow down.
Longinus wiped his eyes with them and could see,
He beat his breast, it was true,
And you pardoned him, Father Jesus.　　3055
Those without faith received their just punishment:
They're lying deep down in hell.
If truly, gentle God, that all of this was true,
I place myself in your hands alone, in those of none other."
He had retained very well his father's advice　　3060
That anyone who seeks him will not be defeated.
Then he shortened the strap of his shield
And drew all his arms towards him —
No count or duke had a more well-built body —
And he swears to the Lord God and his strength　　3065
That he would rather be dead and defeated,
Than not to have struck one or the other of these robbers.

77.

Aiol remounted Marchegai.
A lush jokingly jeered at him:
"My friend, knight, my lord, you with the bay horse.　　3070

❧ Aiol ❦

You've gone far enough, I'm sure of it.
So give me your arms, I'll do the jousting!
I'll do this first joust for you!"
    And Aiol prayed to St. Nicolas:
"If truly, dear sire, my belief is right, 3075
You saved the virgins from the base trial,
The three clerics you raised from the dead, I know it's true,
Put combats on my path — the ones I've wanted —
So that I can help my father, whom I left in the forest,
And Avisse my mother, his faithful wife, 3080
Who fainted away at the thought of losing me when I left.
These burghers are ridiculing me, this I know well,
Because of the luxurious clothing I'm not wearing.
But I believe that, if it pleases God, the glorious one,
They won't see the month of May pass 3085
Before I'll avenge myself of those who are mocking me.
These burghers are harassing me. Well I've seen it."

78.

The robbers were returning along their way.
They spotted the young knight Aiol, who was following behind them.
He's pursuing them calmly, at a nice pace. 3090
He's not pushing the pace too hard, because he knows very well
He'll need his strength for knightly deeds.
    "My lords," said Nivart, "let's stop for a moment.
That burgher is pursuing us — what a mistake!
Have you seen the shield he has hanging around his neck? 3095
I'll have the horse, who's approaching fast,
And Sanse will have the shield hanging around his neck."
    "And I'll have the coat of mail off his back," said Aliaume.
    "And I'll have the helm without gold," said Fouke.
    "If he tries to defend himself, I'll kill him. 3100
Who cares if his body is left lying in a ditch?"

79.

Nivart pulls on the reins of his horse, turning it towards
    the young knight.
But Aiol pricks and spurs his mount, charges to strike him
On his shining gold shield.
Aiol pierced his coat of mail, inflicting serious damage. 3105
Right through the middle of Nivart's heart, he planted his lance.
Along the full length of his lance, Aiol struck him down dead.

⚜ A Chanson de Geste ⚜

A hundred knights are watching them, the big and the small,
Ladies and maidens, elegant and refined,
All of whom had ridiculed him this very morning. 3110
And they're continuing to mock him, they're not stopping!
"Oh, God! Who was that who just fell?
I see that your tarnished shield is still in one piece.
The bay nag is still on his four feet."
Lusiane the fair heard it well and saw 3115
This was Aiol, the young knight, who had struck Nivart down.
She prayed to the Lord God of paradise:
"Sire, merciful father, who made everything,
May you have mercy today
On the youth from afar, who is so poor 3120
He has no friend or relative in this land.
Bring him back safe and sound by your will
So once again he'll be able to speak to me,
Because I love him more than any thousand men God made
And if I can't have him, I won't have a husband." 3125

80.

Foucart called out to his companions:
"My lord barons, let's stop here a while.
It seems to me this scoundrel has caused us great shame
By killing Nivart, our companion.
We'd be better off dead than not avenging him." 3130
He pricked his warhorse with his spurs
And charged swiftly to strike Aiol
Next to the saddle bar, near the saddle horn,
So that Foucart put his lance into Aiol's flesh,
Into the middle of his thigh, a little up. 3135
On the other side Foucart gashes him by his hip.
The brave young knight is gravely wounded.
Bright red blood is trickling all the way down to his spurs,
But Aiol strikes back with such force
That he ripped Foucart's tunic and his coat of mail. 3140
Aiol slashed Nivart's liver and his lungs
And rapidly sliced out his heart,
Finally striking him down dead from his saddle bow.
Louis, Charles' son, is standing at the palace windows,
Up in the tower of his vast palace. 3145
He shouts to his men: "Look at that!
The impoverished knight whom we were taunting!

❧ Aiol ❧

By St. Denis of France, he is worthy!
Go get on your arms, we're going to rescue him!
I don't want him to die because of our disdain. 3150
I'd rather lose Rheims and Soissons
Than to lose such a good knight!"
The French run to arm and equip themselves.
That day, even the emperor armed himself,
Because he wanted to see Aiol up close. 3155

81.

The battle was engaged and the combat.
The French quickly ran to arm themselves.
Even Louis, the king, armed himself,
Because he wanted to see Aiol up close.
But he won't find out that Aiol's his nephew. 3160
Sanse and Aliaume find themselves in a tight spot.
They charge Aiol in great anguish.
Aiol has no chance of getting his lance back,
So he drew his sword, struck immediately,
And shouted "Monjoie!" in a loud voice. 3165
"Sons of bitches, traitors, evil criminals!
You have no right to lay waste to this land.
Today the day has come when you'll pay for it!"
"Sanse!" said Aliaume, "Come on!
May this youth be damned for his foolish arrogance. 3170
Oh, God! What knights he's taken from us!
Let's leave and flee, while we still can!"

82.

Sanse and Aliaume turn their backs to flee,
And Aiol pursues them at a full gallop.
He's retrieved his lance from one of the dead. 3175
They had criticized Marchegai, but he's a swift horse.
He had thin hindquarters and long bones,
And his four well-shod hooves were large and well formed.
Aiol lets him run with great power.
On Sanson's shield he strikes such a blow 3180
That he pierces the hauberk on Sanson's back.
Aiol plunged his huge lance through his body
And strikes him down dead before him.
Aliaume flees towards the woods
And Louis pursues him with his great force: 3185

⚜ A Chanson de Geste ⚜

Seven hundred and ninety-five, all told,
All noble knights with strong shields,
And then the foot soldiers, who brought up the rear.

83.

Aliaume takes off fleeing into the woods,
And Aiol pursues him, spurring his mount. 3190
He brandishes his sharp, naked blade
And goes to strike Aliaume when he reaches him.
Aiol dealt him such a blow as he went by
That he sent his head flying away across the field.
Here comes Louis, spurring his mount. 3195
He found the soldiers of Berry resting in a valley.
Of the surprised household, I don't know anything.*
The French go to strike them immediately
With stout, sharp-pointed lances.
There you would have seen so many sorrel and white-flecked steeds 3200
Fleeing across the countryside trailing their reins
And so many good knights dead and bleeding,
Who remained lying on the field.
Oh, God! What a beginning for a youth!
He shouldn't be ridiculed from now on, 3205
But rather at his will be most lavishly served!

84.

The battle and the strife were very great.
When the count of Bourges saw Louis
And his own noble court surrounded and in extreme difficulty,
You can say and believe that he was distressed! 3210
My lords, this noble count of whom I'm speaking,*
You don't know who he was or where he's from.
There are few minstrels who could tell you.
They don't know the story and have not learned it.
Because of this ignorance, a few people taunt them severely 3215
And the majority considers them as fools,
Because they haven't had a glimpse of the entire, accurate story.
Someone who begins a discourse, I'm sure of it,
When he doesn't know how to finish it once he arrives at the end,
Causes himself to be considered an idiot and a fool. 3220
But I'll inform you accurately as to where the count came from,
And from what lineage, since I've learned it.
He was the nephew of Elye, the noble duke,

❧ Aiol ❧

Who wrongly was driven from his lands,*
The son of Marsent, Elye's sister, with the shining face,   3225
Aiol's first cousin, of whom I'm speaking.
That's why he was waging war against King Louis,
Because he drove Aiol's father out of the country.
Aiol did not know him; he had never seen him,
Because if he had recognized him, he wouldn't have harmed him.   3230
Quite the contrary, he would have helped him bring his war
   to an end.
When the count saw his men killed and slain,
Now you can say and believe that he was distressed.
He shouted to those of his men who were still alive:
"Save yourselves, my lords, whoever can, flee now,   3235
Because I can no longer support you,
I can no longer help or protect you."
He took off fleeing through the middle of the melee.
Never was there a Frenchman, no Poitevin,
No Norman, no Angevin, no Manceau,   3240
Who dared pursue him for even one lone step,
Because they knew full well he was bold and courageous,
Except only for Aiol, of whom I'm speaking.
When he saw that the count was fleeing all alone,
He spurred Marchegai and took off after him.   3245
Aiol caught up with the count on a hillside,
And cried out to him: "This is not the way it's going to be!
I can plainly see that you're the leader here.
You'll leave me hostages before you go.
When you escape from me, I'll have a guarantee   3250
That never again you'll wage war on King Louis."
When the count understood that resistance was futile,
He looked at Aiol and when he saw him
He clearly recognized from his unburnished shield
That he had been dealing blows in the thick of the fray.   3255
"Lord God," he said, "father who never lied,
Here before me is the young knight with the bay nag,
Who today has killed and slain my men.
God, by your pleasure, let me exact vengeance for this.
It's certain I intend to deal him a great blow."   3260
He quickly turns around towards Aiol,
And Aiol rapidly comes back towards him.
Both of them exchange huge blows.
May God, who never lies, protect them now,

❦ A Chanson de Geste ❦

The two first cousins, according to his pleasure, 3265
So that neither the one nor the other be slain there.
They trade wondrous blows when they clash,
Which cause their shields to split.
The count shatters his lance. He'll conquer no more,
But the old, dried-up one he can't parry, 3270
Because there was no stronger one in any land.
Aiol thrusts it with force and it holds up well,
So that the shield hanging from the count's neck is severely damaged,
And the coat of mail on his back is ripped to shreds.
Aiol's lance thrust just passed by the count's side, 3275
It was only by a very lucky accident that it didn't enter into his flesh.
Aiol then struck him with a great knightly blow,
Using the force of the count's warhorse, who was charging towards him.
And the strong, young knight, who's battling so fiercely,
Split apart the horse's front breastplate, 3280
And all the horse's harnesses snapped as well.
Aiol also smashed the saddlebow's rear,
And both the stirrups were badly damaged.
From his swift horse, Aiol strikes him down.
The count is lying all stretched out on the ground, 3285
Stunned by the mighty blows he had received.
Don't be astonished if he was distressed.
Aiol drew his sword and attacked the count.
Upon his head he went to strike a blow
That caused the helm's jewels and gemstones to shower
   down to the ground. 3290
If Aiol had struck another blow with his burnished blade,
He would have severed the count's head from his body.
Just then the count cried out: "Noble knight, have mercy!
I'm surrendering to you the sword I have here,
But keep me from death, with God as your help." 3295
"I don't know what will happen to you," said Aiol,
"Because I'm turning you over to King Louis,
The emperor of France, of St.-Denis.
You've laid waste to all his lands,
Now he'll do with you as is his pleasure." 3300
So that all will witness his act, the great and the small,
Aiol goes over and seizes the count's helm by the nose guard,
And turns him over to Gerard and Amauri,
To Hugon, Nevelon and to Henri.
These are members of the king's court. 3305

❧ Aiol ❧

"My lords, guard him for us," said Aiol,
"And the king will do with him whatever is his pleasure."
These knights replied, "We'll do that!"
"Alas!" said the count, "How I've been betrayed!
Elye, dear gentle uncle, I'm shamed! 3310
Wrongly were you driven from this land
And dispossessed by King Louis.
I'm the son of your sister, so help me God,
Lady Marsent the fair with the shining countenance.
I wasn't able to accept this shame, 3315
Quite the contrary, I sent for my relatives and friends,
The mercenaries from France that I could assemble.
I shared all my treasure with them,
And waged war on King Louis.
More than a thousand of his men I've killed since then. 3320
This war would never end as long as I'm alive,
But it's over now that I've been captured.
I'm sure that if the king holds me prisoner
No ransom can stop him
From having me tortured or hanged." 3325
Aiol, Elye's son, heard all of this,
Because he was near the count and understood it all.
All the blood in his body went racing through his veins:
"Lord God, Sire, Father," Aiol said,
"Who's ever seen such a stroke of fate? 3330
I'm sure that this man is a close relative
If what he's saying is not a lie.
He was the son of Marsent, my aunt, this I've heard.
She was my father's sister, I'm sure of it.
This noble, well-born count I see before me 3335
Has been waging war on the king for my sake
And has fought this brutal war for my good.
It seems to me I've repaid him badly,
When I just now handed him over, when I captured him.
But I didn't recognize him, so help me God! 3340
God, advise me what to do, by your pleasure,
Because if I keep him prisoner, he'll be tortured,
And if I let him go, I'll be in a bad situation,
Because the king of St.-Denis will say
That I've accepted a huge bribe from the count. 3345
I'd always be accused of treason.
I don't want to reveal my identity just yet,

⚜ A Chanson de Geste ⚜

Not until I've done battle and captured counts,
And fought wars and invasions,
But I'll hand him over, it can't be avoided. 3350
But before I do it, it will be agreed
That I'll get a ransom of fine, solid gold,
Horses, palfreys and costly warhorses.
And if I can't reach an agreement,
I'll bring a tough lawsuit against him. 3355
By that holy Lord who made the world,
Before the count is ever killed or executed,
I will have struck a thousand blows with my burnished blade,
Because I can't fail my first cousin."

85.

Aiol forcefully seized the count. 3360
He delivered him to Gerard, a vavassor,
And to Gautier, Hugon and Nevelon.
"My lords," said Aiol, "keep him for us.
I'm entering the battle immediately.
If I can conquer anything there, you'll have your share." 3365
He looked into the melee, into the battle,
And spotted Louis the emperor,
Judging from his costly arms that he was one of them.*
Aiol still isn't able to recognize lances or banners
And doesn't know who is from Flanders or Brabant, 3370
Or who is from Poitou or Gascony.
Instead, that day he is attracted by the most splendid arms.
There where he spots the finest and most costly,
He spurs his mount to approach the best-equipped knights.
He's not concerned to joust against those wearing plain armor. 3375
Armed, he bore down boldly upon the emperor.
He spurs Marchegai, charges directly at him,
And goes to strike his uncle with a great blow.
From Louis' shield, Aiol cuts off the principal flower
And strikes the king down, in front of everyone. 3380
Louis' hauberk saved him from death that day.
Aiol drew his sword and ran towards the king.
Louis vigorously leaped to his feet.
He was filled with terror. He greatly feared his attacker,
Because he was convinced that he'd soon be dead. 3385

❦ AIOL ❦

86.

Louis was standing surrounded by his closest favorites.	
His sister's son struck him and made him fall.	
Aiol drew his sword and ran at Louis.	
The king saw it coming and feared it greatly.	
He covered his head with his good shield.	3390
Aiol dealt him such a blow with his steel blade	
That he split the shield down to its strap.	
Aiol would have knocked him to the ground again,	
But fourteen Frenchmen came running,	
Completely enraged by the plight of their lord.	3395
They were attacking Aiol, Elye's son,	
When Louis shouted: "Hold back!	
Don't touch him or strike him down	
Until I've spoken to him.	
Noble young knight, you're very courageous.	3400
My name is Louis of Mont Laon.	
You've struck me down in front of my entire court,	
You've gravely wounded and shamed me.	
If I'm captured by a knight,	
I should lose my crown and be deposed.	3405
But we're not there yet, be aware of it.	
Before I allow myself to be captured or defeated	
You still have many a blow to strike,	
And you'll have received many of mine in return.	
I trust so much in God, the King Jesus,	3410
That by a single man I won't be defeated,	
And a hard-fought battle you won't be lacking.	
But first of all, tell me where you've come from,	
And from what kind of family stock you come	
That has allowed you today to hold my knights at bay.	3415
You've completely destroyed the Beruiers for me,	
You've captured the count of Bourges for me;	
Never because of Rheims, Beauvais or Laon	
Would I be so happy, you can be sure of it!	
I who am king of France, you've struck me down,	3420
And have wounded me in several places.	
On whose side do you want to be, then, what do you say?"	
When Aiol heard this, he was aggrieved;	
He dismounted, got down off of Marchegai:	
"Sire, for the love of God, have mercy, because I'm your liegeman.	3425
I didn't do it on purpose, may Jesus be thanked!	

⚜ A Chanson de Geste ⚜

Mount up right away and with vigor;
The people of Berry are defeated and ruined.
A valuable war prize has fallen into our hands
When the count of Bourges surrendered to you."   3430
When the king heard this, it caused him great joy.

87.

The battle and the combat were won.
Taking him by the wrist, Aiol turned over to the king
The count, who'd sworn to wage war incessantly.
"You're my rightful lord — I know it's true.   3435
I'm turning him over to you, on your promise
That you will not treat him wrongly or unjustly.
Take ransom for him, this is my plea."
"This I will do, good sir," said the king.

88.

The king took the count of Bourges prisoner.   3440
Louis then turned the count over to Hugon and Nevelon:
"My lords, keep him for us," the king said.
"Take him away to Orleans, my good town,
And let him be left to languish in the depths of my prison.
Because my war has been ended, thanks be to God,   3445
By this noble young knight whom I see before me."
When Aiol heard this, he stepped forward
And spoke in a loud voice so that all would hear him:
"Emperor of France, speak to me,
I'll speak in your stead, since I'm the one who captured him. 3450
If it is pleasing to God, who never lied,
May he not be held prisoner in any country,
Never in any land may he be mistreated,
Neither in fetters, nor chains, nor put in prison.
Instead, take hostages   3455
And let him return to his lands
Until he's back on his feet financially,
And he's united with his friends;
Then he can return with your permission.
He can once again become your liegeman and your friend.   3460
You should be very happy, King Louis,
If you can arrive at an agreement
And receive as your own such a friend
As the count of Bourges, whom I see here.

⚜ Aiol ⚜

You should not mistreat your liegemen, 3465
Rather you should help and support them.
Your justice should uphold both great and small."
When Louis heard this, he was filled with joy:
"Young knight, you're very noble and well born.
I'll do all of this for him, as you wish." 3470
"Sire," said Aiol, "may all thanks be to you
When you're willing to go along with everything I've wanted.
Thus the count will be completely freed of debt, by St. Denis.
It won't cost him two Parisian sous,
Except that he will hold his lands from you." 3475
When the king heard this, he burst out laughing,
And when the count saw this, it made him happy
Because he had been convinced that he was going to die.
He came forward and knelt
At the feet of the emperor and surrendered. 3480
His hands joined together, he became the king's liegeman.
From the king he received his lands and his fiefs.
The emperor of France accepted his homage.
They are reconciled and now are friends
Through the very process that I've just described to you, 3485
And France's betrayers are most distressed.
Makaire of Lausanne, the liar to heaven,
The evil flatterer, when he saw this,
Seemed almost insane with rage and grief.
Immediately, he came running to Louis. 3490
He intends to use some of his flattering ways.

89.

The count was now liberated and proclaimed free of debt.
He immediately went directly to his lands.
With him there remain those of his force
Who after the battle were still alive. 3495
The emperor of France delivers to them a guarantee of safe passage
As far as Orleans, the wealthy town.
Aiol remains with the king of St.-Denis.
Louis calls for him and begins to address him:
"My friend, where are you from? Now, don't lie!" 3500
"Sire, I'm from Gascony, from Mount Olive.
My father's lying there sick, at death's door.
He's lacking food and clothing.
He hasn't done any chivalric deeds for a full fifteen years.

❧ A Chanson de Geste ❧

They call him Gautier of Mount St. Elie. 3505
He sent me to France to seek help,
And I first arrived in this town yesterday evening.
At her lodging, Isabelle, the noble and well-born,
Took me in for the love of God.
May it please the Lord God to grant her the reward she deserves. 3510
But I'm not sure about going to court
Because of my total lack of costly attire.
I have no ermine, no gray fur coats.
I fear that your Frenchmen might well mock me.
So go ahead and retain me, good king, through your largesse. 3515
You'll never receive better service from any man."
"Upon my head!" said the king, "You won't lack for anything!
Because I'm giving you Étampes, free and clear,
The town, the marketplace and the abbey,
The laws, the tribunals and the customs tariffs." 3520
"Thanks be to you, good King Louis, lord!"

90.

"Lord," said the king, "good and noble youth.
I can clearly see that you are worthy and brave.
You've won the battle and the combat.
You've captured many horses and palfreys. 3525
You couldn't have had a better single day.
Of them, I grant you two hundred and eighty horses,
Mont Laon in France and Étampes."
"Thanks be to you, good sire, King Louis,
I'll take the horses, but don't be troubled 3530
When, after having generously made me this grant,
I refuse to accept from you, sire, the two castles,
Because I won't consent to anything at this time
Until I've fought in battles and combats
And ended wars, in the sight of all the French. 3535
And if I can demonstrate my right to even more,
With all of your French believing it as well,
And all men should say that it's my right,
Through your graciousness, my lord, then give them to me."
"By my faith, I won't be found lacking," said the king. 3540
"In front of my entire court, I grant them to you."
Aiol then replied as a well-born man:
"And I will serve you in good faith."
When Makaire heard this he was deeply troubled.

89

⚜ Aiol ⚜

He was a foul traitor of the worst kind.   3545
Rapidly he came to stand before the king.
He drew Louis to one side, into a private corner.

91.

Makaire of Lausanne was a slanderer.
He was insane, treacherous and an evil flatterer.
He runs up to Louis to advise him.   3550
Makaire called to the king and addressed him:
"My lord, rightful emperor, you're making a mistake
By giving that boy all these warhorses.
If he gets two or four, he'll have plenty!
As an exile from afar, this gift will make him arrogant,   3555
And he'll be off tomorrow, just as he arrived only yesterday."
"Be silent, craven," said Louis. "No more of your entreaties.
Whore's son, traitor, foul flatterer,
Never in your entire life did you ever do any good!
You've taken my men from me, making me angry.   3560
Elye, my brother-in-law, the noble warrior,
You had me wrongly drive him out of France
And sever and exile him from my kingdom.
My sister is in exile, and I'm poorer for it:
Wrongly and sinfully you hold your lands.   3565
I don't grant it at all by my own personal decision,
Because if an heir were born to his wife,
The world would know full well that he's my nephew."
Aiol looked at him and became very angry
When he heard what the flatterer was saying.   3570
He'd heard the king use Makaire's name and clearly recognized it.

92.

Aiol, Elye's son, looked at Makaire
And saw that he had disinherited his father,
Who had accurately described the situation to him
When he said farewell to Elye in the dense forest,   3575
How Makaire the traitor had treated him criminally.
When Aiol heard this it made him angry.
It set his blood boiling throughout his body.
Aiol thought that if he could bring it off,
He intended to sever Makaire's head from his body.   3580
However, for now, it's better for him to wait.
He doesn't want to be accused of rushing things.

⚜ A Chanson de Geste ⚜

"Sire," said Aiol, "let's discuss this another day.
Since he's only seeking to do the right thing for you, don't
    blame him."
"My friend," said Louis, "I see it completely differently.   3585
Makaire's trying to do me great harm and bring me down.
Such a worthy man he's taken from me, it makes me angry.
Elye, my brother-in-law, who was so noble,
Through Makaire's treason lost his fiefs,
And now Makaire holds his castles and his estates.   3590
My sister is in exile, I'm fully aware of it,
And it makes my heart heavy with grief.
Never in my life will I have bright days."
"Sire," said Aiol, "hand over to me now
The horses that you say you've taken.   3595
I'll have them led to my lodgings,
Because I've been somewhat wounded in the thigh.
I'll have it treated and regain my health."
"My friend," said Louis, "go ahead and take them.
No matter what anyone thinks, you'll have them,   3600
Because you've won them through your prowess."
Louis had all of the horses led into the square.
Two hundred and eighty of them he separated out of the herd,
Of the very best he could find.
Aiol had them led to his lodging   3605
So all eyes in the city were upon him, and
All the bells were ringing throughout the city.
Aiol will no longer be insulted or ridiculed,
But instead, lavishly served and honored.
He'll yet give back his fiefs to his father.   3610

93.

Now the French begin to reenter the city.
Squires and servants come out to meet them.
They start to talk among themselves:
"Well look at that! Come see the knight who's coming,
Who's brought our war to a close.   3615
Never has any knight on earth done such deeds!"
Hagenon called to his wife:
"Lady Hersent, we're in deep trouble!
Yesterday you ridiculed that knight.
Be aware that your mockery will cost you dearly."   3620
"My lord," said Hersent, "not so fast:

❧ Aiol ❧

I'll patch things up completely with that knight."
She took off running like a devil.
She rushed out through the gate, chasing after Aiol.
At the side of the king who reigns over France,   3625
She went to seize Aiol's stirrup.
In her loud voice, she began to shout:
"My lord, for God's sake, I'm begging you for mercy.
I jeered at you at the beginning of yesterday.
Now I'll willingly set things right   3630
With fourteen barrels from our cellars
Full of costly, well-aged Auxerre wine
And fourteen huge, full slabs of bacon
I had carted over to Isabelle's lodging."
Before Aiol's arrival there they had been off-loaded.   3635

94.

When Aiol first entered into Orleans
Louis himself, who reigns over France,
Rode at his side in a show of friendship,
Passing his right arm around Aiol's neck.
The king loves him more than any man on earth,   3640
Because Aiol has brought his war to a close.
Aiol looked out ahead and saw the gatekeeper,
Who gave him such a hard time when he first rode out.
Aiol called to him and addressed him:
"Had you opened the gate for me, it would have been even
   better for you."   3645
Aiol handed the gatekeeper the reins of a good warhorse,
And the latter bowed down all the way to his feet.
When the king saw this gesture, he became very glad.
He called to Aiol in an affable tone
And started joking with him in a friendly manner: 3650
"Noble, fair youth, lord, upon my head,
I've never seen any man on earth
Pardon ill-will so easily.
To those who were ridiculing you at the beginning,
I see you giving them good warhorses,   3655
And you pardon them too willingly.
You could drive them all out of France,
Banish and exile them from my lands,
And I'd grant it most gladly."*
Aiol answered him sagely and wisely,   3660

❧ A Chanson de Geste ❧

As a man who was raised correctly:
"Sire," said the youth, "you know well
If I wanted to wage war against all of those
Who mocked me yesterday at the beginning,
I wouldn't be lacking for warfare for the rest of my days. 3665
You, personally, insulted me.
I definitely heard you speaking from your solar.
I'd have to wage an ugly war against you."
When the king heard this, he was filled with joy.
He gave Aiol a hug as a sign of friendship, 3670
And to show his affection, kissed him repeatedly.
Aiol left the king and said farewell.
He returned back to his lodging,
At the home of Isabelle, his aunt, whom he won't abandon.
She who helped him in his poverty, 3675
In his riches, he doesn't intend to forsake her.
When Aiol dismounted from his warhorse,
Five knights, who served him gladly and willingly,
Came out to hold his stirrup.
From now on, Aiol will have squires, 3680
Cooks, majordomos and bottle bearers.
Lusiane the fair came out to meet him,
And when she saw him bleeding so profusely,
It caused her so much suffering she fell into a faint.
"Daughter," said Isabelle, "take it easy. 3685
You've let your friendship go too far.
Right away, dear daughter, concern yourself with getting
  him into bed."
"My lady," said Lusiane, "most gladly."
The emperor of France, who held Aiol very dear,
Sent him a hundred pounds of good deniers 3690
And twenty silver goblets and ten of solid gold,
Salted meat, wheat and excellent vintage wine.
The king had all of this carted to Aiol's lodging,
Enough to be able to feed ten knights well,
Pay his expenses and maintain a household. 3695
To his hostess, Aiol delivers such a gracious reward,
To her who had honored and lodged him:
He gives her thirty of the most expensive horses
And twenty silver goblets and ten of solid gold.
Isabelle had all the slabs of bacon stored in her larder, 3700
All the good wheat in her hayloft,

❧ Aiol ❧

The barrels of wine in her cellar,
And then put in her stable the good warhorses.
"My lady," said Aiol, the brave warrior,
"Search throughout the city for me, 3705
The surrounding area and the kingdom.
If there is a nobleman or knight
Who may only possess little wealth, few earnings,
All spent to ransom himself while in captivity,
Have him come to speak to me in friendship. 3710
I'll give him some of the possessions I've won."
"My lord," said the lady, "I'll be glad to do it."
Following Aiol's request, she dispatches messengers,
She assembles the noblemen, the knights
And well-educated foot soldiers, freemen all. 3715
These men came gladly and willingly.
Over two hundred come before vespers.
Aiol sent thirty of the most respected burghers
And he added costly cloaks and clothing,
Tunics stretching down to their feet, 3720
Which the youth gives to the knights,
And after that, gave them the good warhorses.
Now Aiol has a household of knights to support,
And with them he will serve the king who reigns over France.
Elye, his father, will yet be happy, 3725
And Makaire will be angry and irate.
The news was going around the marketplace
And up there in the vast and spacious palace.
A messenger goes to announce to the king
That the knight is showing such great largesse. 3730
When the king heard this he was filled with joy.
He cordially called for his steward
And had a proclamation announced throughout the city.

95.

"Now listen to me," he said, "noble knights.
Merchants and burghers, you of the marketplace, 3735
Who know how to supply merchandise,
And sell costly, rich, gray ermine fur,
Coats of mail, helms and pikes,
And good palfreys and warhorses,
And solid gold, silver and deniers, 3740
Slabs of bacon, wine and costly fish.

A Chanson de Geste

Whatever Aiol, the noble warrior, wants to have —
Throughout an entire year —
Have it all sent to his lodging.
Tell the servants and let it be put into writing: 3745
Don't ask of Aiol a single denier.
The king will gladly pay for everything!"
When the burghers heard this, it filled them with joy.
Now they know that they are going to rake in profits.
Aiol took one hundred marks of gold deniers 3750
And confided them to a messenger with a warhorse,
Along with some luxurious, costly clothes of scarlet
Lined with ermine down to the feet.
He sent them to his host, straight to Poitiers,
To him who, in an act of friendship, had given him a ring 3755
And the shirt and the hose that Aiol needed.
Without delay, the messenger left,
Who was well bred and courteous.
Now he's travelled and ridden so long
That in five days he came straight to Poitiers. 3760
His hardships had been great; he'd endured much.
He searched for the burgher until he succeeded in finding him;
Aiol's instructions were good, and the messenger was well-informed.
He greeted the burgher in the name of the true one of heaven
And on behalf of Aiol, his lord, whom he held dear. 3765
In Aiol's name, he gave the burgher the good warhorse,
And afterwards, the hundred marks' worth of gold deniers
And the very expensive clothes of scarlet.
The burgher received them; he was extremely happy.

96.

The burgher of Poitiers took the deniers 3770
And the scarlet clothes and put them on.
Then he called together his relatives and friends.
When they were together, he said this to them:
"My lords, for the love of God, who never lied,
Do you remember that handsome youth 3775
With the shriveled-up lance and the tarnished shield,
A rusty helm and the bay nag
That you saw pass by here the other day?
He was very poor, in tattered clothes, and distressed,
Since the townspeople were mocking him because of his horse. 3780
I heard you mock and insult him.

⚜ AIOL ⚜

He seemed to me to be a well-born man, and I took pity on him.
I lodged him in my house, as an act of charity.
I had him put on a shirt and breeches.
I gave him my ring when he left. 3785
He's a very good knight, brave and bold.
Now he has a great abundance of furs and ermine
And valiant mercenaries* to serve him.
He captured the count of Bourges the other day
And all alone killed four knights 3790
And brought one of King Louis' wars to a close,
Which had seemed as though it would never end.
He sent me a hundred marks' worth of Parisian coins
And this luxurious robe I'm wearing
And this swift steed you see here. 3795
My lords, I'm showing all this to you to inform you
That if you serve a worthy man, you're well taken care of."
And they all replied, "Well spoken!"
Then Makaire went to Louis.
Discreetly he addressed the king. He said to him, 3800
"My good and gracious king, you've been given bad advice
That has caused you to find such great worth in this boy.
The very first day that he came here,
You gave him fourteen score of horses
From the very best, the most select 3805
Your Frenchmen had captured in the battle,
But he's so treacherous and holds such bad opinions.
Unfortunately, he didn't even want to keep one of them.
He sent them to the freemen of this country
And gave and shared all of them. 3810
Now he's sending for the freemen of your city
And added gray furs and cloaks
And rich fur-lined clothing, making much to-do.
He's having all them divided up equally.
Never did he want to hold back a single one for his own use. 3815
Before this year has passed and is over,
He'll have them all beholden to him.
He'll then become the all-powerful king,
And you'll be disinherited, a poor beggar.
If you believe me, my king, by St. Denis, 3820
Tomorrow you'll drive him out of your country.
What's your business with him? What's he doing here?"
"Quiet, wicked man! Let me be!" said Louis,

❧ A Chanson de Geste ❧

"Whore's son! Oath-breaker! Perjured of God!
You've never done any good in your entire life! 3825
This generosity comes to him naturally, from his good stock,
So that he esteems and values free men.
You've taken such a man from me, and it's distressing to me:
Elye, my brother-in-law, the noble duke,
You had me exile him from this country, 3830
Now he's languishing in exile in another land.
My sister is exiled with him, and that saddens me even more.
I don't know to what land he's fled.
Aiol's one of his kin, this I do know,
Because he's brought my war to a complete end. 3835
May it please God now that he's Elye's son,
And if I knew this to be his true identity right now,
I'd return his fiefs to him to hold.
He'd be the standard-bearer of my country,
And he'd have my entire kingdom in his keeping." 3840
This caused Makaire to become deeply distressed.
His grief almost made him go completely mad.

97.

Aiol took a hundred pounds of Orleans coins,
Had made two pairs of embroidered robes
And placed them in a leather trunk. 3845
Inside he also placed velvet and coverings,
Luxurious bed clothing that he owned,
Solid gold and silver and other possessions.
He strapped the trunk on a swift Norwegian horse.
He sent it to his father by a townsman. 3850
He's made him swear on saints' relics three times,
Upon relics of the Holy Cross,
That he would reveal nothing about his mission,
Nor would he utter a word, as bad as things might get.
The well-mannered messenger departs. 3855
Aiol accompanies him as far as Blois.
He's done so much good in the land
That the French have great love for him.

98.

The messenger turns to leave rapidly.
He was worthy, well reared and very brave. 3860
He'd loaded the hundred pounds on his mount.

❦ Aiol ❦

He first rides through Blois
And came to the great city of Tours.
I don't know how many days he stayed there.
All down his route he travelled, long and wide,   3865
And came to the chapel of Mongaiant.
There he found Elye, the noble Frenchman
And his gracious wife, such a worthy woman.
Right away he asked for lodging:
"My lord, give me shelter, for the sake of God the great,   3870
For the first joy of Bethlehem,
Where our Lord first appeared."
"I'll be glad to do it," said Elye, "come on in."
The messenger dismounted right away.
He sat down on a bench beside the duke.   3875
Now he'll give Elye the news concerning his child,
Which will make his heart glad and joyful.

99.

The messenger dismounts, who was a worthy man.
Elye addressed him, began to speak to him:
"Master," said Elye, "where are you from?"   3880
"My lord, I'm from Orleans, the great town."
"Did you happen to see a son of mine, dear, kind friend,
A noble, well-born youth, his name is Aiol.
I entrusted him with my arms and equipment
And sent him to France, to the king's court.   3885
But he went there quite poor and needy
And lacking clothing and destitute.
I don't know if we'll ever see him again."
"Certainly," said the messenger, "I do know him.
Your son, Aiol, is a very good knight.   3890
The other day he captured the count of Bourges.
Single-handedly, he killed four other knights.
Louis, the emperor, loves him well,
More than any other member of his court.
He sends you this warhorse of great value   3895
And a hundred pounds of deniers. I have them all with me."
When Elye, the noble man, heard this,
For the whole world, he couldn't have kept from weeping.
He wept from pity, overwhelmed by deep emotion.
Both he and Avisse were engulfed by their sentiments.   3900

❧ A Chanson de Geste ❧

100.

When the lady heard about her dear son,
She breathed a heartfelt sigh
And from her eyes flowed tender tears.
"Tell me, brother envoy, may God help you,
Did my child ever talk to Louis, 3905
And did he ever go to the royal court?
He left here poor, in tatters and destitute."
"Yes," said the courier, "so help me God.
Aiol, your son, is a very good knight.
The other day, he captured the count of Bourges, 3910
Killed four other knights,
And brought Louis' war to a close,
Which the king never could bring to an end.
He sends you this costly, swift warhorse
And a hundred pounds of Parisian coins 3915
And a trunk full of garments to clothe
You and his dear father, the gracious duke."
The messenger takes all the possessions and gives them to her.
Avisse the duchess receives them.
The meal was all ready, and they sat down to eat. 3920
They had barley bread in abundance with stream water.
They didn't live on anything else in this land.
When they had eaten, they made up their beds,
But such great poverty had overcome them
That the messenger had neither a mattress nor a cushion 3925
Except for the moss in the woods on which he stretched out,
And he seized a stone and placed it under his head.
He tossed and turned. He couldn't sleep
Until daybreak of the following day.
The messenger leaped to his feet, dazed and dizzy, 3930
His bones were hurting from the hard bed.
He swore to the Lord God, who never lied:
"If I were now in France, in my country,
I'd never try to come to this land.
For a long time now this duke has been exiled. 3935
They all should have been dead by now,
Those who wrongly drove him out of his lands.
Don't be dismayed in the least, noble and gracious duke!
This year will not have passed and gone by,
Before you'll have your lands back, free and clear." 3940

⚜ Aiol ⚜

He left the hermitage and took his leave.
He then returned rapidly to Orleans.

101.

Now Elye was rich and his wife as well,
And the envoy went back to France.
Aiol saw him coming, and it filled him with joy.   3945
He went to greet him and gave him a kiss.
He asked the messenger about his father and how he was doing,
And the courier replied: "My lord, in God's name, well,
But the noble knight is gravely weakened.
For the love of God, I beg you to help him."   3950
"Gladly," said Aiol, "by my head,
But I want to forbid you to say —
If you want to enjoy my friendship —
To utter anything about my father's condition
To burghers, servants or knights,   3955
Nor to anyone on earth under heaven."
"I certainly won't, dear lord, by my head.
I won't say anything to anyone on earth,
To a nephew, an uncle or a wife.
Before I'd do that, I'd let myself be drawn into crime."   3960
Aiol was worthy, wise and well-educated.
He doesn't intend to forget the messenger's reward.
He gives him two silver marks and a warhorse.
The messenger now has a gracious reward for his service.

102.

Now Elye was wealthy and well-supplied.   3965
Aiol was in Orleans, the fortified town.
The king loves him intensely; he does not hate him.
Makaire of Lausanne cannot love him:
He was evil, proud, troubled and angry.
I don't know what devil made Makaire think   3970
The king would seize Aiol's fiefs as he did with his father.
It was now at Pentecost, in the summer season,
That the king held his court, assembling many nobles.
There were very many sovereign lords, princes and peers;
Aiol, Elye's son, serves at dinner.   3975
Makaire of Lausanne was distressed
When he sees the young knight raised so high.

⚜ A CHANSON DE GESTE ⚜

103.

The court the king held was extremely large.
There were a great many powerful dukes and marquis.
Aiol, Elye's son, is serving them wine.   3980
Suddenly there appeared an envoy from the Saracens
That the king of Nubia had sent there.
He was called Tornebeuf* in his country.
Never had an uglier man ever been seen.
He had one large eye and the other was small.   3985
He didn't have a stitch of clothing on him. He wasn't dressed.
He could run on foot faster than a nag
And carried an oaken cudgel.
It had three hundred solid iron nails.
Never did God make any man, great or small,   3990
Who could scarcely move it with his two hands,
If he found the cudgel on a knoll.
The Saracen came to Orleans, the principal town.
You'd have seen people fleeing before him,
Ladies and maidens of noble mien,   3995
Leaning over walls to see him.
Tornebeuf made his way, never stopping
Until he entered King Louis' main hall.
Never was there a gatekeeper or a doorman
Who would deny him passage through those doors.   4000
The emperor of France was seated at the dinner table,
When the dolt raised the cudgel he was holding
And smashed it down on a slab of marble, shattering it.
There was no knight that this didn't cause to tremble,
Even the emperor who reigned over France,   4005
When Louis looked directly at Aiol:
He was the one of all his barons the king most trusted.

104.

The number of courtiers was large; the hall was packed.
There were many princes, high-ranking nobles all.
Then the foul knave appeared — may God do him harm! 4010
He raised his huge cudgel high
And struck a marble slab, shattering it.
There was no knight present whom this didn't cause to shiver.
Aiol stands before the king, goblet in hand.
Rapidly, he set it on the table.   4015
He came over to the foul knave and immediately said to him:

101

⚜ Aiol ⚜

"Get out of here, you cur, may God do you harm!
Don't cause any disturbance in this hall,
Or I'll have you beaten, just like a donkey!"
And Tornebeuf replied, "I'm an envoy   4020
From mighty King Mibrien, who reigns over Arabia.
He sent me to this borderland.
Now, by my head, I'll deliver my message."

105.

"My friend," said Aiol, "are you an envoy?
So tell us what news you bring. What do you want?"   4025
"I'm the envoy of King Mibrien of Nubia.
I shouldn't have to be on guard for good or against evil,
Nor should I be beaten or insulted.
He has sent me to Louis,
And I'll deliver my message from beginning to end.   4030
No man on earth will deny me this."
"My friend," said Aiol, "come and eat first."
And the envoy replied: "I need it."
He throws down his cudgel, then sits down.
Aiol has two knights serve him.   4035
One of them brings him water right away,
The other, a towel to wipe himself off.
Aiol had him brought five whole loaves of bread —
Even the smallest one of them, without a doubt,
Would have made a good meal for a peasant —   4040
And two pork roasts, each two feet long,
A heron, two geese, three golden plovers
And a quart-sized goblet of veined wood —
Aiol had it brought full of aged wine.
Thus the rogue got what he needed.   4045
He completely emptied his huge goblet.
What he left uneaten would not be worth two eggs.
"My friend," said Aiol, "do you want anything more?"
And the pagan replied, "I'm satisfied."
He seizes his huge cudgel and leaps to his feet.   4050
Now he'll deliver his message without delay.

106.

When the rogue had eaten, he sprang to his feet.
He came over to his cudgel and grabbed it.
He called to Aiol and said to him,

⚜ A Chanson de Geste ⚜

"Tell me, noble young man, where is Louis,   4055
The emperor of France, of St.-Denis?"
"My friend," said Aiol, "see, he's right here,
In those great marten furs, in that ermine.
Those noble barons serve him, whom you see here."
When he spotted Louis, suddenly Tornebeuf shouted to him.   4060
"My lord," said Tornebeuf, "let me be heard!
Hear and listen to me, by your grace.
Until I've spoken and delivered my message,
Hear and listen to what brings me here.
This is the message from Mibrien the Arab: 4065
'Wrongly you wear your crown. I challenge your right.
Mohammed and Apolin are more worthy
Than your God whom you serve.
Wrongly you hold the lands that Charles held.'
Mibrien calls you to battle, he's all ready for it.   4070
On leaving Gascony, at Mount Olive,
He won't leave you a castle, tower or city,
House, fortress, vineyard or farm."
When the emperor heard this, he was sickened.
He was ashamed that the French had had to hear this.   4075
Louis summoned four sergeants-at-arms and said to them:
"Take this foul apostate right away, this infidel,
Cut off his nose in the middle of his face immediately
And poke out his right eye, so that he's shamed,
To dishonor Mohammed and Apolin."   4080
When the French heard this, they seized Tornebeuf
By the order of King Louis.
They threw him down on his back
And flung a huge door on to his chest.
With their sharp knives of burnished steel,   4085
They would have cut his nose from the middle of his face
And poked out an eye to shame him.
Aiol stormed in among them and dragged Tornebeuf away from them.
He led him off to his lodging and protected him there.
He had Tornebeuf bathed and then dressed him   4090
In a shirt and breeches of white linen.
A harnessed mule, well-equipped for travelling,
Aiol had brought for his personal use.
He gave Tornebeuf one hundred sous upon his leaving,
And made the pagan swear and firmly pledge   4095
When he arrives in the kingdom of the Arabs,

🌸 Aiol 🌸

He will not speak badly of Louis.
Tornebeuf sets out on his way, all along his road.
He returned as far as Pamplona.
He travelled so many days, that he arrived there.   4100
The pagans were joyous when he arrived,
But their joy was to turn to sadness and grieving.
Mibrien addressed him; he said to him:
"You're arriving all decked out and well equipped.
By Mohammed, who dressed you up in this manner?   4105
Were you in sweet France? So tell me!
How is King Louis doing these days?"
And the envoy replied, "He is very gracious.
He's served by a marvelous court.
No man on earth could afford its cost.   4110
I delivered my message to him without interruption.
Louis immediately had me captured and seized by the French.
They threw me down flat on my back on the ground,
Then slapped a huge door on my chest.
With their sharp knives of burnished steel,   4115
They would have slashed my nose from the middle of my face,
In order to shame Mohammed and Apolin,
If it weren't for a noble and gracious young man
Who recently became a knight.
The French call him Aiol, the young noble.   4120
He's better than all the princes who are here.
The other day, he captured the count of Bourges
And brought King Louis' war to a close,
Which seemed as if it would never end.
The French made him a lord in their country   4125
By the command of King Louis.
He swears to the Lord God who never lied
That he'll send his own liegemen and his allies,
And that they'll come to seek you out in this country.
He won't leave you holding a single castle   4130
Or house or fortress, vineyard or farm.
A giant iron collar with great nails
He'll have put around your neck, so he says,
Then he'll lead you off to France to St.-Denis.
There, he'll have you burned in great torment   4135
If you refuse to believe in the God of paradise,
Who was born of Mary and became man."
These words caused Mibrien the Arab to feel shame

❧ A Chanson de Geste ❧

For the love of the pagans, who had heard him.
He was holding a polished javelin. 4140
He would have stabbed Tornebeuf with it and gravely injured him,
When the pagans seized the king and pulled him away.
"My lords," said the king, "he's surely betrayed me.
Now hear from this rogue how he's lied.
It's not just for nothing that they've dressed him so well. 4145
He did not deliver his message faithfully."
He swears to Mohammed and Apolin:
"King Louis will not be safe in France.
Rather I've sent for my own liegemen and my allies,
Until I've assembled four thousand of them. 4150
Then I'll go off to France to Louis,
And I'll take Orleans and then Paris,
Étampes, Beauvais and St.-Denis,
Hainaut, all of Brabant and Cambrésis.
When I've conquered the valley of Soissons, 4155
At Aix-la-Chapelle which Charles held,
I'll have myself crowned by my supporters."
Now hear about this foul rogue king of the lying god:
It's my opinion that his bragging is insane.
If God protects Aiol, the noble youth, 4160
The month will not have passed or have finished
Before he'll be waging war in Mibrien's country
As far as Pamplona the good city,
Which will make the pagan king's heart heavy with grief.
Aiol will ride off with his daughter, she of the bright visage. 4165

107.

Here we will leave the Saracens
And the arrogant boasts that the foul king was making,
And we will tell you more of Louis,
Of Aiol and of Makaire, who's betrayed God.
Very numerous was the court that the king was holding 4170
By his right in Orleans, his good city.
There was a large number of powerful dukes and marquis.
They bet and wagered on a horse race
And great losses were suffered by evil Makaire,
Just as you will hear as I tell the tale. 4175

⚜ Aɪᴏʟ ⚜

108.

It was at Pentecost at the king's court
When Louis of France held a race.
Oh, God! So many good warhorses were there that day.
Marchegai was not at all among the worst.
Aiol put the bridle on the horse he so loved.   4180
He led him out into the square in the sight of everyone.
With the fold of his ermine robe he wiped his horse's forelock,
His neck, shoulders and hindquarters.
"My friend," said the emperor, "you are so worthy!
Come over here and sit beside us."   4185
This made Makaire of Lausanne angry.
He was evil, arrogant, miserly and treacherous.
Very angrily he called out to Louis:
"Sire, rightful emperor, you're not acting wisely.
Now foreigners have the upper hand at your court,   4190
Who aren't your nephews or the best.
This boy came to France poor and wretched.
Be aware that one of these days he's going to leave.
If one of your vassals causes you grief,
All of us will have to suffer the consequences.   4195
If the French believe what I'm saying, when that day comes,
They'll go off and leave France to you alone.
Never will you have the least help from them.
You've raised up this foul scoundrel to such a place
That fourteen score of the best horses   4200
The French conquered in that battle
You gave them to him, sire, on the very first day."
"Silence, foul rogue!" said Louis the emperor.
"Whore's son! Traitor! Felon! You're green with envy!
I won't love you even one more day!   4205
You drove Elye from his fiefs.
Now he's in some other country — I don't know where —
With my sister, exiled from my kingdom."
Aiol looked at Makaire and was furious.

109.

Aiol, Elye's son, was full of anguish   4210
Because of the slanderous talk by Makaire, the betrayer.
He hated him more than any man alive
And would have immediately begun a fight with him,
But he was not acquainted with Makaire's relatives,

❦ A Chanson de Geste ❦

And he didn't know well yet the king of the Franks,   4215
Nor did he want to reveal his identity in too much haste,
Before he has fought great battles and combats
And brought wars to a close in front of everyone.
That's why Aiol answered him courteously:
"My lord, why are you placing so much blame on me?   4220
I have done you absolutely no wrong.
I'll make amends, where it's appropriate.
I'm ready and able to do so before these Franks.
From today on, if you say anything against me
Or utter anything that is offensive to me,   4225
I won't take it lightly, this you can believe."
"Silence, foul rogue," said Makaire, "don't talk so much,
Because very soon, I'll have you grieving and suffering.
Your horse is not among the swiftest.
The other day he wasn't at all so fiery,   4230
Rather he looked like a peasant's nag
Who's been unhitched from a plow: worn-out, slow-paced,
And three hundred children were making fun of you.
We won't hear from him in today's race."
It hurt Aiol to hear these words.   4235

110.

Aiol, Elye's son, was very distressed
By Makaire's insults that he'd just heard.
"My lord, why are you reproaching at such length
Both me and my horse? It's depressing,
And whatever lies you tell, I've got to listen,   4240
Because you're a powerful man and I'm just a fool.
But as for my horse, it's upsetting that you've insulted him.
He's handsome, well fed and well equipped.
There's none better in this country,
Except for King Louis' dapple gray.   4245
My lord, that horse I'll not criticize one bit.
It's my rightful sovereign's horse. I don't intend to insult it.
But when it comes to your horse, I'll be happy to challenge it,
To race over a league down an entire road,
And if mine can win, then you promise me   4250
A thousand marks of sterling silver and one hundred of pure gold
And I'll have your horse to do my bidding.
If your horse defeats mine, I'll do the same thing."
"By my head," said Makaire, "I accept your challenge,

⚜ Aiol ⚜

Swearing to it by the Christianity God placed within me." 4255
Here's the race wagered and bets laid,
Which afterwards caused such an uproar to be raised in the court
And led to one hundred deaths — indeed, seven score.
"By faith! It's all right," said Louis,
"If Aiol loses Marchegai, I'll completely cover his loss, 4260
Because I'll immediately give him five or six horses
From among the best in this country.
He brought my great war to firm conclusion."
And thus Makaire was quite deeply distressed.

III.

Now the bets on the horse race were made, 4265
And Louis had his horns sound,
His oliphants tuned and ringing out.
Oh, God! So many good horses were led out:
Sorrels, bays, dappled grays and paints.
Marchegai was not at all among the least praised. 4270
Aiol put on his bridle and mounted up.
Very soon he returned to his lodging
With Isabelle his aunt — that's where he went.
Lusiane, her daughter, called out to him.
She ran out to meet him to ask: 4275
"What bets did you make on the race?"
"Fair one," said Aiol, "you'll see very soon —
Before the sun has set."
Right away, he seized arms and armor,
Because the young knight is afraid of betrayal. 4280
Now he dressed himself with them and put them on,
And on top of that, a very costly tunic,
Which was of vermilion scarlet cloth — the folds are wide.
He strapped on a huge sword with a golden hilt
Beneath his tunic — it's not at all visible — 4285
And he swears to the Lord God of majesty:
"Today may you allow my pride to show itself
Down there in that horse race through the meadow.
From the start of the race, You'll be my companion."
He rode rapidly to the racecourse. 4290
He pulled up next to Makaire
Just as Louis had the horns sound:
His oliphants harmonized and rang out.
Whoever has a good horse can't hide it.

A Chanson de Geste

Each one wanted to put his horse to the test. 4295
The emperor himself was in the meadow.
When he saw them all ready to race,
In a loud voice he shouted: "Barons, mount up!
The rider who first comes into town,
And rides up first onto the bridge over the Loire — 4300
If my court has witnessed this deed —
He will have won the race and conquered
A thousand marks of sterling silver and one hundred of pure gold,
And will do as he wishes with the horses."
Then Aiol spoke up as a judicious person: 4305
He said to Makaire, "Ride on ahead.
You're a powerful duke from a noble family.
I'm a foreigner from another kingdom.
I came to the king to serve as a mercenary.
And if you please, because you are worth more, 4310
I'll concede you an advantage through my good nature —
A full two hundred feet of measured ground —
Before I ever move from the middle of this field.
If under these conditions I can catch up with you and pass you,
Then the knights and squires will say 4315
That I've done you a great kindness."
"What, you foul cur!" said Makaire the treacherous one,
"What a perjurer you are and what a traitor!
You really know how to shame and dishonor worthy men."
Then Aiol spoke as a prudent man: 4320
"My lord," said the youth, "you are gravely wrong.
I've listened to your extremely ugly words.
You never seem to want to choose moderation.
But in spite of this, I've given you an advantage.
I'll not hold you back, so get going!" 4325
Then Makaire the traitor took off
When he heard the sound, spurring, in great haste.
Aiol remained motionless in the middle of the field
Until Makaire had ridden two hundred feet of ground,
Or even more if the distance were measured. 4330
And when the king saw this he became very angry.
Full of fury, he shouted at Aiol.
"Brave youth," said the emperor, "what are you doing?
Are you going to let Makaire ride off like that?
If he can arrive first in the city 4335
And ride up on the bridge over the Loire,

❧ Aiol ❧

He'll have won all the prize money,
And it will be very painful for me to lose it."
"Sire," said Aiol, "don't be afraid.
I have such great faith in God of majesty   4340
And in this good horse that you see here
That soon I'll have caught and passed him."
He spurs Marchegai on his flanks
With the spurs of the purest gold,
So that he makes bright red blood spurt out,   4345
And Marchegai carries him off with great pride.
Anyone watching would have seen him gallop by the others,
Splitting stones and causing them to fly,
Making sparks fly from his horseshoes.
The great and the small, he passed all of them.   4350
He drew even with Makaire, then passed him.
And when Aiol had passed him and had left him behind,
He looked around at Makaire fiercely and shouted:
"My lord," said Aiol, "come on, hurry up!
Spur on your swift warhorse.   4355
Ride a little bit faster if you can,
Because I'll assure you it's true,
If you ride so slowly, you're sure to lose."
Aiol, Elye's son, kept riding
Until he came to the city gate.   4360
He stopped up on the bridge over the Loire
And looked back towards the fields.
He saw all the French horses paused,
But Makaire's warhorse is so worn out
That he couldn't take one more step.   4365
Some young knights came along, and as a joke,
Started beating Makaire's horse with sticks and cudgels.
They also threatened to cut his tail off
And called him "worthless nag."
Aiol was in Orleans, the fortified town.   4370
Knights and burghers were watching him
And saying to one another: "This knight is very worthy.
Jesus definitely lighted his way down that race course.
He seems more like Charlemagne than any man alive.
I think it comes from his lineage and his family,   4375
Because may it please the Lord God of majesty
That Makaire have his head cut off
And be turned over to evil devils,

A Chanson de Geste

And that this knight might have the dukedom of France
That Elye held, who was so noble. 4380
Oh, God! How well he'd be endowed with estates,
If he were at the head of such a household."
Now Makaire appears, all overwrought,
Carrying a large, square stick.
He intended to deal the youth Aiol a blow, 4385
But Aiol drew his sword with the gold hilt
That the noble had under his tunic,
And charged Makaire with great ferocity.
Aiol would have severed his head from his body,
When he was restrained by Bernard, Guinemer, 4390
Sanse, Amori and Lord Quare.
"Step away, my lord! Don't do it! Let it be!
Makaire has powerful relatives.
He's duke of Lausanne, the mighty city.
Look, here's his large family, all assembled. 4395
They would soon have wounded and killed you,
You'd have no chance of escaping alive."
When Aiol heard this, he became very angry.
He knows full well that they're telling him the truth.
The young knight backs off a little 4400
When he remembers his father's advice
And the counsels in the dense forest.
One of Makaire's nephews came to them,
The son of his sister — I've heard it said —
A new knight, recently dubbed. 4405
He'd heard his uncle threatened. It made him angry.
He didn't dare assault Aiol with his fists
When he saw him holding the lettered blade.
He seized a large, squared lance
That a squire was holding in the middle of the field 4410
And went to strike Aiol with it.
His blow landed in the middle of Aiol's chest,
And tore his tunic of scarlet,
But he was saved from death by the hauberk
He had donned and put on. 4415
He shatters his lance and broke it.
Aiol, Elye's son, held firm, the bold knight.
He still was holding his lettered blade.
He went to deal the foul rogue a blow
And struck him upon his head. 4420

⚜ Aiol ⚜

Down to his teeth Aiol made the blade glide,
Which knocked him down and killed him.
"You won't be healing from that one, foul rogue!
Whatever shape our quarrel may take, you'll stay right here!
You'll never get up unless they carry you. 4425
I've made peace and reached an accord with you.
Now I have fewer enemies in this kingdom.
God protects me from others through his goodness."
When Makaire saw this, it made him angry.
With his loud voice, he began to shout: 4430
"Where are you, my relatives," he said.
"You who hold towns and cities from me,
Haven't you seen this foreigner
Who wounded and killed my nephew
And before my eyes, he has slain him right here? 4435
If he gets out of this alive, he'll be bragging
Throughout his entire life. He'll be joking about it."
And his relatives replied, "He can't escape."
There were more than fifty members of his family,
The nephews of Ganelon and Hardré, 4440
And the relatives of foul Makaire.
They charged Aiol with great furor,
But they had not brought a single arm,
Intending to batter Aiol with their fists,
While Aiol still was holding the lettered blade. 4445
He charged into the mass of Makaire's relatives.
To his right and his left, he began to slash.
Wherever his blows land, that person cannot survive:
It's not worth sending for a doctor to treat him.
Aiol killed more than fourteen of them on the spot. 4450
His liegemen looked at him,
Those to whom he'd turned over all his riches,
And they said to each other: "Look over there!
There's that noble knight of great goodness.
How his heart is full of fierce pride! 4455
How very well he defends himself.
And we have sworn to him on saints' relics
We would never fail him in our entire lives —
By my faith, we've all solemnly sworn —
When he's attacked right under our noses, 4460
If you want to help him, let's get going!"
There were more than fifty young knights

⚜ A Chanson de Geste ⚜

Who rushed to their houses and lodgings
And got maces and cudgels
And stout lances and lettered blades. 4465
They hurried back to the fight
And dealt great and marvelous blows.
There they rescued Aiol through their great, fierce pride.
There many a knight was wounded and killed.
The king came running to break up the combat. 4470

112.

Louis heard the loud noise and sees the battle.
He shouts to his men: "Take him for me!
Watch out, don't hurt that traitor!
I'll administer my own justice to him, if you don't mind,
According to the role he's played in this uproar." 4475
And the French said to him: "It's your right."

113.

The French all came together there
And immediately seized Makaire.
They all ripped off his equipment.
Louis swore to almighty God: 4480
"Never will he get out of prison in his lifetime
If he doesn't bring back Elye, my brother-in-law, to me alive!
Whore's son! Coward! Foul deceiver!
Deliver a thousand silver marks to Aiol right away
And the gold that was part of the wager." 4485
"Sire," said Makaire, "Who's saying I won't?
I'll give him the warhorses and the equipment."
The agreement was executed according to Aiol's wishes.

114.

"Sire," said Makaire, "by God's mercy,
I'll give him many horses and furs. 4490
I'll respect the agreement as he wishes.
Then I'll go back to Lausanne where I came from.
I never want to enter this country again."
"Silence, foul cur," said the emperor. "That's not the way it will be.
You'll never leave here in your entire life 4495
If you don't bring my brother-in-law back to me alive.
Whore's son! Oath-breaker! Liar before God!

❧ Aiol ❧

You drove him out by force from this country,
And you had him wrongly exiled from France."

115.

Louis addressed his counts and dukes 4500
And shouted to them in a loud voice:
"Seize this rogue! This forsworn of God!
Throw him into my prison, down to the lowest depths."
And they did it right away. They delayed no longer.
The bells ring for vespers, and they all go there. 4505
Throughout the whole city the report spread.
People said they were at the race, that they saw it:
Aiol's good warhorse vanquished all other mounts.

116.

The king came out of church, followed by his courtiers,
And took the youth Aiol by the mantel. 4510
King Louis said to the young knight:
"I've been pleased by the horses you've won.
Now you'll be companions, you and Jobert.
Hilaire of St. Lambert will be the third.
The other day they asked me, by St. Marcel." 4515
"Sire," said Aiol, "according to your pleasure.
If it's what you want, it's fine with me."

117.

Aiol was a brave and courageous knight;
Hilaire and Jobert were very upstanding.
They became companions before the king. 4520
On saints' relics they took oaths, pledged their loyalty,
That one would not fail the other, no matter what happened.
"Barons," said the emperor, "now you are three.
Now you can better wage my war
And impose your will throughout my lands. 4525
I declare to you, French barons," he said,
"The Saracens are attacking me most unjustly
And are in Pamplona — I know it's true.
A pagan said it here, and I believe him.
He came to defy me in front of the French. 4530
Do you think, my lords, that this worries me?
Lords, noble knights, who will go there for me?
Certainly, whoever would deliver this message

⚜ A Chanson de Geste ⚜

Would have my thanks for the rest of my life
And would tell Mibrien that he should be expecting me, 4535
And that he would do well if he were to leave my lands to me."
To this challenge Normans and Hurepois remained silent,
And the Flemish, Bretons and the French.
Woe to him who would dare to raise a finger,
So great is their fear of Mibrien, the mighty king. 4540
Aiol, Elye's son, was well versed in courtly ways:
He led his companions away into a discreet corner.

118.

Aiol addressed his companions:
"Listen to this," he said, "my lords, barons.
Haven't you heard what Charlemagne's son had to say? 4545
He bemoaned in front of everyone
That the fiefs Charlemagne conquered by his spurs
The Saracens are rapidly seizing,
And are all prepared for war. Let's get going!
They're killing huge numbers of Christians, 4550
Ladies, maidens and little children.
My lords, for the love of God, let's be on our way!
We'll bring along our horses and our arms,
And once we're in that land, let's stay there.
I think we shouldn't come back 4555
Until we've done battle with the evil-doers —
Combats, which will cause our fame to echo across the land."
And they replied with great love:
"My lord, we will do your pleasure,
Because for no reason would we fail you, 4560
But rather do whatever you will. We'll grant it."

119.

The three barons went back when they'd finished their counsel
And sat down among the ranks of the noblemen.
The king who reigns over France was still grumbling:
"Barons," said the emperor, "by all the saints in heaven, 4565
Can't I find in my court a knight
Who's willing to go to Pamplona to deliver my message?"
Germans and Bavarians still didn't say a word,
And Normans, Bretons, Flemish and knights from Poitiers.
Woe be to anyone who might rise or stand up, 4570
So great is their fear of the Saracens and King Mibrien.

❧ Aiol ❧

Aiol, Elye's son, leaped to his feet.
In the entire court there was not a more handsome knight,
Nor one who's more ready and ripe for battle.
None could speak better and deliver a message to an
   important personage.   4575
He came to stand before the king of France
And spoke loudly so everyone could hear:
"Sire, rightful emperor, be calm and listen to me.
Saracens are waging war against you, and it makes you angry,
And they're in Pamplona, safely lodged in that fortified town.   4580
My companions and I, who are worthy men —
Whom you've given me, dear sire, and who've sworn loyalty —
We will go to Pamplona to deliver your message
And on your behalf challenge their right to your lands."
"My friend," said the king, "I can't grant this.   4585
You have vigorously brought my war to an end.
I wouldn't want to lose you for the city of Orleans.
I'll find many envoys that I'll be happy to send."
"Sire," said Aiol, "may it please God in heaven
That no one else be sent in my place,   4590
Because no one should hesitate to defend his lord
In that hour when he sees that his sire has need of it."
"My friend," said the king, "I'm even angrier.
You can tell mighty King Mibrien for me
That he wrongly holds the land to which I'm the legal heir   4595
And which Charlemagne conquered, my esteemed father.
Let King Mibrien come to me here in Orleans to have justice done,
In Paris or in Chartres or in Bourg St. Michael
Where I'll be, and my court will be even larger.
Have him and his men baptized,   4600
And if he doesn't want to do it, don't hide it from him:
I'll be coming after him early this summer.
There won't be a city or town that doesn't lie in ruins,
Or tall stone tower or castle that won't be shattered.
If I can seize him, get him in my hands,   4605
No one has ever died an uglier death.
I'll have his body shamed and dishonored."
"Sire," said Aiol, "I'll deliver it well,
And even quite a bit better, God willing."
He left the palace when he had taken leave.   4610
They went back to Isabelle's lodging to spend the night.
They enjoyed a very pleasant evening together

⚜ A Chanson de Geste ⚜

And after supper, went off to bed.
Aiol is asleep in his bed and has painful dreams,
Because Makaire's relatives sought each other out, 4615
And there were as many as ten of them, the evil renegades.
They gathered in a hiding place in an old church.
Said Ferant of Lausanne, Makaire's nephew:
"Now listen to me, noble knights:
How dishonored and shamed we are! 4620
Humiliated and abased by a foul foreigner,
Because through him our uncle's been thrown into prison,
And our entire great lineage, shamed and dishonored.
Now he's the king's favorite and chief counselor
And is going to Pamplona to deliver his message. 4625
Tomorrow morning he's leaving. There'll just be the three of them.
But if tonight we could get going,
We could set up an ambush in the Cinquefoil Forest.
Tomorrow we could hack off all his limbs there.
He would not be avenged by anyone. 4630
We don't know where he was born, what land he comes from."
The ten rogues swore to each other — the great evil cowards —
That they'd not fail each other, even if their limbs were cut off.
They swore Aiol's death on the church's holy relics,
Then they mounted their swift warhorses 4635
And hung their quartered shields around their necks
And held in their fists their stout, sharp lances
And attached their costly standards to their stout lances.
The foul rogues were well armed
With hauberks, burnished helms and steel swords. 4640
During the night they rode out of the city of Orleans.
All night they continued to distance themselves from the city.
They set up an ambush in the Cinquefoil Forest.
May the Lord destroy them, he who sits in judgment over all!
They were there all night long, up until daybreak. 4645
The next morning, our messengers got up at dawn.
Lusiane worked hard to get them ready to go.
Isabelle assigned to them three valiant squires,
And they carried their shields and their sharp swords.
They were born in Soissons, sons of Count Gautier 4650
And Aiol's first cousins, but he didn't know it.
Before vespers, he's going to have great need of them.
They put the burnished steel helms into arms chests,
Put into coffers their double-layered hauberks,

Led with their right hand their good, swift warhorses 4655
And carried their shields and their sharp swords.
The lords mounted on prized mules.
Very joyfully they rode out of the city of Orleans.
The emperor of France rode beside them
And had sixty knights in his entourage. 4660
He addressed Aiol in great friendship:
"My friend," said the emperor, "I hold you so dear.
If the Lord God allows you to return safe and sound,
I'll give you four castles in France as your fief."
"Sire," said Aiol, "may you receive great thanks, 4665
But I don't want to lessen your holdings.
Instead, I'll advance you and serve you well.
If the Lord God permits me to return here,
According to the counsel of your most trusted advisors,
If you give me what they have dared to decide, 4670
Certainly you will be strongly entrusted* because of it."
Thus they left each other and took leave.
The king prayed to the righteous Father to protect them,
That he might defend them from death and injury.
Had he known about the plans of the deceivers 4675
Who were waiting for them in the forest, to hack them to pieces,
He wouldn't have let them ride off unescorted.
Isabelle's eyes were filled with tears.
Lusiane, her daughter, could not console herself
So that, fainting, she wouldn't keel over on her solid gold
   saddle horn. 4680
"My daughter," said Isabelle, "stop this mourning!"
Her mother, a proud expression on her face, pulled her upright.
Thus they began to ride and departed.
The lords and ladies turned back to Orleans,
And the envoys departed, may God give them counsel. 4685

PART TWO

120.

Now Aiol is riding. The three noble lords
And the three squires, in all they were six.
A light rain is falling; it was very quiet.
Aiol sang a song to raise their spirits.
When the song was finished, he began to ponder. 4690
"My lord," said Hilaire, "listen to me.

❦ A Chanson de Geste ❦

Last night I had a dream, which has me very distressed:
Once we had entered aways into the Cinquefoil Forest,
I saw two bear cubs come out of the bushes.
They were trying to dismember us, tear us limb from limb,   4695
When God in his mercy came to our aid.
And we had with us three very prize brachet hounds,
Who rapidly helped us drive them away.
Makaire's relatives were never Aiol's friends:
They'd be lying in wait in the Cinquefoil Forest.   4700
If my advice were heard and believed,
We'd take out our arms and have them ready on our prize warhorses.
We'd be more at ease, safer and better prepared.
And if we get through this forest and we're not attacked,
By God, we can't do worse than disarming."   4705
"My friend," said Aiol, "what you say makes sense.
Anyone who refuses to accept advice, should be ashamed."
They dismounted on a hillside,
And their noble squires served them gladly.
They put their shining hauberks on their backs,   4710
Laced on their heads their burnished green helms,
Girded their swords — whose blades were polished clean —
Hung from their necks their stout, arched shields
And then mounted their swift Arabian horses.
When Aiol had mounted up, he began to look around,   4715
And muttered between his teeth so no one would hear:
"May it please the Lord who endured the passion,
That Makaire and his six relatives are here!
Today I'd make them pay with my bright steel blade
For my father's great suffering, who was forced into exile."   4720
Oh, God! Why is the good young knight boasting?
Before it's vespers and the sun is setting,
If he can't distinguish himself by his knightly prowess —
He'll be grieving before nightfall.

121.

Now all three of the noble barons are armed   4725
And have unfurled into the wind their red banners.
Aiol looked around and leaned on his saddlebow.
He began to speak to Rainald, his squire:
"Now do what's right," said Aiol, "worthy man.
If we have a battle and you see a fight,   4730
Keep a grip on your harness: don't be a fool."

❧ Aiol ❧

"By my faith, sire," the squire replied,
"If we have a battle and I see the need,
We won't have any discussions about holding the harness.
All together, acting as one, we'll do it.   4735
Between me and my brothers, both of these young nobles,
We're the sons of Gautier, the count of Soissons,
And he was the brother of Elye, the noble baron,
Who was forced from France through evil treachery.
Each of us is a worthy man, it's in our blood."   4740
When Aiol heard this, the noble knight was filled with great joy.

122.

Now all three of the noble knights are armed,
And they have unfurled their pennants into the wind.
Aiol, Elye's son, looked over to his right.
He prayed devoutly to the Lord God and his names.   4745
The ten were in the forest — may God do them harm!
Ferant of Lausanne called out to Agenon
And Garin, Richard, Hugues of Monbart,
And Jofroi of Verson and his brother Gontard,
And Guillaume Le Brun and his brother Gontard,   4750
And he called to Bernard from Roimorentin:
"Now's the time for vengeance," he said. "Lords, barons,
Look over there at those three armed knights, each on his horse.
Jofroi and Hilaire are loyal knights.
It would be an evil deed to kill those two.   4755
They are from very noble lineage: a great war would result.
But let's three of us go over onto that slope.
We'll make an agreement with those noble knights
That we'll give them a horse loaded down
With pure gold, silver and many costly silks,   4760
And in return, they'll let us take vengeance on the foul cur."
"I'll go!" said Richard, "And Hugues of Montbart
And with us, from Roimorentin, Bernard,
And you, Reinard, each one here on his horse.
If we need you, don't delay,   4765
But come to rescue us as soon as you can."
And they answered: "Don't worry.
You can go over there feeling safe. We won't fail you."
The three of them rode off down the slope.
Aiol saw them coming and recognized them.   4770
By their arms he saw that he'd never have any love for them.

A Chanson de Geste

He called to his companions, calmly shows them who's coming.
"What do you intend to do, free loyal knights?
Do you want to help me, or will everyone fail me?"
And they replied: "Never say such a thing! 4775
Anyone who thinks that, should be cursed a hundred times!
We won't fail you for anything on earth."
When Aiol heard this, he didn't waste any more time.
Damned if he'd speak or listen to another word!
He spurs Marchegai, who carries him swiftly, 4780
And brandished the hilt of this stout lance he's carrying.
In front, Aiol struck Hugues of Monbart on his shield,
Smashing it above the golden boss and shattering it.
The blow broke through the hauberk on his back, ripped the mail,
And Aiol thrust his lance straight through Hugues' body. 4785
The deep thrust of Aiol's lance knocked Hugues down off his horse,
And Aiol shouted: "Monjoie!" like a worthy knight.
"Whore's son! Coward! You'll never heal from it!
This is Aiol himself who's recognized you,
He'll make peace with you with a sharp sword!" 4790

123.

Aiol, Elye's son, struck down the first attacker.
Hilaire and Jobert were both good knights,
Courageous and bold in the use of their arms.
They don't want to delay. They let their mounts run,
Give whatever each horse can give with golden spurs. 4795
Each one struck his adversary and did not spare him.
Their adversaries' arms would never again be of any use to them,
Because they had fallen to the ground, dead.
Now you'll hear about the three squires:
When they saw the three dead, how glad they were! 4800
Immediately they came swiftly riding that way.
They quickly got off their nags
And unlaced the green helms from their heads.
Off the dead knights' backs, they removed the gleaming,
    double-mailed hauberks.
Rapidly they put them on. They laced up the helms 4805
And girded the swords with burnished steel blades
And hung around their necks the quartered shields.
Then they left their mounts to wander in the meadow
And leaped into the saddles of the swift war steeds.
From now on, there will be six to begin the battle. 4810

❧ Aiol ❧

The seven were in the woods, suffering and angry.
They'd gladly flee, but it would do them no good,
Because they have no stronghold in which to seek shelter.
They came out of the woods, the vile rogues.
The three squires came rushing down, full of fury. 4815
In front of them, on their shields, they struck the first three rogues,
So that neither cinch nor breast strap did them any good
In keeping them from falling down to the ground.
And Aiol and Hilaire and Jobert, the warrior,
Let their good, swift warhorses run, giving them free rein, 4820
And go to strike the three on their quartered shields.
They pierced and split them upon their golden boss.
They pierced and ripped the mail of their hauberks
And had the wood and steel of their arms bathe in bodies.
Down over the path's slope they struck them dead. 4825
"Oh, God!" said Aiol, "By your holy mercy,
How richly have I been avenged of these foul curs!"
They took one of them alive and bound his wrists.
They quickly stripped the others of their hauberks.
They dragged them by the tails of their horses. 4830
They hanged all ten of them. They took no ransoms for them.
Bernard was hanged there, the rich landholder.
He held Roimorentin, a great, vast castle,
Which lies seven days' travel from Orleans,
South through Berry. It's stoutly constructed. 4835
He was Makaire's nephew and Rainier's brother.
After that, Aiol would encounter great problems,
Before he entered France or before he saw Orleans,
Which made him afraid that he would have his head cut off,
So that he'd not want to be in that danger in exchange for Orleans. 4840
Aiol, Duke Elye's son, spoke first:
"My lords, noble companions, be still and listen to me.
Isn't the role of envoy mandated to the three of us?
That's why we shouldn't take with us any more knights.
Since these three squires have equipped themselves, 4845
Shamed be the neck, beard and head of anyone
Who ever denies to them the name of 'knight'!"
And if they were to serve us any longer, it would be a sin.
They shouldn't do this since they're knights,
But now let them take the war prize that we've won here 4850
And return to the city of Orleans
And tell Louis how we came to have what we've won."

❧ A Chanson de Geste ❧

And Hilaire and Jobert answered: "What you're saying makes sense."
But when the young nobles heard this, they became very angry.
However, they esteemed their lord and didn't dare protest,   4855
And so back they went, grieving and angered,
And they kept the war prize that they had won:
Ten hauberks, ten helms and ten quartered shields.
Before the day's end, they arrived in Orleans
And went to Louis to deliver their message.   4860
When the emperor heard them, he became very angry,
And on the other hand, his heart rejoiced greatly
From the fact that the rogues were dead and hacked to pieces.
As a result, Makaire's case has been severely weakened.
Now Aiol rode off, the noble warrior,   4865
With his two companions, joyous and glad
Because they've won the battle with steel blades,
And they're taking with them a strong pack horse
Loaded with equipment and deniers.
Lords, Jesus should certainly help such a man,   4870
Who for so long seeks to accomplish God's vengeance.
From Orleans to Pamplona took five whole days;
I'm not able to give an account of their days —
They came to Belquare and were lodged there.
They stayed there two days and all the third.   4875

124.

Aiol stayed at Belquare for three days.
Together with him were Hilaire and Lord Jobert.
They burnished their helms and their hauberks,
Took care of the horses, had them shod.
In the morning the three young nobles started out.   4880
Foucart was the name of their host in that castle.
Between noon and three in the afternoon they drew close
To the city where the young knights were headed
And found a flowery, beautiful grove.
Mibrien had had it enclosed with new stakes.   4885
There were many wild boar, deer and stags in that place.
"My lords," said Hilaire, "noble, young knights.
We're close to Pamplona, the fortified stronghold.
What do you have in mind? What course will we take?"
And Aiol, who was prudent, said then: 4890
"We'll stay here for today, Lord Jobert.

⚜ Aiol ⚜

Until tomorrow when it's broad daylight,
We can't lay an ambush or start a battle."

125.

Now the noble barons are together in the woods.
They saw long stretches of Pamplona: 4895
The walls, the solars and the louvered shutters,
And in front of the city were pagans and Nubians,
Who were riding out for their amusement.
"My lords," said Hilaire, the affable,
"How shall we handle these Persians?" 4900
And Aiol, who was prudent, answered right away:
"Here's what I think: we'll stay right here
Until tomorrow when it's broad daylight,
Then we'll go straight to Pamplona
To seek out knightly deeds and great jousts, 4905
And if it pleases the Lord God, he'll advance our cause."

126.

"My lords," said Hilaire, "we're here
Near our life's end, if God doesn't protect us.
Either you go ahead or you stay here,
But you need to leave your horse here. 4910
Tie up Marchegai under this pine tree.
He bites and kicks, neighs and whinnies.
He can't stand to have other horses next to him.
We can't predict the moment when we might be seized,
Because we're in a bad fix if the pagans spot us." 4915

127.

"My lords," said Aiol, "you stay here.
You shouldn't have to move just for my horse's sake.
If it's alright with you, I'll go on ahead
To that thick stand of brush you see over there.
By early morning, be all prepared: 4920
Have your warhorses cinched up tight.
We'll bring a battle to the city.
If some Saracens ride out full of arrogance,
Make sure they don't have anything to joke about.
If we can carry off three of them, 4925
That would appear as riches and great war prizes,
And we would be better praised in France."

❧ A Chanson de Geste ❧

He spurs his warhorse on his flanks,
Then he took leave and left them.
Aiol rode through a good four parts of the woods   4930
And came across a fountain where the stream ran clear.
He got down on foot in that leafy glade
And tied up Marchegai very well,
Held tight and fast with his leather halter.
He gave him some oats that he'd brought   4935
And propped up his shield and lance beside him.
He lay down on the grass in the leafy glade,
Because he was exhausted and worn out
From having carried his arms and his shield.
The young knight quickly fell asleep   4940
Until broad daylight the next morning.
He was in such need of sleep
That he wouldn't have awakened for the gold of ten cities.
Hilaire and Jobert became frightened.
They saw the sun shining and the brightness   4945
And heard the cries of the birds above them
And looked back into the leafy wood.
They saw seven knights from the city
Who had come to joust for sport in the field.
These two were completely dressed and equipped for war,   4950
So they went to their horses, mounted up,
And took up their gold-striped shields.
They charged towards the pagans at full gallop.
Oh, God! What a shame that Aiol doesn't know about it!
He had fallen asleep in the leafy glade.   4955
If the Lord God, through his goodness, doesn't protect him,
He'll never see them again and will be saddened.

128.

Now the two barons charge with great fury
And say to each other: "Where is Aiol?
By faith, he's still sleeping alone in the woods!   4960
We'll never do knightly deeds in friendship with him.
Look, here's the battle and the combat is ready.
If we go back for his help,
We'll lose this opportunity completely,
But let's make Jesus our liege Lord,   4965
Of the Lord God, the glorious Father.
And if God is willing to give us his great aid

⚜ Aiol ⚜

And give us victory in the battle and the fight,
We'll go straight back to Aiol,
And we'll let him be the lord and master over our war prize." 4970

129.

Jobert and Hilaire said, "This can turn out well.
Whoever would fail you in this, let him have no honor on earth!"
Ingernar calls out to Ingresain and Ingran:
"Have Tabrin and Haston of Tudele come over here,
And Tabor will be the sixth and Rustran the seventh. 4975
I see two knights whom our companions have surrounded.
By the faith of Mohammed, who reigns over this world,
It appears they're from France, that glorious land."
"I'll attack one of them at once," said Haston of Tudele.
"Sad news about him will go to France." 4980
Then he spurs his warhorse and gives him his head,
And Hilaire spurs his own horse on — lets it run.
He plants his lance in the pagan's body, on his sternum,
And Hilaire's lance knocked him down to the grass dead.
Then he shouted his war cry, "Monjoie," loud and clear. 4985
"Aiol! Lord and dear friend, if only you were here!
If there were thirty-four of them, they'd be headless!"

130.

Tabrin, who has no love for God, spurs his horse,
And Jobert spurs his own horse who gallops off straightaway
And goes to strike the pagan on his painted shield. 4990
He split the shield apart above its golden boss
And split and ripped the hauberk on his back.
Through the center of his heart Jobert thrust his naked standard.
His lance then pierced Tabrin and struck him dead from his horse.
Then he shouted his war cry: "Monjoie! With God's help! 4995
Aiol! Lord and dear friend, if only you were here!"

131.

Tabor pricks and spurs the warhorse under him,
A pagan of foul lineage who never believed in God.
Hilaire proudly spurred his own mount
And went to strike the pagan. His aim was sure, 5000
So that he struck the shield hanging from his neck, split it through
And ripped and tore the hauberk on the pagan's back.
Through the center of his heart, Hilaire thrust his lance,

⚜ A Chanson de Geste ⚜

Which then pierced Tabor and struck him dead,
Then he shouted St. Denis' war cry: "Monjoie! 5005
Dear lord and friend Aiol, if only you were here!
If there were thirty-four of them, they wouldn't escape alive!"
And Jobert strikes the fourth pagan with his burnished steel blade
Above his shoulders so that he takes his head off.
Ingresain, Ingernar and Ingran* took off — 5010
They turned back fleeing down the paved road
Straight to the city of Pamplona to take refuge there.
They entered the city sad and doleful.
The Saracens inside the city got in an uproar.
Seven score of them went to arm themselves. 5015
They put on their hauberks, laced on their burnished helms,
Girded their swords whose blades were polished,
Hung from their necks their gray-brown shields
And mounted their swift, rapid steeds.
Boldly they rode out together through the gate. 5020
All along the paved road they pursued our envoys.
When they came to the woods, the pagans turned back around
Because they were afraid an ambush awaited them there.
There was an ambush, but it was very undermanned:
There was only Aiol who had fallen asleep. 5025
And Jobert and Hilaire, the noble knights,
When they saw that the pagans were turning back,
Fiercely forced them to turn down a hillside slope.
In front of Mibrien, they killed two pagans.
Mibrien called out and began to speak to them: 5030
"Where are you from, you knights who have attacked me?
You've caused me great grief and killed my men."
"Sire," said Hilaire, "we don't intend to lie to you.
We were born in France, in Louis' kingdom.
It's on his behalf that we've challenged this realm. 5035
Wrongly you hold the land that Charlemagne held.
This is the command we bring you from the king of St.-Denis:
That you should come to Orleans or Rheims to serve him,
To Beauvais or Chartres or to the town of St.-Denis.
And you should have yourself baptized at the holy font, 5040
Adore and serve holy Christianity.
And if you fail to do this, you can be sure
That he will come to see you in May after April,
With forty thousand bold knights.
If he finds you in his lands, you will be humiliated. 5045

⚜ Aiol ⚜

He'll have you hanged and everything laid to waste.
If you want a fight, it won't be lacking.
There's our ambush waiting in that leafy woods.
If you come any farther, you'll be captured and killed."
When Mibrien heard this, it caused him distress. 5050
He called to the pagans and Saracens:
"My lords, turn away from this battle, for our faith in Apolin.
Mighty King Louis has assembled his people.
I think that they're all gathered and prepared in these woods.
In my opinion, there are more than thirty thousand of them. 5055
If the king gets hold of us, we'll be killed or captured.
No one can defend himself against the blows of the French!"
When the pagans heard this, they turned back
And didn't stop until they had reached Pamplona
And entered into the city to save their lives. 5060
The pagans within the city were in an uproar
And built up earthen barriers against both gates and posterns.
Aiol was still sleeping under the leafy tree.
Marchegai heard the sounds made by the Saracen rogues,
And he heard the clanking of shields, helms and lances. 5065
The horse felt such grief that he almost went mad.
He scratched the ground with his right hoof, whinnied intensely,
And continued to make so much noise that it woke Aiol.
He saw the sun shining brightly above him,
And he heard the small birds sing as they rejoiced. 5070
He called out to his companions: "We're in a bad fix!
Get to your horses right away. It's nearly noon."
He put on his hauberk, laced on his burnished helm,
Girded his sword, seized his stout shield
And mounted Marchegai, whom his father had raised. 5075
He took in his right fist the stout, polished lance
And began to make his way straight though the forest.
Never did the noble knight take a path or a road
Until he came under the over-arching boughs
Where he had left his companions resting. 5080
When he did not find them there, he thought he'd lose his mind.
In his heart, he began to lament most intensely
And declared himself to be grieved, sad and sorrowed.
"Oh, my companions, how you've treated me with contempt
When in this foreign land you've gone off and left me. 5085
Never should anyone trust anyone else!"
In the midst of his great sorrow and his extravagant outbursts,

❧ A Chanson de Geste ❧

Here come his companions with the war prize they had taken:
They were leading four swift and rapid horses
And on each one was the head of one of the Saracens 5090
They had cut off with their burnished steel blades.
When they saw Aiol, they began to speak to him:
"For God's sake, lord and companion, why are you carrying on so?
We'll swear to you five or ten times on saints' relics,
In Paris or in Chartres or in the town of St.-Denis, 5095
That we never intentionally forgot you.
Go ahead and take this war prize you see here.
Be lord and master of it. Do with it what you wish.
We'll certainly make everyone believe, both the great and the small,
That you've won all of this by your knightly prowess." 5100
When Aiol heard this, he almost went mad:
"My lords, may it not please God, who never lied,
That a lie be told concerning your possessions!
I'll win my own war prize if it pleases God and I live.
But it's fitting for us to part company now. 5105
You will go back to France where you came from.
Tell Lusiane the fair with the bright countenance,
That God save and protect her, he who never lied,
And for Isabelle, her mother, for all the good she did for me,
May the God of glory pay her back, he who never lied. 5110
When I first got there, I was completely destitute,
Because I didn't have a tunic or an ermine cloak.
Greet the king, who reigns over France, for me —
I won back his land and his country —
Because I'll remain here among my enemies, 5115
In this vast forest among Saracens.
I've sworn to this, you can be sure of it,
That I'll never leave here, not even for a day,
Until I've done battle and won such a war prize
That I can show to mighty King Louis." 5120
When the barons heard this, they were deeply distressed.
And they said to each other: "We're in a bad fix."

132.

Jobert and Hilaire said: "For Lord's sake, good sire, have mercy.
Please don't be so angry with us!
We'll swear to you on saints' relics ten or fifteen times, 5125
In Paris, in Chartres, in a town or a city,
That we never neglected you on purpose,

But take this war prize — be the lord and master of it.
We'll get the barons of the empire to believe completely
You've won it through your knightly deeds." 5130
When Aiol heard this, he became extremely angry:
"My lords, may it not please God, St. Mary's Son,
That a lie be told because of your possessions.
I'll win my own, if God gives me life.
But it's fitting now to part company." 5135

133.

Said Jobert and Hilaire, the noble and the brave:
"Noble man of high birth, you've put us in a bind.
Louis will declare and believe to be true
That we have killed, murdered and strangled you,
Captured you by treachery and delivered you to the pagans." 5140
"My lords," said Aiol, "you're wasting your breath,
Because I wouldn't do it for the gold of ten cities.
I'll remain here and you two will leave."
Jobert and Hilaire said: "Noble lord, please come along with us!
But if you don't want to do it, there's nothing else we can do." 5145
They turned away, angry and incensed.
The two knights started the journey back, irate and depressed,
Travelling rapidly all along the paved road.
They knew the route well, for they were born in that region.
They travelled and journeyed so much during their days 5150
That they came to Orleans, the marvelous city.
The king was holding his court with his powerful courtiers.
When he saw them arrive, he asked them:
"Tell me, my lords, what made you separate from Aiol?"
The two knights had anguished hearts. They didn't want
    to blame Aiol, 5155
Rather they praised and extolled him as much as they could:
"He's such a knight — never has his equal been seen!
He killed four pagans the other day in a joust.
You can see here the horses, won in the joust, that he's given us.
We've brought the pagans' heads so that you can better believe us. 5160
But for a high-born man, Jesus has reserved another destiny:
Aiol's had to wage war against one of his peers,
And he's remained with him until the first day of summer,
Until he's won back his lands and his kingdom.
Then he'll come to serve you gladly and willingly." 5165
When the king heard this, he almost went mad:

⚜ A Chanson de Geste ⚜

"Whores' sons! Foul curs! Just the opposite, you've taken him from me,
Captured him through treachery and delivered him to the pagans!"
In a loud voice he shouted: "Barons, now seize them!"
The king had them seized, tied and bound to the ground,   5170
Huge iron rings locked around their necks,
And on each one's legs a chain was fastened.
Then they were thrown into the depths of his stone prison.
He would have had them hanged, if he wouldn't have been blamed,
But these were powerful men from influential families.   5175
They won't leave prison until Aiol returns.
Throughout the city you could hear the mourning,
And ladies and maidens start to weep.
Lusiane was close to going mad:
"Oh! Dear lord Aiol, it is hard to imagine   5180
That our great friendship would end like this!
If I'm not allowed to have you, may it not please God
That I have a husband in all of my days!
I'd rather be sent off to one of those holy places
And foreswear any earthly honor."   5185

134.

My lords, great was the mourning throughout the great city of Orleans,
Where knights, maidens and young girls are weeping,
As well as monks, canons and clerics in abbeys.
So deep was Lusiane's mourning that she almost went mad:
"Oh! Dear lord Aiol! Bold, noble knight!   5190
How you have left all the land free
From those of Berry who had laid it to waste.
Through your great chivalry you have emancipated it,
And you ought to be king of France the bountiful.
I wish to God, Mary's son,   5195
That I had been left pregnant and heavy with his child!
Oh! Poor suffering girl — what a sad state I'm in!
Never can I have his love or love's pleasures."
Her intense mourning causes her to fall down in a faint.

135.

You've often heard it said, such grieving doesn't last long: 5200
They soon forgot him who wasn't anything to them.
Aiol, whose suffering continues, was in the woods.
He climbed upon a brown rock,
Looked down and saw Pamplona:

⚜ Aiol ⚜

The walls, the solars and the high towers. 5205
"Oh, God! Woe to you, Pamplona," said Aiol,
"It was a sad day, after white-bearded Charles had conquered you,
When our Christian men suffered your loss.
Alas! Won't I be able to do anything to help good men?"
The anger he was feeling caused his blood to boil. 5210

136.

Aiol was in the woods, despondent and angry.
He suffered all day and never left
Until the arrival of vespers and nightfall.
He girded his sword and took up his stout shield
And came to Marchegai, mounted up by the stirrup 5215
And took in his right fist a stiff, sharp lance.
Then he started out down his grassy pathway.
He didn't stop until he reached Pamplona.
When he arrived in front of the city gate, he raised his shield,
So that no one inside could launch arrows or sharp spears against him. 5220
He looked at the palace that was Charlemagne's.
"Alas," said Aiol, "how badly it's turned out for me!
Oh! My companions, you've let me down
And left me aggravated in this foreign land.
It could well be that I'll be here until I'm old and gray — 5225
In my opinion four score years or more —
Before I do anything that becomes known in France!"
He started riding around the city and doesn't speak any more
And found a walled grove that belonged to Charlemagne,
Of cypress, pines and small laurel trees. 5230
And Aiol went inside through a old ruined entry.
When he got inside the grove, he got down on foot
And attached Marchegai to the trunk of a tree.
Aiol tied his head up high — he wasn't confident at all —
He was afraid that the horse might whinny and that they'd be noticed. 5235
If the Saracens found out, they're in deep trouble.
He put his shield and his lance down on the ground,
Then went walking through the grove, sorrowful and angry.
Intensely, Duke Elye's son laments
And looks off to his right down a beaten path. 5240
He spots two Saracens, misbegotten curs.
One of them was Kikernart, the other Barbarus.
With their polished and sharpened steel knives
They've pierced the wall and made a large hole in it.

❧ A Chanson de Geste ❧

The misbegotten curs intended to enter 5245
In order to carry off a maiden — never such a beauty had been seen.
A king had sent them, who had come for her.
His name was Gorhan: he was lord of Africa,
And he was waiting for them elsewhere in a leafy thicket
With a hundred Saracens wearing shining hauberks. 5250
She had sent for him: everything's all arranged.
She won't wait any longer for permission from her father,
The old and white-haired Mibrien of Persia.
Whatever the outcome of her plea, she'll go to her lover.
Aiol, Elye's son, figured out by himself what was going on. 5255
Then, after the pagans, Aiol went inside
And swore to the Lord God and his virtue,
That if he can act, they've gone on a fool's errand:
The misbegotten curs are surely condemned to death.
He'll carry off the lady before daybreak. 5260
He placed himself out of the way, between the chamber and the wall,
Near a pillar, beside a vaulted arch.
He understood very well what the Saracens were saying,
And he heard the lady clearly and what she replied.
When Aiol understood what she was saying, never had he been
 so joyous. 5265

137.

The two pagans stayed in the shadows of the chamber
By the main window, to deliver the message.
Aiol was in another place — in the shade of a small tree —
And he saw the brightness from the candles and the lamps
And saw the maiden, who was of such noble bearing. 5270
In Christendom there wasn't a more beautiful woman.
The pagans greeted her according to their custom:
"May Mohammed be with you, sister, noble, sweet friend!
My lady, we're envoys from the king of Africa.
He's informing you by letter and through personal trust 5275
That you should come to him: everything is ready for him
 to take you.
My lord is a mighty king. He doesn't want to break his pledge
 to you.
He'll conform to all of your stipulations.
He'd rather be dead than not take you as his wife."
The maiden replied with very great sophistication: 5280
"It's true that I ought to care for him, when he tells me this.

⚜ AIOL ⚜

Go right away and tell your lord to wait for me a bit.
You can take me away by way of Otrente Street.
My father will be upset, that's for sure!"
When Aiol heard this, his heart was filled with joy, 5285
And he swore to the Lord God and his proud power,
Softly, between his teeth, so no one could hear,
That if he can pull it off, he'll steal this woman from them.

138.

Aiol turned back, he'd learned what they were plotting.
He went out through the hole in the wall: he doesn't want to delay. 5290
He came to the grove and rapidly picked up his arms.
He equipped himself as a bold man should,
Then mounted Marchegai, his swift horse.
He went out of the grove, going out onto the plain.
The two pagans came out — may God destroy them! — 5295
They came to their lord, who was waiting for them in the bushes.
Kikernart spoke first, who was aware of the scheme,
And said to his lord: "Consider yourself proud and strong.
Mibrien's daughter is getting herself ready."
"Go on then," said the king. "Ride quickly. 5300
You two bring her to me, just you two alone,
Because Mibrien hates me, and I'll hate him until death.
I want to leave his land so that he doesn't find even a trace of me.
For Mirabel, the worthy, whose nobility is so great,
I'm leading this palfrey. There's never been a better one. 5305
I wouldn't give up its saddle for sixty gold marks."
The Saracens went back swiftly and rapidly.
From the king to their hole, they didn't leave the straight path.
They found Mibrien's daughter waiting outside.
They lifted her onto the palfrey quickly and rapidly, 5310
But Aiol followed them, who was in on the plot:
May God protect and guide him!

139.

The two pagans were leading the noble Mirabel.
She rode sidesaddle on the swift palfrey.
The saddle on the palfrey's back is worth a castle's income. 5315
The halter on its head was entirely newel worked,
With precious stones — never was a more beautiful one ever seen.
Aiol, who was astute, was following behind,
Until they had gone over the summit of Montinel

A Chanson de Geste

And crossed a small bridge over a stream. 5320
Then Aiol pricks and spurs his mount: he doesn't want to
  wait any longer.
He rapidly places himself between them and the castle.
Loudly he shouts to them, "You won't be seeking shelter there,
  fiends!
It will be a long while before you take the maiden to a city
  or a castle!"
He struck one of the pagans with the full force of his charge, 5325
So that he shattered his shield and ripped open his hauberk.
Through the thickest part of his body he broke open his heart,
And the thrust of his lance knocked the pagan down dead.
And when the other pagan saw this, it wasn't pleasant for him,
Since he knew well and expected that his death was close. 5330

140.

When the Saracen sees his companion on the ground,
Who was slain and killed, bleeding out on the green grass,
Then his heart was filled with such grief he almost went mad.
He'd gladly have avenged this foul cur if he had dared,
But he saw the noble knight who was so battle hardened, 5335
Seated on a warhorse of which there was no better on earth.
On the fair mountainside, Aiol charged at him more rapidly
Than a deer runs, or a stag, a wild boar or any beast.
The foul cur goes fleeing across the hillock.
Aiol spurs his horse, loosens the reins 5340
And brandished his lance, his beautiful standard.
He goes to strike the pagan on his round shield,
Upon its golden boss. Aiol sliced it into quarters,
And he completely rips apart the hauberk on his back.
Into the pagan's heart he puts his new lance. 5345
Aiol strikes the pagan dead, who is lying stretched out on the grass,
Then he drew his handsome sword
And cut off the heads of the two dead pagans.
Then he said something that was full of power and pride:
"Whoever will search these dead men, it's fine with me. 5350
Let them take the hauberks and the handsome arms.
I'll lead off the warhorses back to my homeland."
He got back his lance and went over to the maiden.
Aiol reached out his hand, and took her palfrey's bridle.
Smiling, he said to her: "You've been captured, fair one! 5355
You're not going any farther with the enemy.

⚜ Aiol ⚜

You'll come with me to France, the good country.
You'll be baptized and converted to God.
Then I'll take you as my wife, I don't know anyone so beautiful."
When Mirabel heard this, she almost lost her mind.   5360

PART THREE

141.

Now Aiol's riding toward his home country.
He's leading away the maiden that God has given him.
Now hear how she is lamenting,
How much she's complaining about her bad fortune:
"Now it can be truly said that I've been mistreated!   5365
To what a sad end you raised me, my lord and dear father!
I've been separated from you wrongly and sinfully.
I'll never be the wife of the king of Africa now!
My lord, let me go for the sake of your father's soul.
I'll go back to my country.   5370
Tomorrow, before noon they'll have me back."
"Upon my head," said Aiol, "you'll do nothing of the sort!
You'll come with me to France, to that honored land,
And you'll be baptized and raised over the holy font.
Then I'll take you as my wife and you'll be my spouse."   5375
When Mirabel heard this, she almost went mad,
And the maiden replied: "That thought has never crossed my mind.
I'll never be tempted to commit such a great sin.
Mohammed's law will never be shamed by me.
I'd much rather be killed   5380
Or destroyed and dragged behind horses by their tails!"

142.

Now Aiol sets out leading the maiden.
All night they rode without stopping
Until the next morning at the dawn's first light.
Mibrien's daughter was in somewhat better spirits.   5385
She came over to Aiol and began to speak to him:
"Who are you, my lord, who have taken me by force?
Never have your eyes ever seen such a rich prize,
Because I'm a king's daughter, and my mother is a queen."
"Fair one," said Aiol, "I won't hide my identity from you.   5390
I'll tell you everything, if God blesses me.
I have never revealed this to any man or woman alive.

❧ A Chanson de Geste ❧

It's true that they call me Aiol. My father is Elye.
I'm the nephew of the emperor who reigns over France.
I'm the son of his sister, the worthy lady Avisse,   5395
But she's been driven from France and exiled
Through the counsel of Makaire — may God curse him! —
An evil flatterer, a foul cur and a traitor.
If God grants me life, it's going to mean his death.
With Jesus' help, I've already managed   5400
To have him thrown into Orleans' stone prison.
He'll never get out of there in his entire life.
Instead he'll be shamed and delivered to the executioner.
By joining my family's lineage, you'll hardly be losing out.
You'll come with me to France to that bountiful land,   5405
Then I'll take you as my wife, if that's what God has destined for me."
And Mirabel replied: "I don't agree to this in the least,
Because Mohammed is my god; his justice is boundless,
And nothing can trouble anyone who completely trusts in him."
When Aiol heard this, he was filled with sorrow and anger,   5410
And he shot back through ill humor and annoyance:
"Woe to Mohammed and anyone who trusts in him,
Because his powers aren't worth a rotten apple!
And I swear to the Lord God, St. Mary's Son,
That if you ever speak of Mohammed, you'll lose your life!"   5415
When the maiden heard this, she became very docile.

143.

Now Aiol's riding off to France, his country.
He's leading the maiden with the high-born, noble bearing.
Suddenly she had the urge to eat and drink something:
If this beauty doesn't have something, she thinks she'll die.   5420
She was fluent in fourteen languages:
She knew how to speak Armenian and Greek,
Flemish, Burgundian and all Saracen dialects,
The dialects of Poitiers and Gascony came easily to her.
She came over to Aiol and seized his reins.   5425
Politely she began to speak to him:
"Do you know, noble youth, what I'd like to admit to you:
I'd really like to eat and drink a little something.
Yesterday evening, I didn't eat much at all.
No, today's the third day I haven't had a speck of food.   5430
I was in such fear for that king, my friend —
He was supposed to have me as his wife, and I him, as my husband.

❦ Aiol ❦

I'll never see him again, alas, and he'll never see me again.
So much the more my heart is distressed and angry."
"Fair one," said Aiol, "I've never heard of such a thing.   5435
With God as my witness, I don't have anything to give you.
We'll not find either bread or meat or wine for sale."

144.
"Fair one," said Aiol, "suffer and bear up!
By the faith I owe you, I have nothing to give you.
See this desolate land and despoiled countryside: 5440
We aren't in a village, a town or a city
Where we might find bread, wine or anything else for sale."
At these words, they entered a meadow.
They found a fountain under a spreading tree.
Aiol, the noble knight, got down from his horse   5445
And helped down the noble, high-born maiden.
He put the horses to graze, took off their bridles,
And let them drink the water and graze on the grass.
Then Aiol lay down on the meadow's green grass;
The maiden lay down beside the young knight.   5450
She was shapely and bright faced,
And you will never see a more beautiful rosy color.
Aiol, Elye's son, began to look at her,
And in his heart, he began to love her deeply.
Had she been a Christian, he would have wanted to kiss her,   5455
But because she was a pagan, he didn't want to touch her —
He didn't want to shame his Christian faith —
Instead he wanted to have her baptized and raised above the holy font.
Then he would take her as his wife, spouse and peer.
He was aching and suffering intensely   5460
From the shield and the arms he had been carrying,
And he had ridden and travelled all night long.
Immediately he forgot everything and fell asleep.
The maiden kept watch, whose heart was so heavy,
She couldn't have fallen asleep even to keep her limbs from
    being cut off.   5465
Instead, she kept looking back all along the paved road
And did not see a single man, coming or going,
Who might be coming after her to take her back.
God! Why did the sensible knight lie down?
Without the protection of Jesus, who was delivered to death,   5470
Soon he will be shamed and dishonored.

⚜ A Chanson de Geste ⚜

The city of Pamplona, from which he came, was in an uproar,
And the Saracens searched for the maiden, but they couldn't find her.
Instead they found the wall where it was pierced and broken through.
Then you would have seen the pagans consumed by great mourning: 5475
Mibrien and his wife tearing their hair out,
Saracens and pagans running to arm themselves.
Over seven thousand laced on their helmets.
They rode out through the good city's gate.
Rapidly they spread out all over the kingdom, 5480
Because they didn't know where they might find her.
Four of them rode out following the maiden's trail:
Above all the others, these were the boldest and the most esteemed.
They won't give up the search if they haven't found Aiol,
Who'd fallen asleep under the spreading tree. 5485
The maiden, whose heart was heavy, kept watch
And was looking back where they had come from,
When she spotted the four pagans born in Pamplona.
She identified them with certainty by their horses and their arms.
It's not necessary to ask if she felt great joy, 5490
Because one of them was her brother, newly dubbed.
He hadn't been bearing arms for two weeks yet.
Another one was her uncle — she loved him dearly —
And with him, two of her cousins, close relatives.
"Oh, Mohammed!" she said, "How great you are! 5495
Anyone who believes in and adores you will have his way much more
Than any man's heart would ever think or say.
Now you've rescued me through your goodness!"
Afterwards, she began to reflect, with great nobility —
Never will you hear such thoughts spoken by a Saracen woman. 5500
"Alas!" said the maiden, "What was I thinking?
How could I ever commit such a great betrayal
That I would let this noble knight be slain in his sleep!
He's already won me through his great prowess.
He's a good knight and a battle-hardened noble. 5505
Since I've now been rescued, I'll let him go.
May Mohammed give him his life in France safe and sound!"
So she drew near him on his left side
And whispered in his ear quietly and discreetly:
"Noble youth, my lord, you might be resting too long. 5510
By this great faith that I should show you,
Here come four pagans born in Pamplona.
These are my father's close relatives — I know them well.

🌼 AIOL 🌼

They'll kill you, I'm very sure of it!
Go right away to your horse and quickly mount up.   5515
Turn back along this great paved road,
Because — by the faith that I owe to Mohammed —
It's better to make a good escape than to perform poorly.
When they see me, I'll have them stop.
I'll tell them so many lies and truths   5520
That you can save yourself, if you'll believe me."
"Fair one," said Aiol, "five hundred thanks and appreciations.
By the faith I owe you, you've spoken through great goodness.
There'll never be a single day in my life when I don't love you,
But may it not please Jesus, who was hung upon the cross,   5525
That I would flee from four pagans before I've had a joust.
I would be reproached by all of my great family line."
He jumped to his feet, crossed himself,
Took up his arms, got ready
And came to Marchegai and got him prepared.   5530
He put his bridle on his head and mounted by the stirrup.
He's gotten completely ready to defend himself.
Here comes one of the pagans born in Pamplona —
I've heard my master say it was the oldest one:
He was the uncle of the maiden, whose bearing is so noble.   5535
He was riding more than a bowshot in front of the others,
Astride a good, swift and rapid horse.
In a loud voice he shouts: "Foul cur, there's no protection for you!
You've done a great wrong by abducting Mibrien's daughter
Without his men's consent. You had no permission.   5540
Today the day has come when you'll pay dearly for it.
You'll not avoid having your head cut off!"
Aiol, Elye's son, had no mind to quarrel now,
Because he wasn't used to arguing.
Instead, he spurred Marchegai with great nobility,   5545
And brandished the shaft of his stout, squared lance.
He went to strike the pagan — he didn't put up with any more talk.
Aiol split apart and broke the pagan's shield hanging from his neck
And ripped and tore the hauberk on his back.
He thrust the lance's iron tip straight through the pagan's body.   5550
With the entire length of his lance, he struck him down
   dead on the meadow.
"Foul cur," said Aiol, "you've paid for it!
As far as you're concerned, I've paid in full for this prize.
May God protect me from the others by his goodness!"

⚜ A Chanson de Geste ⚜

The three Saracens quickly came so close to Aiol   5555
That the noble knight could not use his lance,
Or pull it back out of the pagan's body.
Then he drew his sword whose hilt was golden
And went to strike another pagan, whom he joined in combat.
Aiol made the pagan's head fly off his shoulders.   5560
The other two pagans were two hundred measured feet away
  from him.
Aiol saw the two of them together and fears them all the more.

145.

Aiol spurs his horse, proudly gives him his head.
The pagans were a full two hundred feet from him.
He saw the two of them together and feared them greatly.   5565
He had neither pike or lance, the noble knight.
The two pagans thought that he was fleeing from them,
So they could lead the maiden away without being challenged.
This was a foolish idea on their part, for Aiol had no such intent.
Before he would give up, he'd make them pay dearly.   5570
Aiol spurs his horse, proudly wheels about.
While making this French maneuver, he recovered his lance:
With fierce daring he pulled it back out of the dead pagan.
He went to strike another whom he joined in combat.
Aiol broke and shattered the shield hanging from his neck   5575
And ripped and tore through the hauberk on his back.
Through the center of the pagan's heart he thrust his lance.
With his lance, he struck the pagan down dead from his horse
"Oh, God!" said Aiol, "Now we're equal!
Woe to anyone who would leave the maiden to this pagan,   5580
Until that hour when he will have paid dearly!"

146.

Aiol spurs Marchegai; lets both reins go free
And goes to strike the fourth pagan on his golden shield.
He deals a marvelous blow from which there's no protection,
Which breaks and shatters the shield hanging at the pagan's neck   5585
And rips and tears the hauberk on his back.
Aiol thrusts his good, sharp lance through his body.
Right in front of him, he strikes the pagan down dead to the ground.
Mibrien's daughter watched him from a low hill.
Intensely, she proclaimed herself to be pitiful, sorrowful and
  distraught: 5590

141

⚜ Aiol ⚜

"What an insane act you did when you awoke the Frank!
He's a very good knight and courageous in armed combat.
Now he's killed my brother — and I'm distraught —
And also my cousins and my uncle. I'm to blame for this!
In my opinion, even if our pagans had numbered twenty-four,   5595
He would have killed all of them because of his knightly prowess."
You've heard it said by many
That a woman is quick to love a man who strikes well in battle.
She called out to Aiol so that he heard her on the hill:
"My lord, so come over here now you've boldly wielded your arms.   5600
For you, I'll believe in the God of heaven."
When Aiol heard this, it caused him great joy.

147.

Aiol, Elye's son, had understood the lady.
He cut off the heads of the three Saracens
And ties them on the horses. He doesn't want leave a single one.   5605
He has them hanging down by their hair from the saddle horns.
Mibrien's daughter has seen the battle,
So she knows that Aiol has won her by force.
She calls out to him so that he'll hear her:
"My lord, come on over here, because I'm your beloved.   5610
For your sake I'll believe in God who was placed in the sepulcher,
And I will be baptized and held above the sacred font,
Because Mohammed's powers have been dashed to earth,
When all alone you cut off the heads
Of these four Saracens, who don't believe in God.   5615
How I'm suffering in this wilderness, in this dense forest!
We don't have a trail or a beaten path.
May God help us now, who is seated high above.
I greatly desire to enter joyfully into your land.
If such is your desire, I'm completely your beloved."   5620
And Aiol shouted: "Monjoie! May God help us!"

148.

Now Aiol rides off leading his war prize.
The maiden was exhausted and oppressed by the heat.
She came over to Aiol and began to speak to him:
"Noble lord, baron, what will become of me!   5625
I didn't eat last night and not for three days now."
"Fair one," said Aiol, the bold and the loyal,
"I don't have anything to give you, by the faith I owe St. Thomas!

❦ A Chanson de Geste ❦

Look at this desolate land and this scorched countryside."
Aiol, Elye's son, looked out ahead of him 5630
And spotted a pilgrim who was going to the shrine of St. James
And was coming from sweet France. He was struggling intensely.
Aiol spurred his horse and rode towards him.
The pilgrim saw him and became very afraid.
He feared that this was some evil man come to do him harm. 5635
Then Aiol rode up to him and greeted him politely
In the name of God of holy glory who created the world.
When the pilgrim heard God mentioned, he felt greatly relieved:
"May that Lord, who formed the whole world, protect you!"
"Friend," said Aiol, "where are you coming from, what region?" 5640
"My lord, I'm coming from Orleans, the mighty royal city.
There I left the king very angry and despondent
Because of a favorite knight of his, Aiol, whom he'd sent to Spain.
His companions, whom the king assigned to accompany him, had killed him,
And the king has seized them, has thrown them down 5645
Into the depths of his prison and says that he will hang them.
If Aiol doesn't come back, he'll have his justice done."
When Aiol heard this, he was very astonished.
For his two companions, he was filled with fear.
Reverently and courteously he prayed to the Lord God 5650
To protect them from death until he arrives in France.
If he can get there in time, he'll certainly free them
From the king's prison. He'll get both of them out
Once he's in Orleans and sweet France.

149.

"My friend," said Aiol, "may God preserve you from harm. 5655
Pilgrim, dear friend, be my advisor.
Would you have anything to drink or to eat,
Or anything that could help me?
I'm leading a lady here, who's exhausted from riding.
She's so consumed by hunger that she thinks she'll go mad." 5660
The pilgrim said, "My lord, I won't hide from you
That I have here half a loaf and a large whole loaf of bread.
Take as much as you want, I'll grant it to you,
Because I've never refused my food to any free man."
"By God," said Aiol, "may you be thanked for it! 5665
I wouldn't be so happy for thirty marks of silver."
Aiol dismounted onto the grass, the noble knight,

⚜ Aiol ⚜

Came over to the maiden and helped her down without delay.
Both of them sat down under a leafy tree.
The pilgrim was judicious, courteous and well educated. 5670
He freely shared his bread in large quantities.
Aiol and the maiden ate a great deal of it,
But unfortunately Aiol had nothing to drink.
The pilgrim had some water drawn from a pond
That he carried in a flagon to slake his thirst. 5675
Aiol and the maiden drank from it without harm.
"Oh, God!" said Aiol, "Now my heart is glad
For the love of this lady, who's eaten a little.
Pilgrim, dear friend, you've done a very good thing.
Never has a dinner ever been put to a better use, 5680
So I'll give you a good, swift warhorse.
You see here six of them, dear brother, all equipped.
Then take the best one — choose the one you want —
And take from that chest a hundred sous of my deniers
To take with you in the warhorses' straps, 5685
To help you along your way. You're going to really need it."
The pilgrim said, "My lord, don't waste your breath.
I don't need your possessions, because I'm loaded down with
    my own.
I've brought along plenty to support me along my way.
And I also don't need your swift warhorse, 5690
Because before tomorrow at vespers when the sun has set,
I could travel and ride through such a spot
Where I would be quickly killed to get that warhorse.
You are near the borderlands where the pagans live.
You should think about spurring your horses and getting away, 5695
Because if the pagans spot you, your lives won't be worth much!"
With that, they commended each other to the Lord God of heaven.

150.

Now Aiol started off and leaves the pilgrim.
The noble knight rode all day,
Saw vespers approaching and the day coming to a close. 5700
The sun setting, he's turning towards the sunset.
Reverently and courteously he prayed to the Lord God
To provide him good lodging, because he really needs it.
Aiol, Elye's son, looked off on his right.
Between a woods and a field, the noble man searched. 5705
At the edge of the forest, he looked closely

⚜ A Chanson de Geste ⚜

And spotted a house where there were seven robbers
At the great turning bridge: high were the gates,
And deep a huge moat where much evil had been done.
Whenever an honest man would pass by on his way to St. James —   5710
Knight or burgher, who were making their way there —
The robbers made them think that this was a pilgrim's hospice.
No one could pass by without being robbed.
Aiol spurred in that direction and his horse started off.
Out in front, under a tree, he found the seven robbers.   5715
Now here's Aiol, who greets them courteously,
In the name of God of holy glory, who formed the whole world.
No one answered him; they just looked at each other.
When Aiol saw this, he became extremely angry.
Mirabel the maiden was astonished.   5720

151.

Now Aiol has greeted all of the robbers together.
However, these foul curs didn't answer him,
And when Aiol saw this, he became very incensed.
Proudly he addressed them as you can hear:
"My lords," said Aiol, "you're making a huge mistake   5725
Not answering when someone greets you in the name of God!
Watch out if you're contemplating some evil act towards me!
I swear, in the name of that holy saint pilgrims seek in Nero's Fields,
With this sword of mine that's hanging at my side,
I think I'll be fighting you before vespers.   5730
Then the best of you won't be able to brag
That he doesn't have his head and all his limbs cut off."
When the robbers heard this, then they did begin to speak.
Even the boldest among them started to tremble in fear.
Robaut, who was their master, got to his feet.   5735
He was their leader and had the others in his care.
He had, in his lifetime, passed four score years.
He had a long beard down to the knot of his belt.
He had murdered and strangled many a pilgrim —
The sins from these crimes remained within him.   5740
He came up to Aiol and began to speak to him:
"Noble young man, you're very wrong about that.
We've never done a bit of harm to you,
And yet you're threatening to cut off our heads!
We're converts to monasticism and live under its rules,   5745
So we're not supposed to speak or converse with anyone.

🏵 Aiol 🏵

It's prohibited and forbidden in our chapter.
We don't want to violate our monastic vows of obedience."
"My lord," said Aiol, "this well may be true.
If I've offended you, then pardon me.   5750
I'm a knight from the city of Orleans.
I'm a liegeman of Louis, the mighty crowned king.
I'm coming from Pamplona, the magnificent city.
If you please, tonight share with me your hostel
Until tomorrow at daybreak.   5755
Any one of the best horses that you see here,
You may take, my lord, as payment for the lodging,
Except for only mine with which I was dubbed,
Because I wouldn't give him to any man alive."
When Robaut heard this, he was filled with great joy   5760
And whispered between his teeth, discreetly and secretly:
"As far as I'm concerned, when you leave me,
Never again will you steal away someone else's beloved!"
Oh, God! If only Aiol, the noble youth, had heard this,
He would have already cut off Robaut's head with his steel blade.   5765
"Baron," said the robber, "don't worry!
You'll be lodged exactly as you wish.
Never have I seen anyone in my family,
Who, if he gave lodging to a noble man or gave him hostel
For a single night, would have charged him for even his supper,   5770
And I won't charge you, for you appear to me to be noble.
But rather ride on ahead. Go and disarm yourself."
"My lord," said Aiol, "five hundred thanks."
Oh, God! If Aiol only knew the robber's thoughts or what was
    in his heart,
He wouldn't have stopped for the gold of ten cities.   5775
If the Lord God doesn't keep Aiol in his thoughts, by his goodness,
Never before did Elye's son have such an evil hostel,
As they will make him pay for before sunup!

152.

Aiol spurs Marchegai and rode on ahead
Without stopping until he reached the house.   5780
He didn't see a fire burning, a woman or a child,
Or any equipment for cooking.
"Oh, God!" said Aiol, "By your will,
What kind of people can these be, Father of Bethlehem,
Who live here within these woods so out of the way?"   5785

⚜ A Chanson de Geste ⚜

"My lord," said Mirabel, the lovely maiden,
"Don't believe me ever again in all my life,
If these aren't robbers, treacherous betrayers!
Watch out that they don't surprise you, noble, valiant knight,
Because a man who's caught off guard isn't worth one glove!" 5790
"Fair one," said Aiol, "why do you chatter so much?
By that apostle penitents seek out,
I'll not unlace my helmet or take off my armor.
Instead, all night long I'll have my sword girded at my side.
If they try anything against us, either pride or outrage, 5795
I think I can deal with them with my steel blade.
From my sword's blows they won't have any protection from death."
He got down from his swift warhorse,
Then he came to the beautiful and comely maiden.
He took her in his arms and gently helped her dismount. 5800
Inside the house he seated her on a bench,
Then saw to his horses. He set about tying them up
With leather straps. He was taking good care of them.
He found some hay and set it in front of them.
Then he sat back down beside Mirabel. 5805
The foul curs were still out under the tree.
I'll name them, if you'd care to listen:
There's Estous and Harpin, Piniau the Norman,
Magegos and Henri, the sixth is Sorant,
And the seventh is Robaut, the treacherous cur. 5810
The latter is the master of the others; they're dependent upon him,
Do his bidding and obey his commands.
They would not fail him even if it meant the loss of limbs.
The robber addressed them; he's beginning to advise them:
"Listen to me, noble valiant knights! 5815
By God, this knight is very much afraid of us.
However, he is a very valiant knight.
Have you seen the sword that he has girded at his side,
The heads of the pagans he's slain on the battlefield?
We won't attack him at all, that's my advice, 5820
Until he's eaten and drunk all he wants,
Once he's comfortably fallen asleep in his bed,
Beside the attractive and comely maiden.
I'll take off his head with my steel blade,
Then we'll divide up the booty equally among ourselves 5825
And deal with the lady as we like.
We're all companions, to this we've sworn oaths:

That we will not fail each other, no matter what happens."
And they all replied: "We'll do as you say,
And whatever you desire and all your commands.   5830
We won't fail you, even if it meant the loss of our limbs."
Then they all rapidly entered the hostel.
Each one goes about, hurrying to prepare the meal.
They give the warhorses hay and oats.
They want to take off their saddles, but Aiol stops them,   5835
So that they will be ready if he really needs them.
Now they put themselves into Judas' role,
Since they intend to kill Aiol in his sleep that night!

153.

Aiol sat down beside Mirabel,
And the robbers entered the hostel, all seven of them.   5840
Robaut, who was the master, approached the youth:
"Noble youth, my lord, I'm glad you came.
So unlace that helm and take off your hauberk!
If you were disarmed, it would please me more."
And Aiol replied: "By my head, I will not!   5845
When I left Orleans, from the main fortress,
I pledged to Louis and swore on saints' relics,
That from that moment until the hour of my return,
I would not unlace my helm or remove my hauberk.
Instead, I'd travel completely armed and endure the armor."   5850
When Robaut heard this, he almost went mad.
He takes Aiol's lance and his new shield,
And swore to the Lord God, who saved Daniel:
"With this one you'll not fight with me tonight."
When Aiol heard this, he almost lost his mind.   5855
Angrily, he swore on the body of St. Daniel:
"I wouldn't believe in you for all the gold in a castle!"
He drew his sword with its sharp blade,
To the Lord God he swore by the body of St. Marcel:
"If you don't put down the shield now, I'll strike such a blow   5860
That my steel blade will bathe in your brain!
Foul cur, put down my arms, I've no desire for violence!"

154.

Aiol, Elye's son, quickly leaped to his feet.
He came over to Robaut, the foul, treacherous cur,
And swore by the Lord God, the redeeming Father: 5865

⚜ A Chanson de Geste ⚜

"Whore's son, foul, treacherous old man,
If you don't put down my arms immediately,
You'll lose your head. There'll be no protection from death!"
When the robber saw him angrily jump to his feet,
He began to tremble down to his toenails.   5870
Aiol's good lance suddenly dropped from his hand.
"Noble knight," said the robber, "you're very valiant,
Bold in spirit, worthy with rapid reflexes!
Here are all of your arms. Do with them as you please.
I don't want to keep them an hour in my entire life."   5875
The other robbers were a little apart, fearful and trembling;
They called out to Aiol and started flattering him:
"Noble youth, baron, have pity for God the great.
Never have we seen a sole living man
Who acted towards his host with such hostility!   5880
How rudely you're behaving towards our master!
We haven't done anything to displease you;
Instead we're serving you with everything you desire."
Then Aiol remembered the Lord God the great.
Because they were his hosts, he let the matter drop   5885
When he heard them speaking so politely.
He thrust his sword quickly back into its sheath.
He sat back down beside Mirabel on the bench.
Never in all his life had he done such a great folly,
If the Lord God doesn't protect him through his worthy will!   5890
Because the robbers, who tortured God's body,* turned away,
They brought the meal into the main room.
When they were supposed to serve it, they went to arm themselves.
They had no hauberks nor helms and not a single sharp sword.
Instead, they went to equip themselves as peasants would,   5895
They had kettle caps, leather body armor protecting their chests,
And they girded on swords with poor blades.
They had no shields or lances, but rather heavy cudgels.
Mirabel, the maiden, was observing all of this,
Because she was worthy, astute and well-educated.   5900
She addressed Aiol and quickly spoke to him
In his right ear, rapidly gave him this advice:
"Don't ever believe me again in all my life,
If those robbers aren't arming themselves in that room.
Make sure they don't surprise you, noble, valiant knight!"   5905
And Aiol sprang to his feet, rapidly and quickly,
And spotted an axe hanging behind the fireplace.

⚜ Aiol ⚜

A full measured foot in length was its blade
Of iron bound to the handle up to the front grippings.
This was Robaut's axe, the treacherous cur.   5910
Aiol went over there and seized it with both hands.
Above his shoulder, he raised the blade,
He swung and brandished it, continued to wield it.
He came up to Robaut, the cursed tyrant.
He swore to the Lord God, the redeeming Father,   5915
That if Robaut doesn't have all of his companions come forth,
Bring the meal and present it right away,
"You'll lose your head — you'll have no protection against it —
To this Danish axe that I'm holding right here."
When the robber heard this, he was seized by fear.   5920
He shouted a few words loudly for all to hear:
"Barons, come on out, what are you waiting for?
Bring the meal, because I want and command it!
For God's sake, this knight's full of distrust:
He'd not be reassured even if it meant losing his limbs."   5925
When the robbers heard this, they began to disarm themselves
And to bring the meal, plotting among themselves.
If they can capture Aiol while he's seated at table,
They'll tie his hands. He'll have no protection from death.
Then they'll lead him to a prison in the deep forest.   5930
May he be protected by the Lord who formed all people
And was born to the holy Virgin in Bethlehem!

155.

The large table was set and Robaut stood up.
He turned to face Aiol and began to speak to him:
"Noble youth, lord, listen to me now: 5935
You will be seated at this high table
Next to the lady. Each one of us will serve you."
And Aiol swore by his head that he wouldn't do it:
"When I left Orleans, the mighty royal city,
I pledged to Louis, my lord by birthright,   5940
That I would not eat at table until I returned,
So my lady and I will both eat over here."
He took up the shield with arm straps he greatly loved
And his sharpened lance, which he greatly trusted,
And kept the Danish axe very close at hand.   5945
He turned towards his horses that were in the hostel
And called Mirabel over beside him:

⚜ A Chanson de Geste ⚜

"Dear sister, sweet friend, come close to me, over here.
You'll be my companion as long as it pleases Jesus."
She was worthy and astute. Quickly she went over there,　　5950
And when Robaut saw this, he almost lost his mind.
With arrogant rage he swore to the Lord God:
"I think that this knight considers us all to be complete fools.
To hell with the danger, I won't put up with him anymore.
Go arm yourselves. We'll attack him from both sides."　　5955
The robbers ran out of the great room into the chamber and rapidly
　　armed themselves,
And Master Robaut fled, leaving his companions,
Straight down across the main bridge and plunged into the woods.
He went straightaway to Malrepaire, his hideout,
Where he had left his arms and his swift horse.　　5960
And Robaut swore to the Lord God who made the world
That as soon as he was armed, he'd track down the bold knight.
But as long as Aiol's free, he'll stay away from him.
If he sees Aiol at all incapacitated, he'll not hesitate to attack.
Robaut covets the maiden: his lust for her is strong,　　5965
But before he'd have her, he'll pay for her dearly.

156.

By my faith, my lords, I won't conceal from you
That many an entourage does much that is to blame!
Robaut's a case in point, the foul cur.
He has really left his companions in the lurch.　　5970
He'll never rescue or help them.
Now let's tell you about Aiol, the noble knight,
And about the beautiful, attractive maiden,
Who are lodged inside with the robbers.
If they can't enter into combat against the six robbers,　　5975
They'll have bad lodging that night at bedtime.
Mirabel, the maiden, spoke to Aiol first:
"By the saints of heaven, my lord, noble youth,
Hand me that axe because I want to help you.
You know well how to deal blows with your steel sword."　　5980
"Fair one," said Aiol, "it will be as you wish,
But watch out that you don't let anyone take it from you."
"My lord," said the maiden, "don't waste your breath.
They'd have to hack off all my arms and legs
Before I would let anyone else wield it."　　5985
Aiol goes to pass it over to her by the planed handle,

⚜ Aiol ⚜

And she received it willingly and gladly.
Now here are the robbers all armed.
They come out of the chamber close together in ranks.
Mirabel steps forward, the maiden with the proud expression. 5990
At the chamber door, she advanced to meet them.
She struck the first one with the Danish axe:
On his left shoulder she dealt him such a blow
That she sliced him down his front as far as his waist.
His intestines spilled out from him down onto his feet. 5995
She delivered her blow and struck him down dead.
"Oh, God!" said Aiol, "May you be thanked!
Now I have a good companion, who really knows how to help me,
And if Jesus lets me return to France,
She'll have the mighty city of Angers as her dowry!" 6000
"My lord," said the maiden, "may you have a hundred thanks."
Aiol thrusts out the shaft of the stout, sharp lance
And goes to strike another robber, not sparing him at all,
Because he made the steel pass straight through his body.
In the middle of the room the robber fell down dead. 6005
Then Aiol drew his sword with its sharpened steel blade
And went to strike another robber who was coming out of the room.
Through his helm's laces Aiol makes the robber's head fly off.
Then he strikes yet again the fourth robber, whom he cut in two.
The two remaining robbers are in the room, suffering and anguished. 6010
Through a large window, which opens onto an orchard,
They turn in flight, the renegade curs,
Down across the main bridge, and then they plunged into the woods.
But Aiol didn't want to prolong the chase very much.
Instead, he closes the gate and pulls up the drawbridge. 6015
Using the iron chains, he bound it and made it fast.
From the drawbridge back to the house, they went without stopping.
Aiol came to the four robbers who had been hacked to pieces.
He dragged them from the house by their feet, one by one.
Then he threw them into the water off the main bridge. 6020
Back to the house he then went, he didn't want to delay.
At that point, that night Aiol was lodged there,
But he didn't dare to rest or lie down.
Mirabel, the maiden, began to speak to him:
"Noble youth, my lord, for the saints in heaven, 6025
Don't unlace your helm, noble knight,
Don't take off the breast plates of your twice-mailed hauberk.
It would be great madness for you remove it too soon;

⚜ A Chanson de Geste ⚜

We don't know yet what this place is where we're staying.
I'll give you the water. Let's sit down to dinner. 6030
Look here, there's lots of food that's all prepared.
The robbers thought that we would pay dearly for our meal.
Thanks to God's mercy, we've earned our keep.
Let's eat with the assurance that our part is paid in full."
"Fair one," said Aiol, "we'll do what you want." 6035
He ran to embrace her, appreciative of her axe blow.
If she were a Christian, Aiol would have wanted to kiss her,
But because she was a pagan, he didn't want to touch her.
He didn't want to shame the faith in the King of glory;
Instead, he will have her baptized and raised above the holy font, 6040
And then he will take her as his wife, peer and spouse.
Because of these acts on earth, he's now a saint in heaven.*

157.
Aiol, Elye's son, was very worthy and noble.
He unlaced his helm and put it on the table
And removed the breast-plates of his shining, thrice-woven hauberk. 6045
Mirabel worked hard to serve him
And gave him water. They sat down to dinner.
Aiol ate a lot, but drank little wine,
Because he's very much on alert, the noble knight.
When they had eaten and drunk their fill, 6050
Aiol had Mirabel, the maiden, lie down in a bed,
And he made a large fire — he didn't want to sleep in a bed —
Until the next day when dawn was breaking.
He put the halters back on the prize warhorses,
Then he drew his sword and put on his shield. 6055
He searched thoroughly throughout the house.
There he found much silver and pure gold
And rich cloth, fine silks and ermine-lined cloaks.
This booty was worth more than thirty marks of pure gold.
The noble knight loaded it on the horses. 6060
Mirabel led them as far as the drawbridge.
Aiol was in the hostel. He set fire to it in four places,
Then he retreated back across the drawbridge.
The fire was going strong even before he left.
The breeze blew with force. Soon everything was charred and burned. 6065
The robbers who had fled to the woods watched this.
So great was their fear of Aiol that they didn't dare fight.
They turned away in tears. Now may God curse them!

⚜ Aiol ⚜

They didn't stop until they had reached Malrepaire.
Robaut, their master, saw them coming and went out to meet them. 6070
He spoke to them, as you will now hear:
"How have you been doing, noble, worthy knights?"
And they replied: "Things have gone badly for us!
And in your companionship, we trust very little.
Your house and your drawbridge have been completely burnt up, 6075
And our companions are dead and hacked to pieces."
When the robber heard this, he almost went mad.
He took up his arms and seized his horse.
Straight through the wide woods he began to ride.
He didn't stop until he had reached the house, 6080
And he found it and the main bridge all burnt up.
He saw his companions lying in the moat,
And when the robber saw this, he almost lost his mind.
He returned to the others and began to speak to them:
"Come with me, noble, worthy knights, 6085
And we will follow the rogue who has outraged me so.
If I can catch up with him on a hill or hillside,
In a ditch or on the ground where he's fallen asleep,
I wouldn't trade that chance for all the gold God's made,
Because I'll take off his head with my polished steel blade!" 6090
The robbers answered: "It's astonishing you'd say that!
Master Robaut, dear lord, you've failed us.
The first time we needed you, you betrayed our trust.
We've completely abandoned your company.
As long as we live, we'll no longer go with you." 6095
When the robber heard this, he thought he'd lose his mind:
"What! You whores' sons! It's you who've failed me!
You'll have to pay for it, by the saints that God made."
Robaut was well armed and the others had no arms.
He spurred his horse, brandished his lance 6100
And struck the first one of them in the middle of his chest.
Robaut's blow left him lying dead stretched out on the ground.
Then he drew his sword and went to strike another one
Above his shoulders taking off his head.
This was the kind of companionship the evil man provided them. 6105
Then Robaut took off after Aiol all along the paved road.
He'll yet make him angry and depressed,
If Aiol doesn't stay alert as he travels his road.

A Chanson de Geste

158.

Now Aiol journeys forth along his wide road.
He's leading the maiden and the swift warhorses. 6110
All day long the noble youth has travelled and ridden
Until it was vespers again and near nightfall.
"Oh, God!" said Mirabel, of the noble bearing,
"So far away is that France where we have to return!"
"Fair one," said Aiol, "now don't be disheartened. 6115
Right ahead on a hill is an old, small castle
And the ruins of a town. Its walls are all tumbled down,
But not a living soul remains there.
If I can, I'll gladly head in that direction.
Today we've a good chance of finding shelter by the walls. 6120
Tomorrow we'll have help, if God grants it."
"My lord," said the maiden, "may God grant it."
They found the town to be in ruins, where they were to take shelter.
It was at the top of a hill at the edge of a steep cliff.
Down below there's a meadow and a wide pond. 6125
They got down on foot from their swift warhorses.
Aiol, the noble knight, set them out to pasture.
The horses grazed on the grass and drank from the pond.
The maiden lay down beside the knight.
Here is a well-born man poorly lodged, 6130
Since Aiol and the maiden had nothing to eat that night.
For a loaf of bread, he would have given up the best warhorse
Of the seven that he had won and conquered.
He was wearing his hauberk and had his helm laced on,
His large sword was girded on, his shield over his head, 6135
His lance beside him, his spurs on his feet.
If a battle comes to him, he'll be ready,
Because he greatly fears the robbers he's left in the woods.
He was extremely tired and exhausted,
Because he'd journeyed and travelled all day, 6140
And the night before in the hostel, he'd kept watch for the robbers,
And the night before that, he'd spent in the saddle.
Aiol hadn't slept for three entire days:
The length of time it takes any man to go a half a league on foot.
Quickly the noble knight fell asleep, 6145
And also the attractive and comely maiden.
But that night such a horrible misfortune happened to him!*
Never has such a disaster befallen one lone knight,
Because the devil wants to trick him in the end.

155

❦ Aiol ❦

Then a foul-lineaged serpent came out of a rock, 6150
Which was easily nineteen feet in length:
Very black, hideous, awesome and fierce,
Its eyes were set easily a half a foot apart.
It had ravaged all of the pagans of that land.
It had never found a beast that could stand up to it. 6155
Rapidly it threw itself down from the rock,
Right down to where it reached Aiol, the noble knight.
It completely swallows up his entire leg,
His thigh, his knee, up to the knot of his belt.
Gently it holds him, it doesn't want to eat him. 6160
Thanks to the power of heaven, it doesn't dare touch him any more than that.
Our Lord of heaven had forbidden it,
And due to the truce of God, it can't hurt him any more than that.
No one can be shamed whom God wants to help!
This was on the Friday, when God was insulted, 6165
And when he was hung upon the cross to rescue us from hell.
From then until the next day, Aiol couldn't wake up.
Mibrien's daughter was the very first to spot it
And saw the serpent, big, huge and whole.
Such revulsion did the lady feel, she almost lost her mind, 6170
So much that she didn't dare move or cry out.
But she drew near to Aiol, right alongside his head;
She spoke into his ear, politely and calmly:
"Noble young knight, my lord, we're in a bad fix.
A serpent has swallowed your entire leg, 6175
Your thigh and your knee up to the knot of your belt.
For God's sake, noble youth, my lord, don't make the slightest noise.
Don't make the slightest move, or else you'll be eaten!"
When Aiol heard this, he was utterly astonished.
Then he looked at his leg and saw the enemy: 6180
Never in his life did he have such fear of death!
He began a prayer, which he needed badly;
He called on the Lord God, the glorious one of heaven:
"Glorious Lord, Father, who was and eternally is,
You took on flesh and blood in the worthy woman, 6185
And you were born of her — I refuse to disbelieve it —
And on the holy cross you let yourself be crucified.
All day long you had to suffer and agonize.
When Longinus, who failed to keep his watch,* struck you,
From the lance wound in your side the blood gushed forth. 6190

⚜ A Chanson de Geste ⚜

It streamed down the thick lance until it splattered on his fists.
Longinus wiped his eyes with it, and your blood enlightened him:
He admitted his sins and sincerely repented.
God, then you graciously pardoned him completely,
As far as Golgotha you made your blood flow. 6195
And on the mount of Calvary it shattered the stone.
Pilgrims all see it, who go there to kiss it.
We have hard evidence of this because of your death.
Throughout the world, everything was trembling: the earth, the meadows,
And the high mountains and all the stones. 6200
Birds could not fly that day, nor sing joyful songs,
Nor any living beast — this we know very well.
They were sad and mournful. There was only anguish.
You had yourself lain in the most holy sepulcher.
Pilate had you guarded, and there were many soldiers, 6205
But all of their surveillance wasn't worth an iota.
You arose on the third day, dear and righteous Father.
You descended into hell, all along the ancient path,
You had all of its gates and doors shattered.
You had no fear at all of the enemy's power. 6210
You brought out your friends whom you held so dear.
Just as this was factual, true and righteous God,
Protect me today from death and injury,
And deliver me from this foul enemy,
That I may depart safe and sound and whole!" 6215

159.

Aiol had his leg in the serpent's body.
Don't be astonished if he was afraid of death!
Very quietly he prayed to St. Mary's Son:
"Glorious Lord and Father, who made the whole world,
And established heaven and earth and all creation, 6220
And in the beginning made Adam and Eve
Who ate the fruit that you had forbidden.
Just as this was true, glorious Lord and Father,
Protect me today, my limbs and my life!
What a misfortune to have followed me, high-born young maiden! 6225
You must have little esteem for my great knighthood,
When our great friendship will already have been severed.
Mount up on your horse, my dear, sweet friend.
Turn around back along that old, ancient way.

❦ Aiol ❦

Stay right on your path, don't make a mistake and stray.　　6230
May God give you to a man who can truly help you!"
And Mirabel replied: "You've wasted your breath, my lord.
Because I have rejected Mohammed and his idols,
May it not please the Lord God, St. Mary's Son,
That I should abandon you for anything alive!　　6235
Instead I'll die with you in suffering and pain."
Her great anguish causes her to fall down in a faint.

160.

The maiden is in distress because of the good knight,
Whom she can't save as she would have wished.
She appealed to the King of majesty:　　6240
"Lord God, Lord and Father, Redeemer of all,
And you make men and women hear and speak.
St. Abraham," she said, "you were so worthy,
So the good Christian clerics told me and recounted.
Jesus, who took on human flesh, commanded you　　6245
Within an orchard, where you had entered,
That you should give him the thing you loved most.
This was Isaac, your son, whom you had begotten.
By sacrificing him, he wanted to test you.
This was then the custom throughout the kingdom　　6250
To burn the tenth that they had given.
And you began preparations with such great loyalty
That you intended to kill the child and cut him to pieces.
On a donkey you had him mount up.
Straight to *Dominus Videt*,* you had him carried,　　6255
Outside of Jerusalem, on the mount of Bel Cler.
There you caused a fire to start up and blaze.
You brought a sword to sacrifice your child
And you intended to burn and sear him in the fire
And offer to God his bones and ashes　　6260
When a holy angel appeared beside you,
Who whispered in your ear: 'Dear sweet friend, desist.
The Lord God has certainly put your friendship to the test.'
He gave you a sheep with horns and thick wool,
And said: 'Dear, sweet friend, take this sheep　　6265
And sacrifice it, sweet friend, on the altar,
As you were going to do with the child of your flesh.'
He took the sword from you and the child was saved.
Just as this was true, glorious God and Lord,

⚜ A Chanson de Geste ⚜

Protect Aiol today from all harm. 6270
For the sake of his love, I'll take on holy Christianity.
Above the holy font, I'll have myself raised and baptized."

161.

Mirabel was suffering intensely because of the young man,
Whom she could not help from near or from afar.
Now here comes Robaut right across the wilderness. 6275
The robber from evil stock had followed them closely.
He was old and white-haired; in his eyes was the look of an evil serf.
However, he wasn't so poor that he didn't have a castle,
But he always lived from robbery. He had no other livelihood.
He spurred his warhorse and rode up to Mirabel. 6280
She didn't recognize him because of the swift warhorse
And the expensive armor the foul cur was wearing.

162.

The old man was big and strong and full of evil ruses.
When he spotted the maiden, he quickly rode towards her.
The first word he said to her was: "Fair one, who are you?" 6285
"Dear sir, I'm an unfortunate woman. I've lost my lord.
We left Spain the other day at dawn,
From the house of my father, a rich vavassor.
Saracens, evil and arrogant, pursued my lord.
They killed all our men, not even one of them is left, 6290
Only my lord and I. We were fleeing from there
To this ruined town where we had to stop yesterday evening.
We lodged right here by this tower.
This morning we saw this huge, arrogant devil
Who was holding my lord by his foot in great pain, 6295
And he was suffering great anguish from the foul odor
That this serpent gives off, that's causing me such fear.
So please go ahead and kill it now, my lord, through love freely given.
I'll give you three marks of silver immediately."
When the old man heard this, he was filled with great fear. 6300
He coveted the money, but he was terrified of the serpent.
"May God never help me, not a single day," he said,
"If I'd ever give him any help or aid,
Because he burned my house and inflicted immense pain.
He killed my companions, and that's caused me great anger. 6305
Instead, let's take that booty and go off, you and I."

⚜ Aiol ⚜

When the maiden heard this she was seized by such distress
That she fell into a faint four times before Aiol's eyes.

163.

The old man had great fear of the serpent he saw.
It held Aiol by the thigh: he was in a bad spot.   6310
However, Robaut pointed his finger at him.
The old man swore to God, who is seated on high and is farseeing:
"You won't be saved or rescued by me!"
He came over to the maiden and arrogantly said to her:
"Mount up right away on that black horse.   6315
We'll go off together, you and I, and we'll take that wealth."
When Mirabel heard this, don't you think she was outraged?
"Oh, you treacherous old man! May God destroy you and your kind!"
She lashed out with her palm and struck Robaut so hard
Her five finger marks appeared on his right breast.   6320
The old man drew his sword and angrily came towards her,
But she was so afraid that she fell in a faint.
Then Robaut had her mount up, whether she liked it or not,
Whether she wanted to or not, on the black, spotted warhorse.
He rounded up the other horses and placed them in front of him,   6325
Except for Aiol's warhorse, who remained out of his sight
Away from them, in a thicket, grazing under a tree.
May Aiol be protected by the far-seeing Lord God who is seated
   on high
And give him back his lady love who's rightfully his!

164.

The old man's name was Robaut, who was leading off the young
   woman.   6330
He shouts to her: "Ride on, dear friend!
Now you'll lie with me under my blanket.
I'll keep you ten, twelve, thirteen or fifteen years.
Don't get angry at all if I take someone else,
Because I've already shamed a hundred as beautiful as you.   6335
Never has God or man ever called me to account for it."
When Mirabel heard this she almost went mad from anger.
"May God, St. Mary's Son, never, ever help me
To provide you, in any place, with my company.
Oh! Evil foul cur, may God curse you!   6040
Go over there to my lord and fight the serpent!
I'll give you wealth and riches in France."

❧ A Chanson de Geste ❧

And Robaut replied: "That's crazy talk!
May the Lord God, St. Mary's Son, destroy me
If ever he gets any help or aid from me!" 6345

165.

Robaut took the maiden by her sleeve of rich fabric.
Quickly, the robber begins to speak to her:
"Get down on the ground fast!
Let's have a little pleasure in the shade of that tree!
It seems to me there's no escape for you." 6350
When Mirabel heard this, she almost went mad with anger.
"Oh, traitor, old man, may your line be destroyed!
I'd rather be dead than to do such things with you!"
She reached out with her two fists and seized him by his beard.
She yanked and jerked it violently again and again, 6355
With such force that she ripped out a hundred hairs.

166.

Aiol had his foot in the serpent's body.
He confessed to God what was in his heart and his desires,
And made a good confession quietly, between his teeth
To God of holy glory, not holding anything back. 6360
Then the young man with great resourcefulness drew his sword
And thrust it into the serpent's maw,
All the way in, down between the serpent and his own thigh.
He struck violently due to his own strength and his anger,
Pulling the sword back towards him and plunging it in again. 6365
He slashed the serpent's throat and its nerves inside.
Down to the ground flowed the bloody blade,
Along its path, it plunged through the serpent's heart,
And it died, letting out a great bellow.
Aiol rapidly pulled out his foot. 6370

167.

Now the serpent is dead, completely drained of its power.
Aiol, Elye's son, pulls out his foot from the serpent.
He comes to the serpent and cuts it in two.
Nineteen feet was its length all stretched out.
Then he picked his sword up — he didn't feel like cleaning it. 6375
He quickly slipped the blade back into its sheath
And goes through the orchard, suffering and distressed.
Duke Elye's son is grieving intensely:

⚜ Aiol ⚜

"Oh, alas," said Aiol, "what a misfortune!
That well-born maiden, what a prize I've lost! 6380
So wrongly he's leading you off, the evil, white-haired old man!"
Aiol sees Marchegai grazing in the shade of a tree.
Don't bother to ask if he was filled with joy!
He worships God for this and all his power:
"Lord, glorious Father, I hail you for it, 6385
That you've saved this horse and given him to me.
Now let me have the other horses by your power!"
He came up to Marchegai and mounted him by the stirrup
And seized in his right fist, his stout, sharpened lance.

168.

Aiol, Elye's son, was mounted on his warhorse. 6390
Never had he been so happy and joyous
That God had delivered him from the body of the enemy.
He started to follow the trail of the maiden and the old man.
He hadn't gone but the distance of two crossbow shots,
When he saw them together in a flowery valley. 6395
The maiden was exhausted: she couldn't defend herself any longer,
When Robaut knocked her to the ground to lie with her.
He had pulled off his breeches to free himself.
The maiden stepped forward, she didn't want to wait.
Between his two thighs she plunged her hands, 6400
So far in that she grabbed him by his balls.
She yanked on them violently, rendering him powerless.
Robaut fainted four times before he could sit up!
When he raised his head, he saw Aiol come riding up,
And he said to the maiden: "Fair one, let me go! 6405
I swear to you in the name of God the righteous Father,
By me you'll never have shame or hardship."
"My lord," said Mirabel, "thank you in the name of God in heaven,
Because you've taken pity on an unfortunate woman!"
She relaxed her grip and Robaut stood up. 6410
Had she seen Aiol, she wouldn't have let him go.
Woe to the robber now, even if he flees a half a finger or a whole foot!
He knows well that fleeing will do him no good.
Instead, he heads towards Aiol down an ancient path.
Aiol pricks Marchegai with his spurs of purest gold 6415
And brandishes the shaft of his stout, sharp lance.
He goes to strike the robber and does it so well
He breaks and shatters the shield hanging from his neck

❧ A Chanson de Geste ❧

And rips and shreds the hauberk on his back.
Right through his body, Aiol thrusts its steel tip. 6420
With the entire length of the lance he strikes him dead on the path.
Then he drew his sword and cut off his head
And hangs it with the others on the warhorses.
When Mirabel saw this, her heart was filled with joy.

169.

The maiden became joyful when she saw the young knight, 6425
Because he had been freed from the serpent.
She came up to him and began to speak to him:
"Tell me, my lord, how were you freed from the serpent?"
"Fair one," said Aiol, "it's dead with God's help.
Let's go back now. I want to show it to you." 6430
They went back all along the beaten path
And saw the serpent, maimed, killed and slain.
The horses under them were terrified,
And the horses in front of them turned towards France.

170.

Now Aiol rides off leading the maiden. 6435
He has loaded the heads on the seven horses.
The Saracens' heads are decayed and ugly,
But the Christian's head was the best-looking of all.
They came out of the forest onto an open plain.
They saw towns and cities, castles and dwellings. 6440
They didn't stop travelling until they came to Mongraile.
Geraume, the lord of the castle, lodged them that night.
He was Elye's nephew, a well-born, upstanding duke.
They didn't know each other, which was the source of
    much trouble.*
Geraume summoned his household's high steward: 6445
"Go get cranes, geese and fresh venison,
Because I'm lodging this noble knight.
To honor his friendship, we'll organize a feast.
Tonight my townsmen from Mongraile will be with me."
"My lord," said Aiol, "by my head, you're a worthy man! 6450
You'll be fully reimbursed before I leave your lands."
"My lord," said his host, "may it not please the heavenly King,
The glorious one of heaven, who rules the world,
That we should have even a hawberry's worth of what's yours.
Never did my father nor did my ancestors, 6455

❦ Aiol ❦

If they provided lodging for a free man or an honored knight,
Ever charge him for a hostel or a place to stay.
And if it pleases God, I'll never besmirch my family's name.
I have four sons by my wife. Tonight I want them to serve you.
The fourth one is a knight. He's already taking off your saddles, 6460
And he'll clean, curry, water and put the horses at their ease."
Geraume's four sons are very worthy and courteous,
They come to Aiol and serve him in a courtly manner.
They remove his spurs, pull off his hose,
Clean his hauberk and burnish his helm. 6465
"My lord," said Aiol, "by my head, you're a worthy man!
What a distinguished household you have, and so dignified!
Those squires I see here could all be knights."
"My lord," said his host, "they're true to their family line.
I'm Elye's relative, there's not a better duke on earth. 6470
Never a better knight could ever mount in a saddle,
But he became embroiled in a dispute with the king who rules
   the French,
Who drove Elye from his lands, following bad advice,
Which came from Makaire — may God grant him harm —
An evil, flattering advisor, a foul cur from bad lineage. 6475
He deserves death, if I had my way!
The noble duke fled far away to a foreign land.
If I knew where he was, I'd set out to search for him."
"My lord," said Aiol, "by the eyes in my head!
He's still very much alive. I know exactly where he's living. 6480
He will be reconciled with the king, and he'll get his lands back."
"Oh, God!" said his host, "If this were only true!
I'd give a hundred gold marks to bring about that pact."
The good news about Duke Elye caused the host such joy
That he had his arms brought to him, with his hauberk and his helm 6485
And his sharp sword and his shield from Biterme.
He looks at Aiol and courteously begins to speak to him:
"My lord, look here; there aren't any better arms on earth.
I'm still not at all so old or so weak
That, if there were any knight between here and Bordeaux, 6490
And I were to deal him a mighty blow on his new shield,
My lance would not shatter, and he would not empty his saddle."
By this Aiol knew very well that his host was of his own lineage.
"My lord," said Aiol, "if you consented to it,
I could bring your sons with me to my land. 6495
I'd give to each one of them more than he ever would have
   in Mongraile.

⚜ A Chanson de Geste ⚜

These seven Spanish horses I'd give them free and clear,
Gladly and willingly, but I'd want them to serve me."
"My lord," said his host, "may it not please the heavenly King,
The glorious one of heaven who rules the world, 6500
That we should have a hawberry's worth of what's yours.
I'll get arms for them that are handsome and fine looking.
I'll wait until Pentecost, the glorious festival,
Then I'll have them dubbed in my ancestral palace,
Before my household and my closest companions, 6505
Who will be more enthusiastic about it than in a foreign land,
And you'll make your return to France, my lord.
If you need any help if a war against you should break out,
We'll come to your aid with whatever we can do."
When Aiol heard this, he became joyful at the news. 6510
His whole heart in his breast leaps and quakes with joy.

171.

Aiol spent that night in the city of Montgraile.
Geraume, the lord of the castle, who was noble and worthy,
Had a great banquet prepared for him.
There was no knight, burgher or maiden 6515
Who didn't eat with them. All were summoned and invited.
They looked at Mirabel the maiden with astonishment and wonder.
The ladies of Mongraile began to say to him:
"By God, dear, sweet friend, Aiol, look at that maiden.
In our entire lives we've never seen anyone more beautiful." 6520
"By my head," said Aiol, "I won't fail her in the least.
I won her the other day by my knighthood.
I'll bring her with me to France, land of plenty.
I'll have her baptized and raised above the holy font,
And I'll take her to wife if God grants me life." 6525
And the maiden replied: "Five hundred thanks, dear lord."
They spent that night there in the midst of great rejoicing,
And they were served in an extremely lavish fashion
Until the following day, when dawn was breaking.
Geraume's four sons put his saddle 6530
On his Spanish horse, they did it very willingly.
And the lord of the castle mounted up. He accompanied them himself,
Gladly and willingly, for an entire league.
He gave them a kiss of friendship when they separated
And commended them to God, St. Mary's Son. 6535

The noble knight is sadly ignorant,
This is his first cousin and he doesn't know it.
Before it's vespers and night has fallen,
Aiol will have a great fear of death and need of help.
Never will he have seen such a bitter day in all his life! 6540

172.
Now Aiol rides off. He's taken leave.
He's leading the maiden and all his warhorses.
Geraume, the lord of the castle, has turned back.
When he came to Mongraile, his vast palace,
He summons his four sons and speaks to them: 6545
"My sons," said Geraume, "we made a grave error
When we let that knight ride off alone.
My heart tells me that he's definitely of our lineage.
I'd not believe any man on earth
Who'd tell me this is not the son of Elye, the mighty, noble duke. 6550
I'll outfit you with arms and warhorses,
And you'll follow the young knight all along the wide highway.
If he has need of you, it's your duty to help him.
I'm especially afraid for him in the Cinquefoil Forest.
You'll guide him through it and as far as Orleans." 6555
When the young men heard this, never had they been so glad.
Geraume, the castle's worthy lord, equips them
With shining hauberks and helms and swift warhorses,
And he, himself, put on armor — he doesn't want to delay.
Then they ride out of the city together in close ranks. 6560
They aren't bringing with them either foot soldiers or squires,
Except for four grooms to care for the horses,
Because they think they will return that night by vespers.
Now may Jesus guide these new knights,
Because, before it's vespers and the sun has set, 6565
If they want to help their cousin Aiol,
They will be able to prove their knighthood and put it to the test,
And no other quintain will be needed for them.
Now I'll tell you about Aiol, the noble warrior.
All day long the worthy knight has traveled and journeyed 6570
Until evening, when vespers comes again.
Then Aiol calls upon the righteous Father
That he may guide him to a place where there is something to eat.
He looked out in front of him along the great wide road
And spotted a monk who wore a tonsure. 6575

❦ A Chanson de Geste ❦

Under his ears he had cut off his side whiskers.
He wore a frock, an old long skirt and a light wool garment,
And he was shod and booted with a monk's big boots.
He did seem to be fully ordained — wide was the tonsure
   on his head —
And he held in his hands a pick-axe and a lever. 6580
In that spot, the road's paving was all torn up,
And the monk was making a great show of repairing the road bed.
Now here comes Aiol, who greets him courteously
In the name of God of holy glory who reigns over all.
The monk answered Aiol when he had raised his head. 6585
The monk lifted up his cowl and bowed to him:
"May the Lord, who sits in judgment over everything, protect you!
Where do you come from, from what region, noble knight?"
"My lord, I'm coming from Spain," Aiol answered him.
"I'm bringing with me a lady who's exhausted from riding. 6590
We have ridden hard and driven ourselves.
I see this forest growing dusky before us.
I don't see city walls or a house, moats, palisades, houses
Or rich men's dwellings where we can seek lodging."
"My lord," said the monk, "I can give you good advice. 6595
There's an abbey here in this great, vast forest.
If you please, tonight you can certainly seek lodging there.
You'll have a great abundance of everything you need,
And bread and meat and wine, as much as you desire,
Hay and oats for your swift warhorses, 6600
And you can stay there as long as you want —
Four or five days, if you need to.
And when you're ready to travel and ride on,
We'll gladly and willingly accompany you, following behind,
Until you've left the forest, four leagues or more. 6605
You won't have to spend even a denier's worth of your possessions.
Four ladies, who do much that's praiseworthy
And who have come to this retreat for the love of God in heaven,
Will be able to better tend to your wife's wants,
And do what she wishes and all that's good for her." 6610
"Oh, God," said Aiol, "may you be thanked!
My lord, take these hundred sous in coins worth a denier each.
By holy charity, I'll give them to you willingly,
So that for a month you can hire four workers
To repair the road, which is in great need of it." 6615
"My lord," said the monk, "you're wasting your breath,

❧ Aiol ❧

Because we're rich men and have plenty of deniers.
We're repairing the roadway for the love of God in heaven.
We want to discipline and punish our bodies.
I came here today because my turn has come.   6620
Tomorrow another will come, and a third the following day,
And afterwards a fourth without any delay.
Even a prior or an abbot will not be spared.
But go ahead and take that lady and have her dismount,
And let her sleep under that leafy tree.   6625
I'll go on ahead, noble knight,
And I'll tell my lord abbot that I have lodged you,
So you'll have everything you need in abundance.
It will be much better for you tonight at dinner."
Aiol came up to the lady and helped her down without difficulty,   6630
And Mirabel lay down beneath the spreading tree.
Aiol was worthy, courteous and well-taught.
He folded up an ermine cloak and placed it under her head.
Afterwards, he returned to the monk he had left:
"Mount up quickly, brother," he said, "on this swift warhorse.   6635
Let this one be yours. I'm giving it to you gladly and willingly.
It's strong and swift and a good ambler.
I took it the other evening from a mighty pagan king.
With it, the lord abbot can care for the needs of his monks."
"My lord," said the monk, "you're wasting your breath.   6640
When we were out in the lay world, we were knights.
For the love of God, we left it quite some time ago.
I promised the Lord God when I was tonsured
Never would I mount on a mule or a warhorse
Or on any four-footed animal.   6645
I wouldn't ever mount one, even to save my limbs from being cut off."
Then he whispered between his teeth so Aiol wouldn't hear:
"I don't know if I took them in when I said that:
Certainly you won't take away anything worth even a denier!
Instead you'll lose your head, there's no avoiding it."   6650
God! If Aiol had heard this, the noble knight,
He would have cut off the monk's head with his steel sword.
These aren't monks at all, who are lodged there,
But rather twelve robbers, traitors and outcasts,
Who are living there in order to deceive people.   6655
They murder pilgrims cruelly and sinfully
And seize their gold, silver and their deniers.
My lords, all of these robbers were once knights,

⚜ A Chanson de Geste ⚜

But they've been exiled and banished from their lands.
They came together here; they don't know how to earn a living. 6660
Instead, robbing and stealing has become their trade.
They love stolen goods more than any possessions on earth.
Each one had good arms and a good, swift warhorse,
And he doesn't ever want to sell or pawn it.
I'll name them all for you, if you'd like me to. 6665
They are named Gonbaut, the foul renegade,
Who, because of treason, caused himself to be banished;
Moran, Allivin and the rogue Galien,
Constan, Gonsellin, Ricier and Rahier,
Flohar of Val Lievre and Hagenon of Orleans, 6670
Clarenbau of Val Brune, Corson of Val Rahier.
This final robber was the leader of the others, their lord and chief.
He was very strong, rash, arrogant and fierce.
Gonbaut went off — may God grant him trouble.
As long as he's in Aiol's sight, he walks along slowly and calmly, 6675
But when he's reached a point where he's some distance away,
He hurried along the path rapidly and swiftly.
His boots were really weighing him down, so he pulled them off
And ripped off his cape, which was a heavy burden.
He wrapped them all together — the foul renegade — 6680
And shoved them into some bushes to free himself.
He took off fleeing faster than a greyhound.
As far as the forest, he didn't want to delay.
He came to the eleven robbers whom he had left.
Corson saw him coming and spoke to him: 6685
"What have you been up to, my lord Gonbaut?
You're coming in empty-handed, without riches!
Where's the big booty you usually get?
The mules, the palfreys and the swift warhorses,
The pure gold and the silver, the denier coins 6690
That you usually rob from the pilgrims going to St. James?"
"My lord," said the traitor, "I've done very well!
I've got such a booty that there's none better on earth.
A courtly lady and a noble knight,
And seven extremely valuable Spanish horses 6695
That are loaded down with furs and riches.
The lady is paler than the hawthorn flower,
And her tint more rosy than a rose on the branch.
There isn't a more beautiful woman under the canopy of heaven.
You'll have her tonight, this can't be avoided. 6700

❧ Aiol ❧

Whatever you like, you'll have your will with her.
I've granted that the rest of us will have her too.
We're all companions pledged and sworn,
But you are our master, that's why you'll have her first."
"Gonbaut," said the traitor, "you've done extremely well.   6705
You've always deserved my thanks and my friendship."
They entered their road, which was great and wide.
Here we'll leave the robbers, may God grant them hardship.
We'll come back to them soon enough, when it's time and place.
Instead, I'll tell you about Aiol, the noble knight,   6710
And the high-born maiden, shapely and elegant,
Who was asleep beneath the spreading tree.
She was completely exhausted and began to dream
That the ordained monks who had lodged them
Had unleashed upon them twelve evil bears,   6715
Who charged at them all enraged, their huge maws gaping.
They wanted to strangle and eat Aiol
And wanted to rip out his arms with their teeth.
The maiden awakens and leaps to her feet.
"Fair one," said Aiol, "did you have a bad dream?"   6720
"Those aren't at all monks who are living here,
Instead, they're twelve robbers, traitors and renegades
Who came together here to deceive people.
They murder pilgrims wrongly and evilly,
And they take their gold, silver and denier coins."   6725
"Fair one," said Aiol, "you're not speaking well
When you so wrongly accuse men of the Lord God.
They're repairing the roadway for the love of God
And wouldn't betray anyone for any possessions on earth."
"My lord," said the maiden, "let's abandon this plan to stay with them.   6730
I know that if we go there, noble knight,
I will be shamed wrongly and sinfully.
Let's go off in another direction down that great, wide road.
Let's leave this forest. It's making me very afraid.
Across the countryside makes for better riding   6735
To the first stronghold where we can seek shelter.
Then we'll take with us four foot soldiers,
And we'll give them three of our warhorses,
Or four or five if they're willing to accept them,
So that they'll agree to escort us as far as Orleans."   6740
"Fair one," said Aiol, "as you wish, so it will be.
Whoever doesn't want to accept advice, should come to a bad end."

❧ A Chanson de Geste ❧

He takes her in his arms and lifts her onto her warhorse.
Then he mounts up on Marchegai by his left stirrup.
He rounds up all the others; he doesn't want to leave a single one.   6745
They start out along their road, which was big and wide.
With great speed they begin to ride.
The robbers were in the deep, dense forest,
And when they saw that Aiol kept on delaying,
Corsault called to Gonbaut, the renegade: 6750
"What's going on, Lord Gonbaut, have you lied to us?
Where's this big booty that you were supposed to bring?
The beautiful, courtly lady and this noble knight
And seven Spanish horses who are so prized?
If you're deceiving us, you'll pay dearly for it!"   6755
"My lord," said the traitor, "I'm really astonished
That they've delayed so long, by all the saints of heaven!
The maiden is completely exhausted from riding.
She fell asleep under the spreading tree.
Hold on. Wait a bit. I'll go wake her up."   6760
"Go ahead, then," said the robber, "but you'd better not delay."
And the traitor replied: "I won't go on foot."
He took up his arms and equipped himself.
He had a very good horse, and he mounted up by the stirrup.
He quickly turned around and seized his shield and lance.   6765
He didn't slow down until the spreading tree —
The place that Aiol had abandoned and left —
And when he didn't find either Aiol or the woman,
The robber nearly went mad, he had such grief in his heart.
He found the trail of the swift horses,   6770
And he set out after Aiol all along the wide road.
Mirabel the maiden was the first to look back
And spotted the robber who came riding after them
And saw his shining hauberk and helm shimmer and gleam.
She called out to Aiol and began to speak to him: 6775
"Noble knight, my lord, didn't I tell you?
Look at your monk who lodged you.
He's not wearing his black robes. Instead he's left them behind.
He's very well armed on a swift warhorse."
"Oh, God!" said Aiol, "My praise is eternal!   6780
Courteous damsel, you can really help me out.
For this task, you'll be my squire.
Here's what you'll do for me: you'll lead the horses."
And the maiden replied: "Gladly, dear lord!"

⚜ AIOL ⚜

She took the good, swift horses by their reins — 6785
She scarcely goes two paces — she doesn't look back —
And Aiol pricks and spurs his good, fast horse.
And Gonbaut shouts at him: "Vile coward, scoundrel!
The lord abbot just told you that you're well lodged.
Woe to you if you continue on, by the eyes of my head!" 6790
"Oh, foul cur," said Aiol, "may God give you harm!
Before you were a monk, now you're a knight.
You'll pay for it right away if God will help me!"
"By God," said Gonbaut, the foul, evil renegade,
"If you want a fight, you'll have one gladly!" 6795
And Aiol replied: "It will be my pleasure!"
Both of them drew back an arrow's flight apart,
Then they came together, gripping their shields.
They exchanged marvelous blows on their quartered shields,
On their golden bosses, breaking and piercing them. 6800
The hauberks are so strong they can't be torn.
These skillful knights use the great weight of their horses,
Their stout lances made of apple wood,
And with the weight of their swift Arabian horses,
Both of then clashed so fiercely 6805
Neither saddle girth nor breastplate does either any good,
Because they can't keep either one from emptying his saddle.
Each one was sound of body and leaped back on his feet.
If the robber had faith, he'd have been a good knight.
There'd have been no one better from here to Montpellier. 6810
Aiol calls out to him, showing great friendship:
"My friend, for the love of God, abandon this trade.
I'll give you a mighty castle in France as your fief.
No better fighter than you has ever eaten bread.
Never before has any man caused me to empty my stirrups." 6815
"Oh, foul cur," said Gonbaut, "are you trying to preach to me?
The lord abbot sends this message that he's going to lodge you.
You should come back and return to the convent."
Gonbaut drew his steel-bladed sword
And goes to strike Aiol. He doesn't want to spare him. 6820
He deals Aiol a marvelous blow on his green helm,
So that all its flowers and gemstones showered down to the ground.
Gonbaut's sword slides over towards Aiol's right shoulder
And caused twenty links from his hauberk to fall onto the gravel.
The Lord God protected Aiol, because Gonbaut couldn't
  wound him. 6825

⚜ A Chanson de Geste ⚜

"Oh, foul rogue," said Aiol, "you've delayed me too long.
May the Lord God confound me if I consider sparing
You, since now there's no more use for any more entreaties!"
Aiol drew his sword with its steel blade.
With great wrath he started towards Gonbaut 6830
And strikes across the top of his shield, on his helm.
The blade slices as far down as the robber's spine.
The robber staggers, then goes down on his knees.
Aiol, Elye's son, gallantly charges him.
With his sharp sword he deals him such a mighty blow, 6835
Upon the top of his helm of greenish gold,
So that the flowers and gemstones showered down to the ground.
The hauberk's iron cowl was never of any use to him.
Aiol slashed his blade as far down as Gonbaut's molars.
Then the maiden Mirabel came riding up on her horse. 6840
When she sees Aiol, she begins to shout:
"Noble, high-born man, for the love of God of heaven,
Give him his payment according to his service!"
And Aiol replied: "By my head, gladly!"
He held his naked sword whose blade was of steel. 6845
From somewhere in the woods, he fashioned a hangman's noose.
He laced it on Gonbaut. Aiol twists it around his neck.
Mirabel, the maiden, helped him so much
That he was able to tie and hang Gonbaut from the branch of a tree.
Aiol tied Gonbaut's hauberk and helm on his warhorse 6850
And let his burnished steel blade hang from the saddle horn.
They started out along their road, intending to travel.
The maiden rides alongside the knight.
Aiol, the bold and the proud, looked at her.
Through friendship for her, he kept a tight hold on her horse's reins: 6855
He lengthened the stirrup two fingers and a full palm's width.
If any man on earth of mother born were coming for her now,
Who might want, for any reason at all, to challenge the maiden,
Aiol would counter him with iron and steel.
Now may God, he who rules over all, guide him, 6860
Because before he's ridden hardly any time,
It's certain if he doesn't make an effort to rescue and help himself,
Great misfortune will befall him — if he's willing to undertake it —
Because the eleven robbers were in the vast forest.
One of them said to the others: "We've been thoroughly deceived! 6865
I think our companion has been killed and hacked to pieces.
Let's ride after him. We really should help him."

❧ Aiol ❧

And they answered him: "We'll do whatever you want."
They put on their hauberks and laced up their helms
And girded their swords, mounted their warhorses,   6870
Hung their quartered shields from their necks
And seized their lances with their pennons tied to them.
They didn't want to delay from there to the spreading tree —
The place Gonbaut had named and mentioned to them.
When they didn't find him there, they almost went mad,   6875
But they found the trail of the swift warhorses
And found Gonbaut hanged and strung up.
Corsault saw him: the leader almost went mad.
He drew his sword and cut the rope
By which Gonbaut, the false monk, had his neck stretched.   6880
Gonbaut fell to the ground — the foul renegade —
And Corsault turned around and left him there dead.
He set out after Aiol along the wide road.
Aiol, Elye's son, looked around behind him
And saw the eleven robbers come riding towards him,   6885
Their hauberks and helms flashing and gleaming.
If he was in fear of death, you shouldn't be astonished.
He called on the Lord God, the glorious one of heaven:
"Glorious lord, who always was and always will be,
And have the world and the sea under your rule,   6890
Protect me today from death and injury,
That I may not be killed, slain or hacked to pieces.
I could well ride off because I have a swift warhorse,
But I don't intend to leave or abandon this maiden.
I've brought her from afar and should hold her dear.   6895
When the serpent held my naked foot in its body,
She didn't want to ever desert or abandon me.
This I promise to God the righteous Father:
I will never fail her as long as I am able,
And I will take her as my wife, my peer and my spouse.   6900
I'd be extremely cowardly, if I were to fail her,
And by that holy apostle whom pilgrims seek in Rome,
I'd much prefer an honorable death than a shameful flight."
When Mirabel heard this, her heart was filled with joy.
She turned to look at Aiol and began to speak to him: 6905
"Noble young knight, my lord, for the love of God in heaven,
Go on and ride off now down that ancient path!
You have a good horse and you're sure to escape.
I'd rather be shamed wrongfully and sinfully

A Chanson de Geste

Than for you to be killed and hacked to pieces for love of me." 6910
"Fair one," said Aiol, "you're wasting your breath.
I intend to prove you wrong with iron and steel.
By God the righteous, I think I can make them pay dearly,
But stay very calm and take charge of these warhorses
And all the great riches that I've won. 6910
However this fight turns out, I'll strike first."
Now here comes Corsault, the renegade, spurring his mount.
He's the others' master; he's their lord and chief.
He was a giant of a man
And rode more than an arrow's flight in front of the others. 6920
In his booming voice he began to shout:
"Whore's son! Lecher! You've caused me great shame
And hanged my companion, the one I held so dear.
Now the moment is near when you'll be condemned to death."
Aiol, Elye's son, had no mind to quarrel. 6925
He pricked Marchegai with his solid gold spurs
And went to strike the robber, not holding back at all.
None of Corsault's arms did him a bit of good,
Because they couldn't keep Aiol's lance from bathing itself in his body.
Aiol struck the robber down to the ground dead in front of him 6930
And cried out: "Monjoie, God, St. Denis, help me!"
But the other robbers were closing in on him so fast,
The noble man couldn't recover his lance
From the robber's body and pull it back towards him.
Aiol drew his sword, which he well knew how to put to good use, 6935
And went to strike another robber whose head he sent flying.
The nine robbers attacked him from in front and behind.
Aiol defended himself as a brave knight should,
But five robbers struck at him from in front and behind.
Two of them dealt blows on his shield, the third on his helm, 6940
The fourth struck him on his double-mailed hauberk.
Neither cinch or stirrup could withstand this attack.
They struck Aiol to the ground, making him even more enraged.
Aiol dodged their blows, leaped back on his feet
And gripped his naked sword. He held his shield over his head. 6945
Whatever he strikes with a blow is absolutely condemned to death.
The robbers were attacking him, causing him extreme anguish.
They struck him to the ground and laid him all stretched out.
They tightly bound both his hands and his feet,
Then they slung him across a swift warhorse. 6950

🏵 Aiol 🏵

They rounded up the other horses — they didn't want to leave
   a single one behind —
Except Marchegai. They couldn't capture him.
The robbers swore to God, the righteous Father
That before it's vespers and the sun has set,
They intend to exact vengeance on the noble baron for the loss of
   their companions.   6955
Now the foul renegades are saying among themselves
That they'll exact vengeance on the valiant knight,
But they have no idea about the mortal danger
That's about to descend upon them without delay,
Because Geraume, the worthy castellan, is riding.   6960
Between him and his sons, the valiant knights,
They'll rescue Aiol who's in great need of help.
Geraume spotted Aiol tied up on a horse.
He calls out to his four sons and began to speak to them:
"My sons," said Geraume, "by all the saints in heaven,   6965
Look over there at your cousin whom they're leading off all tied up.
He's made them pay dearly with his steel sword,
Because I see five of them whom he's slain and hacked to pieces.
Now it's time for performing well, noble knights!"
He pricks his horse with the spurs on his feet   6970
And brandished the shaft of his stout, sharp lance.
He goes to strike the first robber on the shield hanging from his neck.
Never would the robber need any of his arms:
In front of Geraume, he's struck down dead to the ground.
Then Geraume drew his sword, which he well knew how to use,   6975
And went to strike another robber — the one who's holding Aiol.
From off his shoulders, Geraume cuts his head.
Jofroi, the oldest brother, began to shout:
"What are you doing, my brothers, for all the saints in heaven?
Soon our father will have killed all of them and hacked them
   to pieces,   6980
Before we've been able to even move or lift a finger!
Right now, there are only four of these foul renegades left!"
They prick their horses with the spurs on their feet.
From there, at as great a speed as the warhorses were capable of,
By spurring their horses, down along the hillside   6985
They go to strike the four foul renegades.
Each one of the new knights slays his opponent.
Geraume spots Aiol tied up on the horse.
He drew his sword and severed the ropes.

⚜ A Chanson de Geste ⚜

Gently and courteously he lowered Aiol down off the warhorse.   6990
The first words Geraume said to Aiol when he addressed him were:
"You're not wounded, are you, noble knight?"
"No," said Aiol, "by the grace of God in heaven.
My arms are so good that they couldn't hurt me."
When Marchegai heard his rightful lord speak   6995
He came galloping over to him, because he clearly recognized him.
When Aiol saw his warhorse his joy overflowed!
Geraume's four sons ran to bridle him,
Putting on his bit, saddle and both stirrups.
And Aiol, who loved his horse dearly, mounted up again.   7000
On leaving the forest, he came upon a dwelling:
A nobleman had lived and had been lodged here.
The robbers of foul lineage had attacked them.
They had murdered him and his wife.
The robbers had set up two huge, oak gallows.   7005
Aiol, Elye's son, had taken good notice of it.
He came up to the robbers; he didn't intend to leave them.
He had them dragged to the gallows by the warhorses' tails.
Both Aiol and Geraume, they both had them dragged gladly,
And all four of the sons gave them lots of help,   7010
So that they hanged them all, without taking a ransom.
They hanged the headless robber by his feet.
Now the great men of that region could very well say
Thanks to God and Aiol, because they've been avenged.
Then they returned to the field where the main combat took place.   7015
They didn't want to waste their time with the shields and lances,
But instead, tied the hauberks and helms on the warhorses
And hung the burnished steel blades from their saddle horns.
Aiol, Elye's son, spoke first:
"Noble castellan, Geraume, be still and listen to me.   7020
My share of this war prize I've won here,
I hand over to you free and clear, gladly and willingly,
To help out your sons whom you've made knights."
"My lord," said Geraume, "a hundred thanks to you.
I'll take this war prize. I won't refuse to accept it in the least."   7025
He had it carried back by the grooms.
Straight to Mongraile it was taken and carried.
The castellan, Geraume, was worthy and proud.
He called out to Aiol and began to speak to him:
"Noble young knight, my lord, by all the saints in heaven,   7030
Yesterday evening I provided you lodging in my vast palace

❦ AIOL ❦

And heard you say that you knew Elye.
Now I entreat you, in God's name, noble knight,
By the faith that I owe the righteous Father,
To tell me the truth, if God can help you,   7035
If you were ever in the service of Elye, the warrior,
My uncle from Burgundy, who was wrongly driven out."
"My lord," said Aiol, "you've treated me well,
But I will not speak a word of it to any man on earth
Until I've come to the king who reigns over France,   7040
But I can reveal at least this much of what I know:
If ever you loved the duke, then you will hold me dear."
When Geraume heard this, never was he so happy.
"Noble young knight, my lord, I was sure of it.
It's the absolute truth that you are related to me.   7045
Now I'll never abandon you for all the gold on earth,
Until I've accompanied you to the city of Orleans.
If you're ever in need, I'll come to help you out
Against all men who would put your life in danger."
"My lord," said Aiol, "a hundred thanks to you!"   7050
Now the noble knights start off together.
They bring with them the maiden who's held in high esteem.
Aiol doesn't want in the least to leave behind the seven horses
He had won and conquered in Spain.
They start out along their road that goes straight to Orleans,   7055
But they have no idea of the mortal danger,
Which soon would threaten them before daybreak.
They rode and travelled so long that evening
That they were able to spend the night at Roimorentin.
This was a luxurious castle, worthy of esteem,   7060
Which was located seven short leagues from the city of Orleans
In the direction of the province of Berry. It was well fortified.
That night, Hunbaut, a host, gave them lodging.
He was a rich man of extensive wealth.
He had through usury climbed up and raised himself   7065
And had a high-born wife, the daughter of a knight
Who, impoverished through illness,
Because of poverty, gave his daughter to the usurer.
Thus poverty causes many a man to take ill-advised actions.
Hunbaut had a fine, four-story house.   7070
His noble wife was named Esmeraude.
She had borne to this usurer a clever young man,
His name was Antiaume, and he was worthy of esteem.

⚜ A Chanson de Geste ⚜

Because of his inborn goodness, Antiaume had rejected everything
  that came from his father.
You could have hacked off his arms and legs, and he would never
  betray anyone.   7075
Oh, God! He's making every effort to make his noble guests
  feel comfortable,
To stable their horses, burnish their helms,
To beat out their hauberks, which were in need of it.
He had been taught all of these good tasks so well,
There was no one better on earth to serve a worthy man.   7080

172.

Aiol was given lodging in Roimorentin.
Both him and Geraume of Mongraile, the worthy man,
And all his four sons, the newly dubbed ones,
Their host had them served and honored.
They had seats and cushions and good woven covers.   7085
They had the whole house strewn with wild mint and roses.
Antiaume, their courtly son, got to his feet.
He had a great desire to honor their six noble guests
And the king's daughter, Mirabel, of the bright countenance.
There weren't enough squires to unload all of their harnesses.   7090
They were all laden with sweat and with iron.
Antiaume rushed down the steps of the stairway.
He searched throughout the castle, far and wide.
He searched for his companions so long that he found them.
Through generosity he led them with him   7095
In order to serve the noble men who are in his home.
The young squires were well clothed and well groomed.
You would have seen them nobly bring the wine
In large silver cups whose rims were gilded with gold.
Mirabel, the maiden, and Geraume, the worthy man,   7100
Were seated side by side on a couch,
With Geraume's four sons off to his side.
Esmeraude, their hostess, and Aiol, the judicious,
Were sitting across from them, on an ornate couch.
They began to speak of one thing and another: 7105
"My lady," said Aiol, "for the love of God, don't blame me
If I'd like to ask you something in friendship.
How did it happen that you were given in marriage to this man?
I'm very much astonished that you have this burgher as a
  husband!

❧ Aiol ❧

You should be a great lady with immense wealth." 7110
When Esmeraude heard this, she breathed a heartfelt sigh:
"My lord," said the lady, "for God's sake, don't make fun of me.
Poverty makes a man change how he thinks.
My father was a nobleman with powerful relatives.
Throughout the whole Berry province, you couldn't find 7115
A better knight when it came to bearing arms.
Then he became ill, fell into dire poverty,
And he mortgaged his lands. Very little money remained.
Hunbaut had amassed great wealth through usury.
He paid off all my father's mortgages on his lands. 7120
In return, my father gave me to him as his wife. I couldn't refuse.
Now I have by him a son whom you see here.
He resembles his father about as much as a majestic falcon is like a
    lowly sparrow-hawk.
My son is incapable of adopting his father's way of thought:
He asks for trictrac and chess boards to play board games. 7125
He can't get hunting dogs and birds out of his mind.
You can't get him to abandon the pathway of noblemen."
"Certainly," said Aiol, "there's much to be liked about him."
He called out to Antiaume: "Come over here, my friend.
Stay with me during these four months of summer, 7130
For the love of your mother who's told and related to me
That you're a well-born man of high lineage.
I'd like to make you into a fully dubbed knight,
With arms and a swift, prized warhorse."
When the young man heard this, he bowed deeply, 7135
And gladly knelt at Aiol's feet.
Between Aiol and Geraume, they both raised him to his feet.
Aiol, Elye's son, didn't want to delay any longer,
Because he didn't want to promise without delivering:
The noble man was never accustomed to doing this. 7140
Aiol had brought before him all the arms
He won in Spain with his broad sword.
He equipped Antiaume with all of the best:
On his back, Aiol put a shining golden hauberk
And fastened on his head a green, gemstone-laden helm. 7145
Aiol girded his sword on his left side,
Raised his right palm and delivered the dubbing blow:
"May God grant you faith, peace, honor and goodness.
You've stabled my horses down there for me.
Take the best one of them, because it's my most eager desire, 7150

⚜ A Chanson de Geste ⚜

And tomorrow in Orleans, before it's vespers,
I'll give you luxurious clothing and a stout, bossed shield."
When the young man heard this, he thanked Aiol for it.
Aiol then gave Esmeraude, his hostess, a mantel,
And gave his host a hundred sous to prepare the meal, 7155
So that he would be better served and honored.

173.

Aiol was provided lodging by his host, Hunbaut.
The meal that was served was copious and elegant.
Their horses were provided with an abundance of hay and oats.
Antiaume took off his armor: he was a very noble young man. 7160
He sat down beside Geraume's sons seated on the stools.
You would have seen how rapidly the meal was prepared,
The servants putting the table-tops on the trestles,
And they were ready to serve water from gilded vessels.
Mirabel wiped her hands on a white towel. 7165
They sat down to the meal. Great was the revelry.
But before they get up, there will be great mourning:
Their host betrayed them, which was evil and sinful.
If the Lord who saved the world doesn't look out for them,
Neither courtly Geraume or Aiol, the noble warrior, 7170
Will see Orleans or their dearest friends again.
Their host was filled with the greatest evil intent.
Never did the evil Cain have such a false heart
When he slew his noble brother, Abel.

174.

When they had eaten and drunk copiously, 7175
The noble knights were seated around the table.
"My lord," said their host, "by St. Simon's body,
I don't know if I've sufficiently repaid you
For the honor you've done in my house.
It's as if you were the lord of Rheims or Laon! 7180
Last night you gave me a very expensive gift.
I beseech my son, Antiaume, as a very great reward,
To serve you faithfully, as a mounted knight.
May he be accursed, the day he lets you down!"
"Indeed," said the young man, "and by St. Simon's body!" 7185
Esmeraude isn't at all looking to create a scene.
She turned to Aiol and began to speak to him:
"Noble, well-born man, I want to know your name.

⚜ Aiol ⚜

I'll praise it again and again in many houses."
And Aiol replied, not wanting in the least to cause an uproar: 7190
"My lady, the French and Burgundians call me Aiol.
I came to serve the king as a soldier on Rogations Feast Day.
This knight with the bright countenance is named Geraume.
He's the castellan of Mongraile and is a very powerful man.
These are his four sons, it's certain: 7195
Berenger, Jofroi, Hastes and Nevelon."
When their host heard this, he began to frown
And whispered between this teeth, slyly, like a thief:
"In the Cinquefoil Forest, it's for sure
That you hanged Bernard, my rightful lord,   7200
Who holds Roimorentin, and his brother, Focon,
And Ferant of Lausanne and the worthy Agenon,
And Garin, Richard and Hugues of Monbart.
As a result of this incident, Makaire, their uncle, is in prison.
These were his nephews whom he brought up.   7205
May the Lord God, who formed Lazarus, confound me,
If I don't go tell my lord in his castle,
Who rules this land and the environs all around.
He'll exact vengeance for the death of his two brothers.
You might even kill him, we won't keep it secret."   7210
He slipped away from the table. Never did anyone manage
  such dissembling.
He's plotting such a great betrayal against Aiol.
Never had he ever felt such bitterness during any of his time on earth.

175.

Hunbaut rises to his feet now
And leaves the table — he left the nobles.   7215
He entered his private chamber, the foul renegade.
He calls his courtly wife to him:
"Sweet sister, dear friend, if you've ever held me dear,
Don't repeat the opinion that I'm going to share with you.
It's the devil that's made you give lodging to that foul cur!   7220
In the Cinquefoil Forest — there no use in hiding it —
He hanged Bernard, my rightful lord,
Who held Roimorentin, and his brother Focon
And Ferant of Lausanne and Agenon the Proud.
It's been only a bit more than four whole months   7225
Since he arrived in Orleans naked, poor and wretched.
His lance was black and twisted, his shield was old,

⚜ A Chanson de Geste ⚜

And his horse was scrawny — he could barely keep his feet.
I've certainly heard it said and repeated everywhere,
That in every place he was ridiculed by servants and squires.   7230
And everyone was saying, throughout the city of Orleans,
That he stole his arms from a cart driver,
And he'd stolen the nag they saw him riding.
I don't know by what diabolical means he's managed to rise so high,
Because now he's the king's favorite and leading advisor.   7235
By St. Paul of Ravenna, I'm going to tell them this
Up there in my lord Rainier's palace.
I'll have his men take up arms and put hauberks on their backs;
I'll make sure he's avenged of the death of his two brothers,
Whom this foul cur has killed. I'll make no secret of it."   7240
When the lady heard this, she thought she'd go completely mad.
"What are you saying, foul fiend? Have you lost your mind?
You've loyally provided lodging for these nobles,
And you've eaten and drunk with them.
Aiol's dubbed your son and made him a knight.   7245
He gave me a mantel worth many a good denier.
In return for his excellent favors, you're repaying him evilly.
Right away you're starting the kind of quarrel
For which you'll end up being hanged like a common thief.
Your son will be dragged by horses' tails,   7250
And I will be burnt at the stake in a huge fire.
May the Lord God confound them — he who rules over all —
If they don't have your head shaved instantly,
If you refuse to abandon this talk.
By St. Paul of Ravenna, I'm going to warn them!   7255
I won't let it happen, even if all my limbs were cut off!
I'd never be a party to such a betrayal!"
When the traitor heard this, he thought he'd go mad.

176.

When the foul rogue heard his wife speak so forcefully
He felt such pain in his heart, it almost exploded with anger.   7260
He raised his right hand and hit her in the teeth,
Causing her to fall to the floor in a faint.
The ermine was all bloody from her bleeding.
When she sat up her heart was filled with grief.
"Alas," said the lady, "what a wicked revenge!   7265
May my father and my close relatives be cursed
For having me marry you!"

⚜ AIOL ⚜

The rogue leaped to the sword that was hanging in the chamber
And swore to the Lord God, the almighty Father:
"If I hear you speak a word of any of this,   7270
You'll lose your head right away,
And you'll swear to me faithfully and loyally
That, through you, they will know nothing of this.
From all your relatives, you'll have no protection!"
He held the sword in his right hand; in his left he held her   7275
By her tresses, brutishly by her locks.
He was close to cutting off her head without the slightest
    hesitation.
She was afraid of death and said quietly to herself:
"For God, almighty Father, mercy!
Receive my pledge and then my oath   7280
That I will never tell them on a single day of my life.
Since it can't be otherwise, act wisely now,
So that harm doesn't come to you or to your relatives."
And the traitor replied: "He's false who doesn't consent
To what can be better for him this whole life through!"   7285
Esmeraude replied softly so that he wouldn't hear:
"The emperor be cursed if he doesn't hang you from his gallows,
If you behave in such vile manner towards one of his knights.
By that holy Lord to whom the world belongs,
If I can be eased from it, through some magic spell,   7290
I won't respect either my promise or my pledge to you
Not to let them know swiftly and rapidly.
It's better to break my oath than to do otherwise
And deliver them to be killed in such a foul manner."

177.

The traitor left his high-born wife.   7295
He left the chamber and returned to the main hall.
Hear what the traitor did — may God cause him harm!
How well he knows how to slyly deceive and hoodwink them.
"Barons, take your ease, noble knights!
Have yourselves richly served and looked after.   7300
Dear son, I want to entreat you that concerning your lord,
You should do nothing that might harm him.
I'm going to look around town to seek some fun."
"My lord," said Aiol, "we'll certainly grant you that.
Where did our lady go? I'm quite a bit surprised."   7305
"She has a bit of a headache," said their host,

⚜ A Chanson de Geste ⚜

"So I ordered your beds to be set up elsewhere."
Quickly he turned away, he didn't want to linger.
He ran off towards the main palace as fast as he could.
Hunbaut will soon foment such trouble for Aiol, 7310
He'll have encountered none more vicious in all his days.
Now hear about the lady whose heart was full of grief.
She came to her chamber's door, nodded to her son,
And he came running to her right away.
When he saw her all bloodied, he was astonished. 7315
"My lady," said the young man, "by all the saints in heaven!
Who dared to do this to you? Why is he still standing?"
"Dear son," said the lady, "the devil and evil
Will attack us tonight, be on your guard!
We have loyally offered lodging to these noblemen. 7320
They have eaten and drunk together with us,
And your father intends to deceive and betray them.
Look at Aiol over there, your rightful lord,
Who killed Bernard for us, that wicked rogue,
Lord Makaire's nephew, and his brother Rainier's, 7325
Then he dubbed you. You should hold him very dear,
And serve and support him above all others.
Your father is going to betray and deceive him.
He's going up there to that palace to inform Rainier,
And he'll have his men take up their arms and don their hauberks. 7330
If the Lord God doesn't intervene, he who reigns over all,
You'll see your lord hacked to pieces right in front of you.
Because I refused to go along with your father's scheme,
He hit me in the teeth and made my blood shoot forth.
Then he pulled out his sword and intended to cut off my head. 7335
Thus he forced me to pledge and swear
That I would say nothing to any man on earth.
It's better to fail my oath, than to see them hacked to pieces.
I'll do penance for it, if God will grant it."
When the young man heard this, he thought he'd go insane: 7340
"How the devil can this be?" Antiaume replied.
"What good does it do my father to behave in such a vile manner?
Since he's committing treason, I don't owe him any allegiance,
Because no traitor will ever be spared by me!
By St. Paul of Ravenna, I'm going to inform 7345
Aiol, my good lord, who made me a knight,
That I wouldn't fail him, even if my arms and legs were hacked off."
"Dear son," said the lady, "may God come to your aid,

⚜ Aiol ⚜

He who allowed himself to be tortured on the holy cross
To save sinners from death and destruction." 7350

178.

Antiaume, the courtly youth, left his mother.
He went out of the chamber and approached Aiol,
Damned if he'd call for counsel to anyone!
But in a very loud voice, he yells to his lord.
"Barons, quickly take up your arms and get ready! 7355
There's going to be a great need for those who want to prove
  themselves worthy.
Dear lord, Aiol from France, much evil is coming your way.
My father's betraying you. He broke bread with you.
In the Cinquefoil Forest you hanged Bernard,
Who held Roimorentin, and his brother Foucart 7360
And Ferant of Lausanne, Agenon the Vassal,
And Garin and Richard, and Hugues of Monbart.
My father proved his falsity when he gave you lodging.
Towards you he assumed the role of Judas.
He ran up to the great palace as fast as he could, 7365
To his lord, Rainier, who was Bernard's brother.
If he has his way, you'll never again see
The mighty city of Orleans. You'll never enter its gates."
When Aiol heard this, he rose to his feet.
Devoutly and piteously he prayed to the Lord God, 7370
The King of holy glory, who made the world,
That he might defend him because he was in dire need of it.
"Aiol," said Geraume, "don't yet be dismayed!
He who would strike us up close will have a hundred woes
  on his neck.
I believe our new knights will help us." 7375
"Indeed," said Antiaume, "as long as we can last."
Antiaume, the courtly youth, made extreme haste
To saddle up the horses and attach the harnesses.
"Alas," said Mirabel, "what great treason have we here!"
"My lady," said Antiaume, "don't lose heart yet. 7380
By St. Paul of Ravenna, I'll personally help you.
Anyone who comes after you will pay dearly for it!"
Esmeraude, the fair, made great haste
To outfit all of the barons, lending them armor.
She kissed her son. She put him in God's hands. 7385
He took up an old shield he found in the house

⚜ A Chanson de Geste ⚜

And a big lance he carried in his hand.
He's a new knight and doesn't have any arms yet —
Aiol had promised him that in Orleans he'd give him some.
If God guides him, he'll take care of Antiaume.   7390
Antiaume, the courtly youth, accompanies Mirabel
Straight through the main gate he found open.
He leads away the war prize Aiol won
In the land of Spain where he labored so mightily.
Now may God, who made the world, guide them —   7395
And the moon shone brightly to light their pathway —
Because before daybreak, as you'll be told,
He'll have fear of death, which will seem certain.
Now hear about their host, what he was up to:
He climbed up all the marble steps to the palace.   7400
With his booming voice he shouted loudly:
"Tell me, my lord Rainier, what reward will the person have
Who tonight avenges you for your brothers' deaths
And turns over to you the one who killed him?
Anyone who can avenge himself will have great honor!"   7405
"Certainly," said Rainier, "Anyone who can accomplish this for me
Will be my good friend for all the days of my life."

179.

"My lord," said the traitor, "have your men arm themselves.
There's a great opportunity I'll tell you about.
Well now, before the bells rang out for vespers,   7410
Seven knights came riding up armed and clad in iron,
Straight to my house to seek lodging.
They were marvelously and expensively equipped.
One of them was Geraume of Mongraile, the noble knight,
And all of his four sons, newly dubbed knights.   7415
They were headed to France, accompanying a foul rogue:
His name is Aiol — that's what I've heard him called.
He's coming from Pamplona, where he delivered a message.
He's leading a war prize, never have I seen its equal,
And seven horses loaded with expensive furs,   7420
Gold, I think, and silver denier coins,
And Mirabel, the king's daughter, of the shining visage,
Whom he won through his knighthood.
I didn't know a word of this before vespers,
When I lodged them gladly and willingly.   7425
Right away Aiol gave me a hundred sous' worth of denier coins

❧ Aiol ❧

And a very luxurious mantel to my wife,
And my son gave himself completely over to serving him.
Soon this service was extremely well repaid,
Because Aiol made him a knight at once, 7430
Providing him with arms and a swift, rapid horse.
The horse Aiol gave him is worth a hundred pounds.
When we'd eaten and drunk in great quantities,
I asked his name. He didn't deign to hide it.
Now you can hear and believe that my heart became filled with anger 7435
When, within my house, I'd lodged
The person who hanged my lord, to whom I owed feudal allegiance!
Noble lord, you shouldn't delay exacting vengeance."
"Certainly," said Rainier, "God knows my intent!"
In his voice, which was loud, he began yelling: 7440
"Barons, arm yourselves quickly, if you have any loyalty to me at all!"
And they replied: "Just as you wish!"
Fourteen knights ran to arm themselves
With arms and swift, rapid warhorses.
"My lords," said Rainier, "let's get going! 7445
Go have the main gates of Roimorentin closed,
So that there's no way they can escape."
And they replied: "Lord, as you command!"
Four foot soldiers hasten and hurry there.
When they found the tracks of the well-rested warhorses, 7450
They turned back sorrowful and depressed.
In their loud voices they began to shout:
"In faith, Lord Hunbaut, you're in a bind;
Esmeraude, your wife, has gotten them to leave.
Your son has betrayed us, it's the truth! 7455
He's left with them — that's what we've been told."
When Rainier heard this, he almost lost his mind.
In his tower, he had a great bugle sound the alarm.
Then you would have seen townspeople and foot soldiers
    arming themselves,
And storming all around the city. 7460
Within a very short time, more than two hundred were armed,
Including burghers, foot soldiers and mounted knights.
And they marched out of the city in ranks and iron-clad.
They tried hard to pursue Aiol's party. They went as fast as
    they could.
Geraume of Mongraile distinctly heard them coming. 7465
He called out to Aiol: "Dear lord, listen to me!

⚜ A Chanson de Geste ⚜

We're about to have a marvelous and deadly battle!
Antiaume needs to move on ahead with the horses
And Mirabel, the king's daughter, with the shining countenance,
All the way to Orleans, the magnificent city.   7470
We'll remain behind to deal fierce blows,
And we'll hack them to pieces with our lettered steel blades."
"My lord," said Antiaume, "you're wasting your breath!
You want to turn my knighthood to nought,
But by that holy apostle pilgrims seek in Nero's Field,   7475
I wouldn't do it for the gold of ten cities,
If it meant I couldn't strike fierce blows with you.
And if God will uphold and guide me,
I intend to repay the gift you've given me."
"My lords," said Mirabel, "there's no need to quarrel.   7480
Woe to you if you shrink your numbers, because there are
  very few of you.
I'll take charge of the horses gladly and willingly.
Now I need to change myself into a squire!"
She threw her leg over her horse with great dignity*
And put her feet in the golden stirrups.   7485
Anyone who would have seen the maiden spur her horse
And lead the packhorses and guide the warhorses
Would recognize a most high-born woman.
The nobles stopped there on the paved road.
Now here come the pursuers, who have been making a great effort.   7490
He who ruled over all of Roimorentin
Was riding a bowshot's length in front of the others.
In his loud voice he began to shout:
"Geraume of Mongraile, how in the world could you think
That you would accompany my mortal enemy!   7495
Many times I've had you served and honored.
If you go any farther with him, you'll pay dearly for it!
Barely more than three months have passed
Since this boy came to France to win riches.
When he came to Orleans, the marvelous city,   7500
The only wealth he was carrying with him he could show,
Was a mere five sous' worth of coins,
Except for some ugly arms, a smoky shield
And a scrawny, sad excuse for a horse.
I've certainly heard it said and repeated everywhere   7505
That everyone was mocking him — servants and young men —
And they were all saying throughout the city of Orleans

189

That he had stolen the arms he was carrying,
And he had stolen the horse he was riding.
I don't know by what diabolical means he rose so high 7510
To become the king's favorite and his close advisor.
This past summer he captured the count of Bourges,
And because of him, Makaire was thrown into prison,
And our entire family has been shamed and dishonored."
"Foul rogue," said Aiol, "by my head, you're lying!" 7515

180.

"Worthless cur," said Aiol, "by my head, it's not true!
Never did my family do such a thing,
Committing such a betrayal of which you're accusing me.
I'll do combat with you with my Viennese blade.
Geraume, dear cousin, here's a chance to excel. 7520
By St. Paul of Ravenna, I'll tell the truth right now!
My father's name is Elye, your uncle, the courtly noble,
And if God lets us leave here, as you and I want to,
I'll increase your holdings by ten skilled knights."
"Certainly," said Antiaume, "it's not much to me, 7525
Since from so little — like my father — can come so much pain!"*
"Indeed," said Geraume, "by the faith that I owe the Holy Cross,
Because I wouldn't fail Aiol for all the gold in the Vermandois
 region."
When Aiol heard this, the courtly knight was filled with joy.

181.

When Aiol, the courtly knight, heard these words — 7530
That they were all committed to help him —
You can say and believe that it made him very happy.
He spurred his warhorse and headed towards Rainier,
And Rainier charged towards him unwaveringly.
Both of them came together with marvelous rage, 7535
With as much force as their horses could muster when
 they felt the spurs.
They dealt amazing blows on their vaulted shields,
On the golden bosses, which battered and smashed them.
Their hauberks were so good that their mesh did not tear,
But instead the shafts of their stout lances shattered. 7540
The prized warhorses galloped with such swiftness
That their bodies and chests crashed violently together,
And their helms, heads and vaulted shields.

⚜ A Chanson de Geste ⚜

Their horses carried them five hundred feet
Before each knight could rein in his charging steed. 7545
And when Aiol saw this, he was astonished.
He drew his sword and came towards Rainier.
He dealt Rainier a marvelous blow on his burnished helm,
Which caused the flowers and gemstones to shower to the ground.
Rainier's hauberk was so strong that not a single link was broken 7550
And Aiol's blow was great, cutting down to his saddle.
It cut Rainier's horse's neck in two,
And Rainier jumped down to his feet. He was in fear of death.
But Aiol held up, who was holding his steel blade.
He was about to take vengeance on the cur of evil lineage right then, 7555
When at that moment the men of Roimorentin came to
   Rainier's aid.
Geraume pricks and spurs and brandishes his lance.
Right in front of him he struck Lord Hagenon on his shield —
He was a provost of the land, a guardian of that region.
All his arms weren't able to guarantee, for even a moment, 7560
That Geraume's lance wouldn't be felt within his body.
Right in front of him, Geraume struck him down dead on
   the ground.
And when Rainier saw this, he thought he would lose his mind.
Hagenon was one of his relatives and his first cousin.
"Geraume," said Rainier, "you've killed my cousin! 7565
I intended to spare you; now you're my enemy.
If God wills it and I live, you're going pay for it dearly."
Rainier's men brought him a prized warhorse,
And he mounted up and seized a lance.
"Roimorentin!" he cried, "Knights, go strike your blows! 7570
It's sure to be a disastrous day for these curs of foul lineage."

182.

When Aiol, the courtly knight, saw that the enemy forces
   had increased,
He then spoke these prudent words to his companions:
"We can't continue to sustain this combat here.
We're only seven — each of us wearing chainmail. 7575
I see more than two hundred of the enemy along this beaten path."
But not a word came from Geraume's sons.
Instead, they spurred their warhorses across the grassy plain.
Each one of them struck down his opponent with his great
   pointed shaft.

⚜ Aiol ⚜

Antiaume, who was anxious to strike, pricked and spurred,   7580
And he delivered a blow to a knight whose name was Hugh,
Causing the shield hanging from his neck to be split and broken
And the chainmail on his back to be ripped apart and shredded.
Right straight through Hugh's body he ran his shaft,
Which struck him down dead on the short grass.   7585
"Finally, you foul cur," said Antiaume, "your end has come!"
When Rainier heard this, the color drained from his face.
He was heard to say to Antiaume these words:
"You'll pay dearly for my nephew's death,*
Because you're my liegeman — it's a known truth —   7590
And your father is my serf, by right of birth.
Through usury he rose to be a rich man of wealth.
It would have been better for you to stay true to your upbringing!
Because of this rebellion, you'll need to have your neck stretched,
So you'll think you've been raised to the skies."   7595
"I've clearly heard," said Antiaume, "what you have to say.
Before it's day and the dawn has broken,
I'll have defended my head at a price that will cost you dearly."

183.

Aiol together with all the six knights rides fiercely.
They all gallop, giving their horses free rein.   7600
"My lords," said Antiaume, "let's ride prudently.
Each one of us has a good warhorse. I don't see a one that's sweating.
We've exacted vengeance on ten of their knights.
I'm sure that there are not more than nine left.
Let's ride close enough to them that we can hear what they're up to.   7605
If we could isolate these knights from the rest of their men
So that they could be killed and destroyed,
After that, we wouldn't need to fear their townsmen in the least,
Because they've only learned poorly how to bear arms,
Since it's a trade that they don't exercise often.   7610
There's a huge old castle a short distance ahead of us.
It has a ruined tower, which is extremely dilapidated.
We can take refuge there to have some respite.
There we can defend ourselves for a long time,
Until the king who reigns over France finds out.   7615
I don't think he'll be slow in coming to our aid."
"Antiaume," said Aiol, "by St. Clement's body,
May I always find you completely in good faith towards me,
And if God allows us to leave here safe and sound,

A Chanson de Geste

I believe that I'm yet going to make you an expensive gift, 7620
Which will raise up all of your people."

184.

Roimorentin's inhabitants were making every effort to pursue them.
An arrow's flight in front of all the others,
Spurring his horse, rode their lord, called Rainier.
In his loud voice, he began to shout: 7625
"Aiol, foul cur, traitor, may God destroy you!
I'll give you your payment for the deaths of my brothers,
And with my sword I think I'll shave your head!"
When Aiol heard this, he thought he'd go insane.
He pulled on his reins and turned towards Rainier, 7630
And Rainier didn't hesitate to ride towards him.
Both of them joined combat like angry leopards.
They deal each other marvelous blows on their quartered shields.
They crack and pierce their shields' golden bosses.
Their hauberks were so good that they couldn't rip them. 7635
With the barons' great blows, with the weight of their warhorses
And with their stout, planed shafts of apple wood,
There was not one of them so arrogant or proud
That under the force of that blow he'd not have to empty his saddle.
Both of them, who were fierce warriors, leaped to their feet 7640
And drew their swords whose blades were of steel.
They struck each other huge blows on their quartered shields,
Which caused the gemstones to shower down from their helms.
There wasn't a single gemstone on them that they didn't dislodge.
I think that Rainier would have had the worst of the encounter, 7645
But his men came running up to help and aid him.
There were more than two hundred of them, mounted and on foot.
Antiaume, the usurer's son, pricked and spurred.
In front of him, he struck a knight on his shield
So that all his arms never could protect him 7650
From having Antiaume's lance bathe in his body.
Before him, his foe was struck dead to the ground.
Antiaume drew his sword, which he knew how to put to good use,
And struck a townsman causing his head to go flying.
He met his father on a swift warhorse. 7655
He swore to the Lord God, the true lawgiver:
"If you weren't my father, you'd pay right away
For your high treason with this steel sword."
The inhabitants of Roimorentin ran up all enraged.

⚜ Aiol ⚜

There were more than two hundred of them, mounted and on foot. 7660
Now you would have seen Aiol channel his anger into vengeance.
His huge sword at his side, his shield held over his head,
He formed the image of a valorous knight.
They wounded him so much that they made him get down on foot
And Marchegai fled across the plain. 7665
Geraume seized Aiol's horse by its pure golden rein.
That night Aiol would have been killed and hacked to pieces,
Except that Geraume and his sons rushed to his aid.
There was not one of them who didn't unhorse this opponent.
Geraume led back his warhorse by force 7670
And Aiol mounted up, the brave and the proud.
Then they rode away together, in serried ranks.
Antiaume guided them down an ancient path,
And under a leafy tree, came upon Mirabel
Who had put forth a great effort and exhausted herself. 7675
But before they could take refuge in the tower,
Our knights encountered a terrifying threat.
The inhabitants of Roimorentin came rushing up, all enraged.
There were more than two hundred of them, mounted and on foot.
They slew Geraume's warhorse out from under him. 7680
He leaped up and jumped to his feet
And drew his sword. He held his shield over his head.
Anyone he can reach with a blow is condemned to death,
But what does it matter? His defense wasn't worth a denier,
Because he was captured, taken prisoner and tied up. 7685
They had him sent back to Rainier's castle,
And when Aiol saw this, he almost lost his mind.
Geraume's four sons had good reason to become angry
When they saw their father captured and bound.
Then you would have seen these noble knights 7690
Trying to rescue their father, but without the least success.
They felt the most intense pity for the noble man.
At the castle's entrance the battle raged,
But they weren't able to help or aid Mirabel.
Rainier went and seized her by her pure golden rein. 7695
He had her and the booty sent back to his castle,
Along with all the seven horses that Aiol had won,
Which were laden with expensive furs.
Rainier began to yell in his loud voice:
"Have that whore thrown into my prison! 7700
In the morning, I'll have her turned over to the squires,

⚜ A Chanson de Geste ⚜

And I'll have her pimp hanged like a common criminal.
Geraume will be hanged along with his four heirs,
And Antiaume will be dragged by horses' tails."
When Aiol heard this, he thought he'd go mad. 7705
With his shield on one arm, he held his naked sword blade.
Anyone he reaches with a blow is condemned to death.
He went to strike Rainier upon his helm.
Next to the main bar his blow slices through the circle,
But the helm's so strong that Aiol can't break it. 7710
Nonetheless Aiol stunned Rainier and made him stagger.
Aiol stopped above his fallen foe, holding high his steel blade.
He'd have cut off his head immediately, without delay,
But Rainier's men came running up to help their lord.

185.

When Aiol saw Geraume being captured and led away, 7715
Bound to prison with his bright-faced friend,
No one could begin to describe the anguish he felt.
Geraume's four sons were close to passing out.
Antiaume began to shout loudly:
"Lords! Barons! Good knights! There's no use in feeling distraught. 7720
Never did feeling depressed ever conquer anything.
Get inside that tower, don't delay for a second!
Start defending yourselves. Your lives depend on it!
I think that shortly I'll be able to bring you the kind of help
That will cause those who are attacking you to pay dearly." 7725
Now the five knights went inside the tower
And forced their way up to the galleries
Through a narrow passage inside the tower.
And Antiaume rode off, commending them
To the God of holy glory, who was hung upon the cross. 7730
And when Rainier saw this, he almost lost his mind.
In his loud voice he began to shout:
"Barons, get riding after Antiaume and seize him for me!
If he escapes you alive, I'm a dead man!
He's the person on earth who hates me the most." 7735
"That's right," said Antiaume, "you're going to pay dearly.
You haven't yet chopped down all of the forest:
There's still one straight branch where you'll be hanged.
I think that my father is close to having the same fate.
He's helped you commit this heinous crime 7740
For which you both will be shamed and dishonored."

195

❦ Aiol ❦

"What!" said Hunbaut, "have I sired
Such a child who's threatening to cut off my head!"
"That's right," said Antiaume, "you've deserved it,
Because no traitor is going to be my relative!" 7745
He spurs his horse and takes off
With five knights after him, intent on doing him harm.
What does he care? He wouldn't give a denier for their threat!
He had a strong, swift and well-rested horse,
And when the foul curs saw they couldn't harm him — 7750
That they couldn't catch him at a ford or on a plain —
They turned back, let him go
And turned all their efforts towards attacking the castle.
The five knights inside, who will be in need of help, defended themselves.
They threw down stones, rocks and great, round boulders. 7755
Hunbaut gave great impetus to the assault.
He crossed over the moat by the supports that held the bridge.
He came to the foot of the tower and began to shout:
"Barons, come on ahead! Why aren't you attacking them?
If you'll give me some help, we'll have them right away." 7760
"My lords," said Aiol, "I heard our host speaking
At the foot of this tower. I'm certain that's who it was."
When Aiol, the noble knight, said that,
Jofroi, Geraume's son, let a stone drop
Which was big, huge and heavy, as much as he could lift. 7765
Down on Hunbaut's helm, he let it fall.
It crushed his chest and his intestines,
Just like a rockslide it smashed him to the ground.
Next to the wall it struck him dead in the sight of his relatives.
And Aiol yelled to him, "Dear host, now here's your pay! 7770
Good host, you betrayed me like a proven thief,
But God's mercy should be highly praised."
"It's true," said Rainier, "that you'll pay dearly for this.
Before noon tomorrow, you'll be hanged from the gallows."
"My lord," said Aiol, "may it please God that you're lying." 7775
Now we'll leave Aiol, the noble young knight,
And his companions, who have remained with him.
May God protect and defend them.
We'll now tell you about the messenger who was on his way,
About Antiaume, the noble knight, who was brave and prudent. 7780
He was very familiar with all the passages, plains and waterways.
From there to Orleans, he had no problems or delays.

❧ A Chanson de Geste ❧

He entered the city by the main gate.
It was past midnight and the cock had crowed.
He stopped right in front of the king's door.   7785
He called out to the doorman, "My friend, open the door!"
The doorman replied to him: "By my faith, you're not entering!
You're not at all a worthy man to be out at this hour."
"My friend," said Antiaume, "I'd like to spare you,
But if you don't open this door right away, the harm will be so great   7790
That Louis wouldn't want it for the city of Orleans."
When the doorman heard this, he jumped to his feet.
He opened the peephole and looked enough
That he saw beneath the nobleman a horse dripping sweat,
Because it had been ridden and worked hard.   7795

186.

The doorman got up when he heard these words.
He opened the peephole and saw the noble knight.
"My lord, what do you need? You look very distressed to me."
"Yes, indeed! It's true my dear lord, pity, for God's sake!
Geraume of Mongraile, who is Louis' liegeman,   7800
And all of his four sons, the noble knights,
Were in Mongraile in the magnificent palace,
When Aiol came back from delivering his message
To mighty King Mibrien, where the king had sent him.
Geraume, the valiant, gave him very good lodgings   7805
And, to escort him, came into France.
Yesterday evening, he was lodged in Roimorentin.
Rainier was in his tower and heard the news of their arrival.
Because of loyalty to his brother, he considered Aiol as his enemy
And had all his men summoned and assembled.   7810
When the barons found out, they rapidly prepared their defense —
Between Aiol and Geraume and all his four sons,
They moved all their baggage outside the city gates.
Rainier with all his men quickly pursued them,
And Aiol's party defended themselves as long as they could.   7815
They forced their way into an old castle.
Geraume was seized and bound,
And Mirabel, the king's daughter with the bright visage,
And all the seven horses that Aiol had won,
Remained behind within Roimorentin.   7820
If God doesn't protect them, he who turned water into wine
On St. Archedeclin's* wedding day,

❧ Aiol ❧

Mighty King Louis will never see him again."
When the doorman heard this, he opened the door for him.
Quickly and rapidly, he let Antiaume dismount. 7825
"My lord," said the gatekeeper, "now listen to me.
Wait for me here, by your mercy.
I'll go take your message to the chamberlain."
"Go quickly then," he said, "dear lord. I beg you to make haste."
The doorman went up all the marble steps 7830
And banged the doorknocker. The lord chamberlain came,
And the doorman relayed to him everything Antiaume had told him.
The chamberlain turned away and went to Louis.
He knocked on the king's door, and Louis woke up.
"What do you want, my friend, for God's sake, don't lie!" 7835
The chamberlain recounted to him all the pride, the peril
And the catastrophic situation Antiaume had described.
When the king heard this, he leaped to his feet.
In his clear voice, he began to shout:
"Have your men arm themselves, by St. Denis' body! 7840
Because if I lose Aiol, I'll be crushed!"
Then you would have seen the palace in an uproar
And the noble knights seize their arms and put on battle dress.
The emperor of France left his chamber.
He looked down the stairs and spotted Antiaume, 7845
Because the moon was shining and was reflected off his helm.
Louis asked the chamberlain: "Tell me, who is this
I see down there armed and mounted on a prize warhorse?"
A chamberlain replied: "Sire, from Roimorentin,
He's come straight here to deliver the message." 7850
When the king heard this, he had Antiaume come forward.
He asked about the news, and Antiaume explained to him
Exactly how Hunbaut and his relatives had betrayed them that night.
"By my head!" said the king, "he's committed a grave crime against me."

187.

"My friend," said the king, "you're very brave and worthy. 7855
My seneschal Jofroi will go together with you,
Along with two hundred knights in full battle dress.
Get going right away, because you can show them the way.
Afterwards, I'll have the townspeople of Orleans follow you shortly.
Bring back my noble knights to me before it's evening. 7860

⚜ A Chanson de Geste ⚜

Bring that traitor, Rainier, before me.
We'll administer the justice to him that the French will decide.
As the result of having been loyal to my barons,
I'm going to increase your fiefs, but do serve me well right now."
"Sire," said Antiaume, "woe be to anyone who does less!" 7865
"Mount up, brave knights," said Louis, the king.
"Because if I lose Aiol, it will be a devastating loss.
I'd rather lose Rheims or Chartres or Blois."
Two hundred knights mount up and many a rich burgher —
So many that the congestion was intense trying to cross the bridge. 7870
Antiaume guided them since he knew the roads well.
From all the common people of Orleans and the burghers,
Antiaume had a hundred of them stay behind in case of an ambush.
Until they reach the old castle, they remained mute and silent.
Another hundred fully-armed, dubbed knights 7875
Were led by Antiaume on Norwegian warhorses.
Day was breaking when they arrived at the small castle.
Aiol was inside, distraught and extremely angry.
Since there were only five of them, they're in fear of death,
Because their attackers outside are shooting Turkish* fire-arrows 7880
And the armed men climbed up under the galleries.
Fiercely they press them with their good Viennese blades.
Of Geraume's four sons, three were captured.
They brought them outside and bound them in the field.
Aiol went inside because of his fear. 7885
Jofroi, Geraume's son, went inside with him.
They're so physically exhausted, they've no energy for fear.
Aiol swears to God that he'll not be a failure —
As long as he can hold out, in life or in death.
He knew, as well, that Rainier would kill him instantly, 7890
Because he hated Aiol bitterly due to his brothers' deaths.
And Rainier yelled in a loud voice:
"Aiol, whore's son, evil traitor, renegade,
Because of my brothers' deaths, you'll die right away.
I wouldn't even take all the king's treasure 7895
To keep from hanging you, no matter what!"
The burghers had prepared tinder and flints,
Then they built a fire. They wanted to burn the defenders.
"Oh, God!" said Aiol, "who was hung on the cross,
Have mercy on my soul. I don't think I'll ever see 7900
My relatives or my friends or my uncle, the king.
Oh, Elye! Father, you'll have to remain

❧ Aiol ❧

With Avisse, my mother, who fainted because of me,
In the forest for many years. May God, who sees all things,
Provide you with another form of rescue, because from Aiol,
    your heir, 7905
You won't get a tiny seed's worth of help!"
Now here comes the king's seneschal, spurring his mount
And the courtly Antiaume, who's leading the French.
He yelled: "Monjoie!" It's the king's war cry.
"Foul cur, Rainier! Traitor! By the saints of Orleans, 7910
You'll hang from the gallows before the evening's gone."
The besieged knights in the castle hear this and didn't take it lightly.
They dropped down from the galleries,
Not worrying in the least about possible injury.

188.

Roimorentin's inhabitants saw the French approaching. 7915
They were giving great support to their lord, Rainier.
Armed and wearing a hauberk, he was seated on Marchegai,
Whom he'd won in combat. Most proud of his mount was he.
In such a loud voice, Rainier began to shout:
"Don't be at all dismayed, noble knights! 7920
Let's defend ourselves! We really need to,
Because — by that lord whom pilgrims seek in Rome —
Before I die, I'll have sold myself dearly!"
Now here comes Antiaume, the usurer's son,
Who brandished the shaft of his stout, sharp lance. 7925
He goes to strike Rainier before him on his shield,
On the golden boss, breaking and piercing it.
It rips and tears Rainier's shining hauberk.
Along Rainier's side, Antiaume guided his lance.
The devil protected him, because the lance didn't touch him. 7930
Then Antiaume forcefully seized Rainier and threw him to
    the ground.
Before the traitor could get back up,
Antiaume, the courtly, grabbed him by his helm's nose piece.
He pulled Rainier up, acting like a true warrior.
In his clear voice, he began to shout: 7935
"Where are you, noble knights of France?
I've got the traitor here. Come on and help me!"
Then fourteen knights came riding up,
Who forcefully seized Rainier and tied him up.
They turned him over to the seneschal of France as his prisoner. 7940

⚜ A Chanson de Geste ⚜

When Aiol heard "Monjoie!" yelled and shouted,
If he'd been given all the gold on earth,
He wouldn't have been nearly as joyful.
He comes down from the tower, but he has no horse at all.
He found Marchegai wandering loose just in front of him —   7945
Rainier has just fallen off of him —
And Aiol mounted him. He wasn't looking for a better horse.
He reached down to the ground and picked up a stout shield;
He went to strike a knight in front of him on his shield.
On its golden boss, he broke and pierced it.   7950
All of his arms were of no use to the knight,
He fell dead on the ground in front of Aiol.
Aiol turned around and seized the knight's horse.
He gave it to Jofroi, Geraume's son, through friendship,
And Jofroi mounted it. He was extremely joyful.   7955
Then he drew his sword and with his shield on his arm,
Went off to look for his brothers he'd been seeking for so long
So he could give them back their arms and their swift warhorses.
At that moment, the force consisting of the townspeople of
    Orleans arrived.
Along with the hundred men who had lain in ambush in the thicket. 7960
They surrounded Roimorentin's burghers, both in front and behind.
Roimorentin's townspeople couldn't defend themselves,
Because they weren't used to bearing arms,
Since they rarely plied that trade.
They took themselves all the way back to Roimorentin.   7965
Aiol has the seneschal sound his horn to announce
To the townspeople that they'll forfeit nothing inside the castle's walls.
To the burghers, he returned their houses and their fiefs.
From the tower's gallows they had Rainier hanged.
Then they had Mirabel released from jail   7970
Where both she and Geraume were held prisoners.
Aiol had no intention of leaving behind his seven horses
Or all of the great wealth he had won.
With him he is taking Antiaume, the usurer's son.
He never intends to blame Aiol for the death of his father,   7975
Who died at the foot of the tower, crushed by a huge boulder.
Inside the tower, they leave ten knights,
Who will keep watch over the walled city, the surrounding town and
    the marketplace.
They all started out on the road, in serried ranks.
One of Geraume's sons rode on ahead to announce   7980

 AIOL

That Aiol's returning from Spain safe and sound, joyful and glad.
And the emperor mounts up with a hundred of his knights
And Lady Isabelle and Lusiane of the proud countenance.
When they saw Mirabel riding beside Aiol,
It's clear that neither of them had cause to be glad. 7985
Mighty King Louis, who reigns over France,
Went to hug and kiss Aiol, his favorite.
Now they enter the city of Orleans.
The king leads them into the vast palace.

PART FOUR

189.

Great was the joy that Louis felt! 7990
He hugged Aiol and began to speak to him:
"Noble young knight, lord, your arrival is a wonderful thing.
I've been so worried and distraught because of you,
I thought I'd never see you again,
However, I have jailed your two companions. 7995
If they've betrayed you or failed you in any way,
Tomorrow I'll have them hanged without the slightest objection."
"Sire," said Aiol, "so help me God,
They've been ill-treated in return for their honorable knightly service.
We went to Pamplona — I don't intend to lie to you. 8000
I fell asleep on a Wednesday morning,
And I wasn't going to wake up for all the gold God made.
They won their war prize as worthy and noble knights should.
Since they were in my service, they offered it to me,
But I became angry and ill-tempered with them, 8005
Because I didn't want to take anything that was rightfully theirs.
So go ahead and give them back to me, at your pleasure."
"By my faith, very willingly," the king replied.
"I'll not contradict you, by St. Denis' body,
Even if I had to lose Étampes and Senlis." 8010
Hilaire and Jober are released from prison.

190.

Aiol's companions were very happy
He had testified loyally in their favor.
They show him much joy and great friendship.
Lusiane, the fair, took Oton of Poitiers. 8015
She leads him up to the palace along with Duke Gontier.

🔱 A CHANSON DE GESTE 🔱

She sits down between Aiol her cousin and Mirabel.
She intends to give Mibrien's daughter a hard time:
"Tell me, my lord, Aiol, this lady, what's she here for?
Is she coming to Holy Cross, our cathedral? 8020
This kind of woman must have worked in a tavern.
I know very well how it is with Spanish women.
In this, our own land, they don't know how to earn a living.
It's certain that my mother wasted her gold and her deniers
And her good-natured largesse she showed you recently 8025
When you want to take a wife and leave me!
May God never ever pardon you for this sin!
How I was mocked by soldiers and knights
When I would get up in the morning and in a slip and bare-footed,
I would go to Holy Cross to pray to the Lord God 8030
To protect you from death and danger!
Young Spanish lady, I intend to challenge your right to him,
And I forbid you — in the name of God the righteous father,
Of St. Martin and of the virgins who did so much that was
    praiseworthy —
To take Aiol, the noble knight. 8035
I certainly should have him. I served him first.
And if you do take him, so help me God,
I'll have all of your limbs shamefully hacked off!"
Mirabel behaved as a high-born woman and didn't respond at all.

191.

Lusiane was very angry and distressed, 8040
And when she saw her uncle, the king, she became emboldened:
"In the name of God, my lord Aiol, I wouldn't ever have believed
Our great friendship would be over.
In the past, I was there when you weren't so rich
And Marchegai was only worth thirteen or fifteen sous. 8045
Young lady from Spain, I intend to challenge you,
And I forbid you, in the name of God, Mary's Son,
And the precious lives of the martyrs and the virgins,
To take Aiol, this noble knight,
That I ought to have because I served him first. 8050
And if you take him — if God blesses me —
I'll have you shamefully hacked up and killed."
Mirabel was a refined, high-born woman and didn't respond at all.
When Aiol heard this, he almost went crazy with anger,
Because he saw Mirabel was troubled and distressed. 8055

 AIOL

Angrily, Duke Elye's son leaped to his feet.
Now the noble knight will speak calmly and knowledgeably.

192.

Aiol, Elye's son, rose up from his seat.
He climbed up on a high table, standing on his two feet,
And spoke loudly, so everyone would hear.   8060
"Now listen to me," he said, "noble knights,
French and Burgundians, Germans and Bavarians,
Those who hold the borderlands, the heads of this city.
Help me to appeal to my lord, Louis,
For I'm his liegeman and I hold my fiefs from him.   8065
For him I've done battle and fought vast combats
And ended wars, thus guaranteeing his income.
Never have I asked for anything worth even two deniers,
No more than my horses, which he gave me willingly.
Whatever this assembly decides, that will be my inheritance. 8070
I want to ask him now. May he give it to me quickly."
And the king replied: "Let everything be granted to you.
Tell me what you want. Everything will be granted to you."
"By my head," said Aiol, "first, let it be pledged to me
And very solemnly sworn on saints' relics."   8075
The king took a glove that was held by a bishop.
Then he questioned Aiol as to exactly what he wanted.
On saints' relics the king swore before thirty knights
Of France's highest nobility, of the most worthy,
That he would grant Aiol all that was within his rights.   8080
Now Aiol will speak, the noble and the proud.
The king still doesn't know that Aiol's his nephew,
But now Aiol intended to let him know.

193.

"My friend," said the king, "now I've granted you a boon.
I'd like to know what you want and hear what you have to say." 8085
"I'll tell you," said Aiol, "so that the French will hear it.
I request from you Navarre and Langres and Dignon,
And the cities of Angers, Noble and Besançon,
And Trèves, Plaisance, Cremoigne on the Mount.
And I want Meaux, Provins, Rheims and Chalons,   8090
Amiens, Saint Quentin, Laon and Soissons.
The duchy of France, I ask of you,
From the basilica of St.-Denis, the main standard,

⚜ A Chanson de Geste ⚜

And the post of seneschal for your entire kingdom.
In a short while, I will be gone,   8095
But because you are king, I will honor you.
I'll recognize you. I'll be your liegeman too.
I've asked you for this and I'll tell you the reason
Why I asked for it and what my name is.
My father's name is Elye, with the bright countenance.   8100
My mother is your sister, daughter of King Charles.
You drove him out of France because of an evil cur,
Following the advice of Makaire and other robbers.
May God reward them for this with death!
Never a day of my life will they be without war!"   8105
When the emperor heard this, never had anyone been so joyful.

194.

Aiol held Mirabel by her white hand.*
When the king now hears that Aiol is his nephew,
Never had he been so joyous or so glad.
Quickly Louis runs over to hug and kiss him.   8110
"Noble young knight, lord, why didn't you say so?
Right away I'd have dubbed you, the first thing,
And awarded you your honors, your lands and your fiefs!"
"Sire, I wouldn't have dared, by all the saints in heaven,
Since I was poor, in rags and wretched."   8115

195.

"My lord, noble young knight, that was a crazy thing to do,
Not revealing your identity to me at the very first."
"Sire, I didn't dare do it," said Aiol, "upon my life,
Because I was so poor I didn't have anything to live on.
By my faith, Lusiane is my first cousin.   8120
Now let us give her a man who is rich and powerful,
Since I'm her cousin, she has no hope of having me."
"Sire," said Lusiane, "this revelation has cured me,
But by that apostle pilgrims seek in Galicia,
I love you all the more since you can't be mine.   8125
Oh, God!" said the maiden, "I would be cured
If I were reconciled with the noble young woman.
Maiden from Spain, I've treated you very badly.
I was very wrong to have insulted you.
Don't become the least bit angry about all that I've said.   8130
I'm now ready and prepared. Take me right to Aiol.

205

I'll lead you to him in front of the entire royal court."
The maiden replied, who was worthy and noble:
"I forgive you everything, fair one, everything you said to me,
In good faith, in love and all of it without any baseness." 8135
Now here they are, reconciled, sitting side by side,
Which caused great joy in the magnificent assembly.

196.

Aiol took Mirabel by her white hand;
He came before the king and said, smiling:
"Have her baptized, sire, Mibrien's daughter. 8140
I won her recently through steel and blade.
Since then I've suffered pain, anguish and exhaustion."
And the king replied: "I order and command it."
To the Church of the Holy Cross our French led her.
In the cathedral, there was a basin of shining gold. 8145
They filled the basin with water and blessed it.
They had the maiden baptized right away.
The king acted as her godfather along with the best of his court
And the fair and attractive Lusiane.
They definitely refused to change her name at all, 8150
And they went ahead and confirmed her in the Christian faith,
Her name remaining *Mirabel*, just as before.

197.

Thus she was baptized at the holy font.
The emperor of France loved her and held her dear.
In a magnanimous gesture, he gave her three cities: 8155
They are Trèves, Plaisance and the third, Cremoigne.
"Sire," said Aiol, "so should it be.
From now on, you will be her father before all earthly men.
I'll take her as my wife, if you'll state the waiting period."
And the king replied: "Never will I set a waiting period.* 8160
On the octave of Pentecost, that high holy day,
I'll give her to you as your wife in Aix-la-Chapelle."
And Aiol cried out in his fine voice:
"Now hear me, my lords, noble, honest knights!
Who among you wants gold, silver and fine fabric from Biterme 8165
And mules, palfreys and Castilian warhorses?
Let him come with me tomorrow and serve me well,
And I'll go to take possession of my honors and my lands."

❧ A Chanson de Geste ❧

198.

Then all the noble knights responded to him,
To whom he had given fine gold and deniers, 8170
Mules, palfreys and swift warhorses:
"In the name of God, sire, we'll go gladly
And defend your honor against all men,
So that we'll win it, if God will grant it."
In the morning, at break of day, they got ready. 8175
They rode across the land and took possession of Aiol's fiefs
That he had inherited from Elye, the noble knight.

199.

They rode so far that they came to the city of Nevers.
Makaire had put Pinart and Pinabel there:
Two evil traitors, who were swollen with arrogance. 8180
They were so dissolute, they didn't deign to return the fiefs.
Aiol took them prisoner and gave them their just desserts,
Thus he had seven score of them hanged on the hill of Montidel.
Then he placed his guards inside the castle.

200.

After that, he came to Langres in Burgundy. 8185
Those inside the town yielded it and handed over
The keys to the city, bringing them out to him.
They swore loyalty to Aiol and became his liegemen.
The king came straight to Besançon to meet him.
He called out to Aiol, addressed him proudly: 8190
"How are things going, nephew?" "Very well, thanks be to God, dear uncle.
I'm conquering my lands. No one is challenging my rights.
Anyone who contradicts me will die shamefully.
Now I'll send for my father to come from Gascony."
Aiol sent three counts to Elye right away. 8195
He had twelve packhorses loaded with fine gold and sterling silver
That he sends to the hermitage, straight to the holy man.

201.

Now the envoys leave — they don't dare refuse.
The messenger guides them, who had carried the wealth
Aiol sent there, as you have heard. 8200
They travelled and rode for so many days
That they came to Mongaiant and found Elye there.

⚜ Aiol ⚜

They gave pure gold and sterling silver to the monk.
This site became a place of honor because of God and Elye.
They said to Elye: "My lord, you will come 8205
To the king of sweet France. He's sent his message to you through us,
Because he wants to be reconciled and at peace with you.
And your son, Aiol, the young knight, informs you
He's become acquainted with and beloved by the king of France.
He also requests through us that you no longer remain here, 8210
Because he's won back all of your inheritance."
When the duke heard this, he praised God for it:
"My lords, in that case, I'll go with you, gladly and willingly!"
They had the duke mount up on a good palfrey,
Which will carry him well at a good amble. 8215
They lifted the duchess up onto a mule's soft saddle.
They requested leave of the hermit,
And he commended them to God of majesty.
Let's just say they passed through many countries and kingdoms,
Because I'm not able to tell you about all their lodgings — 8220
It would be very boring for me to name all these lands.
They spent so much of their days riding and travelling
That they came to Orleans, the marvelous city.
Upon arriving, Elye did something noble and courtly:
He went to Holy Cross to worship and pray. 8225
He took out four marks of gold and placed them on the altar.
In this manner, he greatly honored our Lord
For the good he had done him and his goodness.
As they left the church, Elye encountered the king
Who was coming to meet him with his magnificent court. 8230
When Louis saw him, he began to speak to him:
"High-born man of good lineage, it's good to see you here!
May they be dishonored and shamed,
Those who had you leave and be separated from me."
And Elye, the noble and courtly, replied: 8235
"And may you be blessed, as you have well deserved!"
Louis answered: "My lord, you're very wrong,
Because a very good friend causes evil counsel to be averted."*
"Sire," said Aiol, "it's the pure truth,
But now I beg you, my father, as a gesture of true friendship, 8240
And I beg you also, my mother, whom you see here,
That you show the king forgiveness and pardon him."
And Avisse replied: "Gladly and willingly!"
She went over to bow low before her brother's feet,

⚜ A Chanson de Geste ⚜

And he raised her back up, taking her gently in his arms. 8245
Tenderly he kissed her mouth and her cheek,
And then did the same to Duke Elye, in affectionate friendship.
Then the duchess ran to embrace her son.
She kisses his mouth and his cheeks more than a hundred times.
Thus Aiol reconciled the king and his father, 8250
Had each one of them pardon all ill will and rancor.
The king grants Elye his lands and all of his inheritance,
The post of seneschal for his entire kingdom
And named him high counselor to his privy chamber.
Also, as before, he returned to him his honors. 8255
"Dear son," said Elye, "you have certainly done well,
You who have won back all of my fiefs.
Yesterday evening I was poor; now, I'm extremely rich.
Now I'd like you to hand over to me my horse and my arms
That, back in the forest, I gave you upon your departure." 8260
"My lord, said Aiol, "I've never heard of such a thing.
Neither the shining hauberk nor the helm could last long,
The shield and the lance were lost during a joust,
And Marchegai is dead — his life is ended.
A while back, the dogs devoured his carcass in a ditch. 8265
He wasn't able to run anymore. He was completely senile."
When Elye heard this, he was close to losing his mind.
In his wounded pride, he angrily took a cudgel
And charged at Aiol. He intended to kill him.
"Foul cur," said the duke, "woe to you if you dared to think 8270
Marchegai was dead, my well-rested horse!
You'll never find another one as good.
Get out of my lands! You won't even hold a foot of them!
Did you think, false rogue, foul low-life, all conceited
Because of your pierced trousers and pointy-toed shoes 8275
And your blond hair that you wear in braids,
That you're a powerful man, and I'm just some tramp?"
Then the high nobility of France began to make fun of Elye.
Even Louis burst out laughing.*
When Aiol saw his father infuriated because of him, 8280
He instantly and quickly threw himself at his feet:
"My lord, mercy, for God's sake," said Aiol, the noble.
"I think I'll still be able to show you the horse and the arms."
He had them all quickly brought out into the square.
Aiol had had them exquisitely prepared, 8285
Elegantly adorned with pure gold and silver.

209

❧ Aiol ❧

Aiol then had Marchegai led out before Elye:
The horse was fat, his flanks fully filled out,
Because Aiol had provided him with a long period of rest.
Aiol had Marchegai led to his father by two silver chains. 8290
Elye took his ermine cloak in his hand
And rubbed down the horse's flanks.

202.

Aiol doesn't intend to quarrel or argue.
He leads Marchegai to his father by his golden rein,
His hauberk, his shining helm and sharp sword, 8295
His shield — it's plain to see, it's been skillfully painted —
And his lance well-maintained and brightly polished.
"My lord, here are the arms you gave me.
Do with them as you wish and whatever is your pleasure."
"Good son," said Elye, "they're yours, free and clear. 8300
I'll have others sought for me. Soon they'll be ready for me.
For God's sake, don't ever fail yourself or your mother."
"My lord," said Aiol, "may it not please God my Father
That, in my whole lifetime, I should have a denier or any
    material thing
Without your being called its lord and my mother its lady. 8305
Instead, I will serve you as though I were from another land.
Yours are all the lands that I've conquered."
Aiol, Elye's son, then asked for his wife's hand
From mighty King Louis, that the king might grant her to him.
From a stone chamber they brought Mirabel out to him. 8310
He wed her that day in joy and gladness.
The archbishop of Rheims sang mass for them.
Upon leaving the church, she was raised up on a mule.
That day Mirabel was blessed and made holy.
On a mule luxuriously covered and draped, 8315
On a golden sidesaddle was the lady placed,
And they left the city and set out on their way.
I don't know what happened on each day of their journey,
But they rode so long, morning and evening,
That they continued the wedding feast in Langres, in Burgundy, 8320
Because Aiol, the lord of that entire region,
Did not want to celebrate his nuptials in the great, square tower
Or in a house, a castle or a paved hall.
Instead, he had them held outside Langres' city walls, in a
    wide meadow.

⚜ A Chanson de Geste ⚜

There you could have seen many a canopy raised 8325
And many luxurious tents, fringed with gold and silver tassels.
This opulent wedding feast lasted two weeks,
But before they left, they would pay dearly.
Makaire managed to get out of prison, the traitor, the cur,
By bribing his guards, who accepted huge sums of money. 8330
The foul cur journeyed so far that he arrived in his fiefs,
And he won back three cities under his dominion:
Lausanne, Autun and the broad Cremoigne.
He assembled mercenaries from throughout the land.
His treasury was vast, and he paid them handsomely. 8335
A great many Lombards and Burgundians rallied to him,
Until there were thirty thousand of them, each wearing a helm,
Who came to Langres one morning.
Makaire, the traitor, dismounted in the meadow
To set the leadership and organize his people. 8340
They'll serve at the wedding feast with the blades of their swords.

203.

Just outside Langres in Burgundy, in a leafy copse
Of yews, poplars and spreading olive trees,
Makaire, the traitor, dismounted on foot.
He said to his men: "Much evil has come my way. 8345
Louis of France has destroyed and disgraced me,
Seized my lands and awarded them to another."
"Good lord," said his men, "why are you dismayed?
See them over there in their tents, happy, relaxed and confident.
If you can capture Aiol, may he be hanged this morning!" 8350
Then they leaped into the saddles of their long-maned warhorses.
Shortly, they'll serve at the wedding feast with their sharpened swords,
But they're acting foolishly, these unfortunate, wretched men,
Because the day before, the emperor had come
With seven hundred knights wearing shining hauberks. 8355

204.

That evening, Aiol was lying stretched out inside one of the tents
Beside his wife, as was his duty.
But here, the knight had acted prudently and cautiously:
He had himself well guarded by five hundred French.
When they saw the enemy approaching, they became very afraid. 8360
They got ready to defend themselves.

❧ Aiol ❧

Makaire pricks and spurs his mount and goes to strike Jofroi,
A noble knight who was born in Orleans.
He deals Jofroi a marvelous blow on his upright shield,
Which splits and shatters three pleats of his hauberk. 8365
He thrusts his cold iron right through the center of his heart.
With the entire length of his lance, Makaire strikes him down dead.
This death causes the French to become anguished and irate,
Because he was the seneschal of Louis, our king.
The Lombards forged ahead, forcibly and powerfully. 8370
They set fire to the pavilions and got them burning.
The French inside them were sorely distressed.

205.

Joserant of Paris saw his relative murdered.
In his heart he felt such anger, he almost went insane.
He spurs and pricks his warhorse, who's not slow at all, 8375
And quickly goes to strike Bevon of Viane,
Breaking and splitting the shield hanging from his neck
And ripping and tearing the hauberk on his back.
Straight through the middle of Bevon's heart, he thrusts his
    stout lance.
With the entire length of his lance, Joserant strikes him down to a
    bloody death. 8380
Manesier, who was watching them, felt grief because of his brother.
He swears to the Lord God, the almighty,
That if he can get to Joserant, he'll pay dearly.

206.

Full of grief, Manesier pricks and spurs his mount across the field.
He goes to strike Joserant of Paris on his shield, 8385
On his golden boss. He broke and battered it
And ripped and tore the hauberk on his back.
Straight through Joserant's body, Manesier thrust his lance.
With the entire length of his lance he left him stretched out, dead.
Then he shouted his battle cry: "Knights, strike your blows!" 8390

207.

Louis, Charles' son, pricks and spurs his mount.
He goes to strike Oedon the Burgundian on his shield.
On its golden boss, Louis' blow batters and shatters it
And rips and tears the hauberk on Oedon's back.
Right straight through his body, Louis thrusts iron and pennon. 8395

A Chanson de Geste

With the entire length of his lance, he strikes him down
   dead from his saddle.
This caused great grief to Oedon's brother, Garin of Monlaon.
He goes to strike the king on his lion-painted shield,
Which knocked down Louis and his horse on a hillock.
Louis leaped back to his feet, drew his colored sword   8400
And raised over his head his lion-painted shield.
Anyone his blow reaches has no protection from death.
Now here comes Aiol, spurring his warhorse.
He has armed himself very well inside his pavilion
And is seated on Marchegai who's galloping swiftly.   8405
At his side are Jofroi and Hilaire — all three are companions.
They wouldn't separate themselves from him for all the gold
   in this world.
Now they'll rescue the king, no matter who stands in their way.

208.

Aiol sees in the melee Louis, his lord,
Whom the evil Burgundians are pressing hard.   8410
He spurs Marchegai, gives him free rein
And goes to strike Gerin on his new shield.
On its golden boss, he breaks and batters it
And rips and shreds the hauberk on his back.
Aiol thrusts his lance right into Gerin's sternum.   8415
Along the entire length of his lance, he struck Gerin down
   dead on the grass,
Then he seized Gerin's warhorse by its golden rein,
Charges into the melee and hands over the horse to his lord,
And the king mounted it by the left stirrup.
At this very moment dawn began to break.   8420
Mirabel, the maiden, had remained on a knoll.
The fair beauty was barefoot in her nightgown,
Still dressed as she had been on that past wedding night.
She looked down from the knoll and saw the losses,
Saw the hands, the feet, the bodies and the heads   8425
Of the noble knights who were lying dead on the grass.
She prayed to the Lord God, the glorious one of heaven:
"Lady St. Mary, worthy virginal maiden,
If I lose my lord, today, such a war will begin
That will never disappear from this earthly world!"   8430

209.

The day was clear and beautiful, and the sun shone brightly.
The emperor of France was grieving and depressed:
He saw his men dying in pain and anguish.
He spurs his warhorse, which doesn't run slowly at all,
And goes to strike Makaire in front of him, on his shield, 8435
On its golden boss. Louis' blow breaks and shatters it.
The hauberk on Makaire's back isn't worth a bezant.
The devil protected him, as his flesh wasn't touched.
As long as the king's lance held up, Louis swiftly drove him to the ground;
The foul cur instantly and quickly jumped back to his feet. 8440
Louis pulled up and drew his sharp sword —
He would have sliced off Makaire's head, who would have had no protection from death,
But Girber and Guy the German hauled Makaire away.
They pulled him out of the melee away to safety.
Because of this rescue, Makaire wasn't at all silent in battle. 8445
Instead, he charged rapidly through the ranks,
Holding his sword whose sharp blade
Slashes chests, sides and warhorses' heads.
Anyone his blow reaches has no protection from death.
In his loud voice he goes around shouting: 8450
"Where are you, Aiol, evil, foul cur!
Did you really think you were going to take away all my fiefs?
Right now you'll pay for it, if God gives me my wish."
Elye's son heard him and came running towards him.
He dealt Makaire a blow on his shield in front of him, 8455
Which strikes down both Makaire and his horse amid the field.
Aiol stopped above Makaire and drew out his naked blade.
In my opinion, he'd have avenged himself right then,
But Girber and Guy the German rescued Makaire
From the melee and drew him away to safety. 8460
There you could have seen such a great battle
And so many knights killed and fallen, bleeding.
The Burgundians' force was strong, for there were few French.
The emperor of France was utterly heartsick.
Spurring his mount, he heads towards the city of Langres. 8465
Angry and sorrowful, he left so many of his men behind.
Aiol, Elye's son, remained there, still fighting,
And Makaire's allies attacked him from in front and behind.
They did great damage to the valiant knight,

A Chanson de Geste

Because they struck dead right in the middle of the field 8470
Jobert and Hilaire, both of them, before Aiol's eyes,
And also Geraume, the worthy, and Antiaume, the young knight,
Geraume's four sons, all of them most worthy.
Aiol, Elye's son, then withdrew from combat.

210.

Aiol left the battle, spurring his warhorse. 8475
Mirabel, the duchess, had remained on a knoll.
The Burgundians surrounded her and seized her.
They turned her over to Makaire, the evil, foul cur,
And the noble duchess called out loudly to Aiol:
"Will you let me be led away, noble duke's son? 8480
You'll have to endure great shame for it every day of your life!"
When Aiol heard this, it caused him great pain,
And he swears to the Lord God, the Father Creator,
He wouldn't let it happen for all the gold of this world,
And that, at the ford's crossing, it would be his turn to strike. 8485
He pricks Marchegai with his sharp spurs,
Aiol strikes a Burgundian in front of him on his shield.
The shield he shatters, above and below the boss,
And rips and tears the hauberk on his back.
Right through his body, Aiol thrusts his iron and pennant. 8490
With the entire length of his lance, he strikes the Burgundian
 down dead from his saddle.
Then Aiol drew his sword with its golden hilt
And struck again, upon a Lombard's helm,
Whose gemstones and flowers went showering down.
Aiol shifted his blow and struck him down dead on the sand. 8495
At that moment, forty Burgundians arrived.
With more than thirty lances they struck at Aiol.
They bloodied his breastplate, his cinches and his stirrups.
Whether he wanted to or not, they struck him down from his horse.
Then Aiol leapt to his feet and drew his painted blade. 8500
Anyone his blade touches has no protection from death,
But a great misfortune befell him that day,
Because his sword flew into two pieces.
The Burgundians surrounded and seized him.
Now here comes Makaire, the evil traitor, 8505
Holding a naked sword by its golden hilt.
He would have immediately cut off Aiol's head — there'd be
 no ransom —

⚜ Aiol ⚜

When Guy, Aleran and Girber rescued him,
And the noble duchess exclaimed loudly:
"Have mercy, Lord Makaire, for the love of God and God's name! 8510
How could you now kill a man like Aiol?
Since you've already captured us, put us in prison.
You've completely redeemed Burgundy's honor."
And the traitor replied: "By my head, indeed I have!"
He has them turned over to the forty Burgundians 8515
And has their hands tied behind their backs
So tightly that bright blood flows forth.

211.

Makaire captured Aiol and with him his wife.
He had their hands tied behind their backs
So tightly that bright blood dripped down. 8520
Then he had all their possessions loaded and strapped on packhorses:
The tents, tapestries and rich, folded cloths
And the tableware too, which had been set out for a meal.
Rapidly, they secure all this on strong packhorses.
They set out on their way without delay. 8525
I don't know how I ought to relate their story to you!
From there to Lausanne, they made no delay.
They entered the city mounted and on foot.
Makaire, the traitor whom God should punish,
Climbed up all the steps of the vast palace. 8530
He had Aiol brought there along with his wife.
They looked at each other and wept out of pity.
Makaire summons his head jailers:
He has them sent down into the depths of his prison.
Then they lie there so long, in sorrow and sinned against, 8535
That Aiol had by his wife two tiny heirs.
Afterwards, they will suffer many pains and mortal dangers
Before bearing arms and becoming knights.
Now this song will greatly increase in intensity:
Its deals with authentic history. It would be foolish to seek
   a better one.* 8540
But in one way the Burgundians committed an error:
They left Aiol's horse behind.
A Lombard seized Marchegai: he wanted to stroke him.
The horse perceived that this was not at all Aiol
And killed the Lombard with both his hooves. 8545
Marchegai then returned to Langres, completely unbridled.

❧ A Chanson de Geste ❧

The Beruiers opened the gate wide for him,
And Marchegai entered the city — never was there such a warhorse.
He had a much greater knowledge of warfare than a bad knight.

212.

In Langres, Elye lay suffering and anguished;   8550
He is very ill and gravely weakened.
He still doesn't have any idea that his son's been captured.
He heard the noise, the din and the shouts, and
Sends for his seneschal, called Gerard of Valseri:
"Well-born man, tell me, what's that racket they're making?"   8555
"My lord," said Gerard, "there's bad news.
Makaire of Lausanne has managed to get out of prison
By bribing his guards, who accepted huge sums of money.
Yesterday he defeated the king in these fields.
They're leading away Aiol, your son, whom they captured in battle." 8560
When Elye heard this, he almost went mad.
Because of his son, the noble knight fainted four times.

213.

In Langres, Elye lay full of pain and torment.
He's in deep mourning for the son he's lost:
"Noble knight of high birth," said the duke, "how unfortunate
   you are!   8565
May Makaire of Lausanne be confounded!
Marchegai, good horse, I'm distraught because of you,
For if I had you back, I'd be completely reassured."
"My lord," said Gerard, "Marchegai has returned.
The good war and guard horse, never was there better!   8570
He's already eaten a large bushel or more of oats."
When Elye heard this, never had he been so joyous.
He prayed to the Lord God, the Father above:
"Sire, glorious Father, I render thanks to you!
I'll get up tomorrow morning when it's light   8575
And wage war again with iron and shield.
By that holy apostle by whom God does good things,
Those who are now acting joyous, happy and confident,
Will yet for their crimes be hanged by the neck!"

214.

The duke and his wife both feel great pain   8580
And lament Aiol well, with courtly restraint:

❦ Aiol ❦

"Oh! How unfortunate you were, noble knight!
Makaire of Lausanne, may you be shamed.
You've taken from us the finest heir
Who was ever in France or anywhere here below!" 8585
"Lady," said the duke, "let us set aside this intense grieving.
I've never seen anything accomplished or gained from deep
    mourning.
I won't value it one denier's worth since I've got Marchegai back.
Tomorrow morning, if it pleases God, I'll get up first thing,
And I'll start to wage war again with iron and steel. 8590
Those who are now acting joyous, happy and confident,
Will yet, because of their crimes, be anguished and distraught!"

215.

On Saturday morning Elye got up.
He summoned his head chamberlains:
"Bring me my arms, my trousers and my shoes. 8595
Help me up from this bed — I've been in it too long.
To hell with this illness that's stayed around so long!"
And they replied: "As you command!"
Without delay, they brought Elye his clothing.
They dressed him in a shirt and white breeches. 8600
They threw an ermine cape on his back
And over that a tunic embroidered with pure gold.
Then they dressed him in a mantel of scarlet.
"My lords," said Elye, "now listen to me.
Be so kind as to bring me something to eat. 8605
I've not sat at a table for fourteen years now."
And they replied: "Sire, whatever you wish."
They led Elye to the highest table.
To start off, they brought him two cakes of sifted flour
And the large shoulder of a huge wild boar 8610
And small fowl that had been peppered and roasted
And copious quantities of wine, both spiced and claret.
Elye ate it all, the courtly and noble.
There was no chance he'd give any of it away!
Instead, he ate heartily and enthusiastically. 8615
He drank a quart each both of wine and claret.
The young knights began to make jokes
And said to each other: "For the love of God, look at that!
This old man has just eaten so much at his dinner
That it would have been plenty for four other knights!" 8620

❦ A Chanson de Geste ❦

When Elye heard this, he almost lost his mind.
"My lords," said the duke, "you're very wrong about this.
If I eat my own food, what cost has it been to you?
Now just take the four knights you've just mentioned,
Who could be here bringing me my arms and armor, 8625
Have them all armed and dressed in iron,
And just watch me. I'll take them on,
And before vespers and sundown,
I'll have defeated and vanquished all four of them —
Or I'll never eat again in all my life!" 8630
Those who knew him said: "He's telling the truth.
Never a better knight than he is has ever put spurs on!"
When the duke had eaten, he got up
And came back to the main palace.
Mighty King Louis got up to meet him. 8635
He went to kiss and embrace him.
"Dear brother-in-law," he said, "by holy charity,
I never want to be without your loyal support."
"Sire," said Elye, "listen to me.
I beg and entreat you, through holy charity, 8640
To set up a quintain in the meadow,
So I'll be able to deliver a blow to test myself,
To find out if I can still wear armor and bear arms,
And in the thick of the fray, if I can meet a knight in combat."
"My lord," said the king, "it will be as you wish." 8645
Elye, the noble and the brave, armed himself.
He put on a hauberk, laced on a helm
And girded on a sword with its hilt of newelled gold.
He mounted Marchegai, who had been saddled up,
Then rode out of the city surrounded by a splendid entourage. 8650
Elye pricks and spurs, rides over a moat
And strikes such a huge blow at the quintain
That it broke the post right down at the ground
And caused the quintain to fall backwards in front of him.
Those watching said: "He's dealt a mighty blow! 8655
I don't know of any man in all of Christendom
Capable of withstanding such a blow in battle."
King Louis ran to embrace him:
"Dear brother-in-law," he said, "for holy charity,
Never do I want to be separated from your loyal support. 8660
Now I'll assemble my men from all across my kingdom.

We'll rescue Aiol, whom I can't ever forget."
"Sire," said Elye, "may God reward you for it!"

216.

The emperor had his letters and documents written up.
From his entire kingdom, he summoned his knights   8665
And all his town militias, mounted and on foot.
They all came promptly, ready for war.
I don't know how to relate their story to you.
The armies got prepared, without any further delay.
They marched out of Langres in serried ranks.   8670
Elye leads them all, his pennant unfurled.

217.

My lords, from that very hour when the army first set out,
They found no house or town that they didn't burn.
In the hills of Marais, they encountered the enemy avant-garde —
Makaire had left five hundred armed men —   8675
And the French armed themselves with firm resolve.
Now they concentrated on doing their best, because they'd find
   combat.

218.

The Burgundians knew well the roads and paths of that land.
As much as they could that day, they fought against the French.
Elye was very much afraid he'd lose some of his people.   8680
He spurs Marchegai, gives him free rein
And goes to strike Gautier, the count of Valterne.
Neither shield or hauberk did the count a bit of good:
Straight through his body Elye thrust the new shaft.
As long as his lance held up, he struck the count dead from
   his saddle.   8685
This greatly grieved Gautier's brother, Guimart of Letormele.
He spurs his warhorse, gives him free rein
And goes to strike the duke on his new shield.
His blow breaks and shatters the golden boss.
Elye's hauberk was very strong: not a link of chainmail was broken. 8690
The old knight was so strong that he didn't bend over or fall.

219.

The old knight was so strong that he didn't fall or bend over.
Instead, he struck back at Guimart with all his might.

❧ A Chanson de Geste ❧

Upon the golden boss, he pierced Guimart's shield
And ripped and tore the hauberk on his back. 8695
With the entire length of his lance, his immediately struck him
  down dead,
And the Burgundians turned to flee. They deserted the field
  of combat.
All the way to Lausanne, they didn't cease their flight.
On foot and on horseback they entered the city.
Makaire was inside, the foul cur, the traitor. 8700

220.

Makaire was inside, the traitor, the foul cur.
He was deeply grieving over the people he'd lost.
Now here come two messengers swiftly spurring their mounts.
When they came close, they shouted: "Makaire!
In faith, Lord Makaire, things are going very badly for you. 8705
The French have captured the Marais Hills from you.
All this has been done by Elye, the evil traitor.
He's been lying ill: he accomplished this through treason.
The inhabitants of this land consider us to be evil.
Have Aiol burned at the stake, the foul cur!" 8710
When Makaire heard this, he almost went mad.
He drew his sword with the slicing blade.
He came to the prison, swiftly spurring,
And intended to strike Aiol when he got close to him,
But Aleran and Girber held him back. 8715
"Hold back, Lord Makaire. This act will never be tolerated.
Anyone who kills his prisoner should die in shame.
From then on, neither knights nor ladies ought to serve him.
And outside our walls are our closest friends.
If you kill Aiol now, we'll never see them again." 8720
"My lords," said Aiol,* "this Makaire is an evil renegade.
His family has laid to waste so many of my towns and castles."

221.

"My lords," said Makaire, "I've got to spare Aiol for now.
I pray you to pursue my war from this day on."
And they replied: "Whatever you command! 8725
Down there, at that gate, at the main barrier,
We'll bring a fine battle to them!"
And the traitor replied: "I grant and command it!"

221

❦ Aiol ❦

222.

On Saturday morning, Elye got up,
And King Louis and his powerful entourage. 8730
They rode throughout the land, destroying the kingdom.
There remained no town or city that wasn't completely laid to waste.
They didn't return to the main force until afternoon.
The Burgundians rode out, the foul curs,
And the well-armed French were waiting for them. 8735
There you could have seen a fierce battle engaged:
So many noble knights struck down and wounded.
Elye pricks and spurs his mount, crosses a ditch
And strikes a knight he encountered.
Elye's blow cracks and pierces the shield hanging from his neck 8740
And rips and tears the hauberk on his back.
Straight through his heart Elye thrusts his iron tip
And knocks him down dead on the ground.
Then Elye shouted: "Monjoie! Noble knights strike your blows!"
The burghers retreated back into the good city. 8745
They closed all the gates and remained inside.
The French army took up siege positions around the fortified town.
Those inside intended to remain under siege for five full years,
Before they would forfeit anything worth a denier's coin.

223.

Makaire was inside the city, angry and depressed. 8750
He was in deepest grief because of his people whom he'd seen killed.
He drew his sword, the foul cur of evil stock;
He whips around and goes to the prison.
He was about to strike Aiol, the noble knight,
When Girber, Aleran and Guy pulled him away: 8755
"Stop it, Lord Makaire! This act will never be condoned,
Because the king holds our best friends prisoners outside the city,
And uncles, relatives, nephews and cousins.
If you kill Aiol now, we'll never see them alive again."
Aiol heard these words in the prison where he lay. 8760
In his loud voice, he began to shout:
"Whore's son, traitor, now you're done for!
My father and my uncle have laid siege to you because of me.
They won't leave here until there's no one left alive.
Instead, they will have taken Lausanne and shamed you." 8765

⚜ A Chanson de Geste ⚜

When Makaire heard this, he almost lost his mind.
If he weren't restrained by his men, he'd have gladly struck Aiol.

224.

King Louis and Elye concentrate and think hard
As to how they can get Aiol out of Lausanne.
They choose an envoy who was born in Brittany: 8770
"Go to Makaire there in Lausanne for us.
Tell him to turn my nephew and his wife over to me,
And if he doesn't want to do it, I'm coming to get him.
He should make no more attempts to seize any other lands.
I will let him hold Lausanne for the rest of his life.   8775
If not, I'll have him hanged high, in front of all his men."
"Sire," said the envoy, "my troubles are beginning.
Makaire, the foul cur, has no mind for God.
If he becomes angry with me, he'll quickly have me hanged.
To be sure, I'd not abandon the mission, were I to lose all my limbs.   8780
I'd deliver the message, no matter how the embassy might go!"
The envoy mounts his warhorse, takes up his shield and lance
And rides away from the tent and the tallest pavilions.

225.

Makaire mulls it over, then decides to send an envoy to Elye.
He summons a messenger, may God curse him!   8785
His name is Guinehot, and he was born in Lombardy.
He had a big stomach, a curved spine
And drank so much every day he was always intoxicated.
He's never met a noble man he wouldn't just as soon kill.
"My friend," said Makaire, "may God bless you.   8790
Ride out right away for me to the king of St.-Denis.
Tell him to leave me Burgundy free and clear.
I don't want you to hide from him that if he doesn't,
Tomorrow I'll hang Aiol as dawn is breaking,
And Mirabel will be burned in a great fire of thorns."   8795
"My lord," said Guinehot, "I'll be saying it well."
He went to his lodging and took up his arms,
Mounted his warhorse, set out on his way
And rode out of the city by way of the ancient gate.

226.

The king's envoy came before Makaire.   8800
He delivered his message politely and courteously:

❧ Aiol ❧

"Know that Louis, Charles' son, hereby informs you
That you wrongly hold his castles and his borderlands,
And my lord notifies you that you, as your inheritance,
Will have this city, free and clear. You'll have no other fiefs.   8805
You will turn his nephew and his good wife over to him.
Go to speak with him down there at that city gate.
Tell him exactly what you want, because you won't be in any danger."
When Makaire heard this, he almost went insane:
"My friend, what your two lords are requesting of me is an outrage.   8810
Go now and tell the king for me, in front of his whole court,
If I can meet him on the field of combat or in battle,
I'll cut off his head with my slicing sword.
Then I'll wear the crown in Paris or in Chartres.
Tomorrow, I'll hang Aiol from a beech or an oak,   8815
And Mirabel, his wife, will be burned at the stake."
Hervieu,* the envoy, turns away. He's careful not to voice any outrage;
He's fulfilled his mission well. Now he'll start his return,
And Guinehot comes directly to the tent of striped cloth.

227.

Makaire's envoy was so evil, he didn't deign to dismount.   8820
Instead he leaned on his saddle horn and unfurled his ensign.
Haughtily he called out to the mighty king of France:
"I won't greet you,* king, because no one's ordered me to.
I'm brave and bold when it comes to defending myself:
I won't flee even if four men await to do battle with me.   8825
Know that Makaire of Lausanne informs you
That very wrongly you wear the French crown,
Because you never were the legitimate heir of mighty
   King Charlemagne.
The French prove themselves to be extremely evil when they
   grant it to you.
If you don't get out of Burgundy, he'll have your nephew hanged,   8830
And his wife burned at the foot of the gallows."
When the emperor heard this, he almost lost his mind.
If it weren't for Aiol, the envoy wouldn't have any limbs left.

228.

"My friend," said the emperor, "I don't know what you're worth.
With the people of your land, it's always been the case   8835
That they're fools, vain, arrogant and boastful.
My father caused them very great fear.

⚜ A Chanson de Geste ⚜

One day, the French were attacking the Lombards,
Because they made them eat what was scarcely fitting.*
This caused my father grief when he heard of it,   8840
And he came to St.-Domin in his raging fury.
In one day, he had a stone door carved:
He had the Lombards kiss it, both the great and the small.
Then he had them eat rats and big mouse-hunting cats.
Their heirs and all their people are still reproached for that."*   8845
When the Lombard heard this, he was almost bursting
  with rage.

229.

"By my faith, emperor, what you've said is evil and sinful
About the Lombards, whom you're condemning so wrongfully.
They are good knights when it comes to dealing out blows.
Martinobles, my father, was not the least bit stupid.   8850
If he saw a knight who was going to St. Peter,
And he had a beautiful lady my father liked,
You'd never see a man lay them low so fast.
There are still a hundred knights in France who are his bastards.
I heard my father say it, so I know it's true,   8855
That you're my brother, so come kiss me!"
When the emperor heard this, he made a joke of it:
"Then tell me, who are William, Bernard and Richard?"*

230.

The emperor was very amused when he heard Guinehot's banter:
He forged on ahead; nothing held him back.   8860
He came over to the Lombard and cleverly addressed him:
"Now get out of here, Lombard, may God do you harm!
You've eaten so much garbage of mice and rats
And so much compost of tripe and dried-out grape vine stalks,
You look to me like a mare, a donkey or a cow.   8865
I'll always consider a fool anyone who chose you as an envoy,
Because the people of your land are forever frightened
And carry large swords, huge, heavy cudgels
That they quickly throw down when they come to battle.
They grab their adversaries by the hair, yank and jerk,   8870
Hold on to them and drag them down, just like little children."

⚜ Aiol ⚜

231.

"By my faith, emperor, that's sinful talk
About the people of Lombardy you've shamed so falsely!
They are worthy and bold when it comes to dealing blows.
May it please God who never lies, 8875
That you, yourself, be challenged to a duel,
Or old man Elye or Count Baldwin,
So they would fight me with a sharpened steel blade.
Rapidly I'd make one of them scream loudly deep from his throat.
You don't have any right to France and shouldn't be holding it. 8880
Woe to all those who want to put up with you,
Because you shouldn't ever have reigned even a single day!"
And when the king heard this, he almost lost his mind.
If it weren't for Aiol, he'd have gladly struck Guinehot.
Because of his son, Elye greatly fears the Lombard. 8885
He steps forward and politely says to him:
"My friend, good youth, there's no need to attack.
The person who sent you to the king knows you're worthy."*
And the Lombard replied: "In faith, you've told the truth."
Right away he rode away, completely disdaining any leave-taking. 8890
As he was leaving the tent, just as he was going,
He encountered Hervieu, the king's envoy.
Hervieu greeted him politely and courteously.
Before they separate, they'll not be good friends.

232.

The two envoys encountered each other. 8895
Hervieu was very courteous and greeted him politely.
The Lombard heard the greeting, but didn't answer a word.
Instead, through gross evilness, he let out a sardonic laugh,
Then said to Hervieu with very cynical arrogance:
"Who are you, baron, who's going in there? 8900
Are our missions cancelling each other out?
Because of a great deadly war, our two lords hate each other.
I'm considered most honorable and noble,
So my heart's full of very rich goodness:
That's why I won't take the horse you're leading there 8905
And also all the arms you're carrying."
When Hervieu heard this, he burst out laughing
And said to Guinehot: "Baron, you're kidding me!
By that apostle that pilgrims seek in Nero's Field,
If you had stolen or carried off anything of mine 8910

❧ A Chanson de Geste ❧

For which you could get a denier coin,
I'd never remain in Christendom.
I wouldn't stop until I was in pagan lands,
And I'd want to serve and honor Mohammed!
If you really intend to do what you've just said, 8915
Right now, let's each one of us deliver the answer to his message.
Then we'll see each other back here, armed and in battle dress.
You'll have your battle, if you dare!"
And Guinehot replied: "You'll swear it to me!"
"Gladly!" said Hervieu, holding out his hand to him. 8920

233.
Both envoys turn away and leave.
Guinehot returns to Lausanne, to Makaire.
Woe to him if he omits any part of his message!
Guinehot calls out to Makaire. Arrogantly he addresses him:
"Now listen to me, Lord Makaire! 8925
Out there I encountered a Breton, from the outlying islands.
I spoke to him proudly and with great courage.
By my faith, I have pledged to him, and for your sake have given my word,
Out there by right a battle must take place right away."
And Makaire replied: "It's right that it be done." 8930
"Indeed," said Guinehot, "but I'm afraid of harm,
Because he's a knight who's valiant in the use of arms.
But have a hundred armed knights on the square,
Then have them lie in ambush just inside the city walls.
You can have him seized and with him many others." 8935
And the traitor replied: "You are courtly and wise.
It will be done, no matter how this turns out."
And Hervieu came straight to the tent of rich cloth.
When he sees the king, proudly he addresses him.
Politely and courteously he delivers him his message: 8940
"Sire," said Hervieu, "now hear something outrageous:
Makaire's message to you and its contemptible terms.
He notifies you through me that if he encounters you in a battle,
He'll cut off your head — you'll get no other wage —
And also Elye, the brave and courageous duke. 8945
Then he'll go to France, to Paris below Montmartre.
In the great square of St. Germain in the Fields,
There he'll be crowned before his entire entourage.
Tomorrow he'll hang Aiol from the branch of an oak,

And Mirabel, his wife, will be burned at the stake. 8950
As I was returning, I encountered his messenger.
He insulted me vilely. He wanted to challenge me to a duel.
I agreed to combat down there in that meadow."
"My friend," said the emperor, "I indeed want it to take place."
Immediately, the beardless Duke Beuve spoke up: 8955
"Sire, rightful emperor, don't allow this insanity!
The Burgundians are deceitful and the Lombards seething
  with fury.
Let's organize a sortie from our tents of rich cloth:
I'll have a hundred knights armed and ready.
I'll have them lie in ambush in these tents of rich cloth. 8960
They'll observe the combat closely and in good faith,
So that winner will be able to leave safe and sound."
And the king replied: "You are cautious and wise.
These words are sensible, and it's right that this should be done."
Hervieu went off and armed himself. 8965
He went out to the right of the tents of rich cloth.
He met Guinehot by the wall of Pinabel.*

234.

Both envoys came riding, spurring their mounts.
They dismounted from their good, swift steeds.
They cinched them up tightly and quickly remounted. 8970
But Guinehot was cunning and full of deceit.
When he sees Hervieu, he comes over to him and starts
  mocking him:
"I'll brag about it before the Lord God. I've never seen a
  Breton before
Who would dare to attack a good knight,
Because Bretons are in truth very evil people. 8975
They pursued us all across the plains of Lombardy,
All through Pouille and the lands as far as Jerusalem,
And we hunted them down like animals.
We made them lie exposed out in the wind and the rain.
They dug up our vineyards. They fled our fields. 8980
A Breton won't ever be happy without his bran bread
Or a full pot of milk where he can make bread soppings."*
And Hervieu replied: "Foul cur, you're lying,
Because Bretons are worthy and full of daring.
In the army avant-garde, they fought bravely for the French. 8985
There they demonstrated their great skill with arms.

⚜ A Chanson de Geste ⚜

You'll pay for this right away if God allows."
Both of them glared at each other then began to spur fiercely.
The Lombard knew little of honorable arms.
He tried to strike Hervieu in a base and deceitful manner,   8990
But Hervieu struck him back instantly
And dealt Guinehot a marvelous blow on his silver shield,
Which broke and shattered its golden boss,
And the hauberk on his back wasn't worth anything at all to him.
Iron and wood ripped into Guinehot's left side.   8995
As long as the shaft held up for him, Hervieu struck him down, all bloodied.
"Defeated foul cur, may God bring you harm!
You've insulted me enough for today."

235.

The messenger for King Charles' son struck Guinehot very well.
A marvelous blow he dealt the Lombard high on his shield,   9000
Which shatters and breaks its golden boss
And rips and tears the hauberk on his back.
Right beside his flank he thrusts his pennant.
He's not killed him in the least, the evil criminal,
But he's knocked him off his Gascon horse.   9005
And Hervieu, who has the heart of a noble warrior, shouts to him:
"Foul cur, get back on your horse. May God bring you harm!
I'll let you remount, no matter what anyone thinks,
Because a man who's down won't be attacked by me."
The Lombard heard him, but didn't answer yes or no.   9010
Instead, he played dead on the ground, waiting for help.
He kept one eye open, the other squinting.
"Hey, foul cur," said Hervieu, "may God's body give you harm.
Today you've brought us a great betrayal."
He wraps his finger around the lock of Guinehot's right sideburn,   9015
Then drags him along like a common criminal.
Guinehot has well deserved it and has received his just reward.
Hervieu turned him over to Louis, King Charles' son,
And he had him taken to his prison in Soissons.
He's lain there ever since — up until now when we're singing this song.   9020
His ransom was set at his own weight in silver.
The Lombards rode out from the city and the evil Burgundians,
And the French, who were well prepared, met them in battle.

⚜ Aiol ⚜

There you would have been able to see a great combat begin,
And so many brave knights being struck down and killed. 9025

236.
The battle was great and the combat intense.
Makaire pricks and spurs his mount and strikes Godefroy,
Louis' seneschal, who held the county of Vermandois.
Makaire deals him a marvelous blow, straight on his shield,
Which rips and tears the pleats of his hauberk. 9030
Right through the center of his heart, he plunges his lance's cold iron.
Along the entire length of his lance, he immediately knocks him
    down dead.
He shouts his battle-cry: "Strike, noble knights!"

237.
Now here comes Hervieu, who conquered Guinehot,
And goes to strike Morin of Plaisance, the strong. 9035
He breaks his shield and rips his hauberk,
And thrusts his lance straight through his body.
Along the entire length of his lance, he strikes him down dead from
    his warhorse.
Now here comes Makaire, who felt great grief,
And right away shouts his battle-cry in a loud voice. 9040
They deal each other marvelous blows on their golden shields,
Which they shattered, split and battered.
It's not at all a question of falling, because each one holds strong.
And when Elye saw this, he felt wondrous grief.
Quickly and rapidly, he drew his sword 9045
And goes to strike Makaire on his golden shield,
So that the flowers and gemstones fall to the ground.
The hauberk's coif wasn't worth anything to him.
From his face, he slashes his flesh down to the bone.
Makaire, who thinks he's mortally wounded, turns to flee. 9050

238.
Makaire turns to flee, wounded in his face,
And the Burgundians entered the city by the wide gates.*
All around they pitch their striped tents.
Then the siege lasted five full and long years.
King Louis never was able to breech the wall 9055
Or to take the city or to capture Makaire.
Aiol, Elye's son, was in the depths of the prison.

⚜ A Chanson de Geste ⚜

He experienced great sorrow at Christmas and at Easter:
"Oh, alas," said Aiol, "this is a great shame!
Dear sister, sweet friend, what a curse was my great nobility, 9060
My person, my prowess and my knightly feats,
But by that apostle that pilgrims seek in the ark,*
It hurts me more because of you than any of my own troubles."

239.

Aiol was in the prison, distraught and depressed,
And Mirabel, his wife, began to pray to God, 9065
Because she was pregnant and great with child.
"My lady," said Aiol, "it's no use for you to grieve;
I've seen very little accomplished through intense grieving.
Outside of the city is my father, the bearded Elye,
And Louis, my uncle and his powerful force. 9070
He'll never leave here, you can be sure of it,
Until he's conquered Makaire and his city."
"Oh, God!" said the lady, "the wait's too long for me."

240.

Now the noble Aiol was in the depths of the prison,
With Mirabel, his wife, the courtly and the wise. 9075
There her labor pains began: she was sick and suffering.
Her labor lasted three days in the depths of the prison.
Never did she have the help of a midwife,
Other than Jesus, the heavenly Father,
And her lord, Aiol, son of Elye the wise. 9080
Never was a taper or candelabra lit.
God gave her two sons in the depths of the prison:
You would never see such beautiful children born to mortal woman.

241.

For three days, Mirabel labored in the throes of childbirth.
Never was there lit a candelabra or a lamp. 9085
Never did she have the help of a man or a woman,
Except for the Lord God, who has all in his power,
And her lord Aiol, who's experiencing sympathetic labor pains.
God gave her two sons in the depths of the prison:
You'll never see more beautiful born to man or to woman. 9090
When the children were born, Makaire found out right away.
He drew his sword and went down to the depths of the prison.

⚜ Aiol ⚜

In a loud voice he yells, the evil-minded coward:
"Where is Aiol, foul cur, who did away with so many of my
   noble people?
May it not please the Lord God that such a child be safe."   9095
When Aiol heard this, he almost went berserk:
"Have mercy, Lord Makaire, for the sake of God and his angels.
Let my children live. This gesture won't create any trouble for you.
I'll swear to you on saints' relics, between me and my wife,
I'll always serve you with my shield and my lance."   9100
When the traitor heard this, he took it to be sycophancy
And swore to the Lord God and his fierce might
That he'll never eat again until he's cut off their limbs.

242.

"My lord, noble knight," Aiol said to Makaire,
"For the love of God, the heavenly Father,   9105
Let me keep my children, you'll never have any harm from me.
I'll give you all my lands and my inheritance, free and clear.
I'll swear to you on saints' relics, and my wise wife too,
I'll always serve you, armed and on horseback."
When the traitor heard this, it only made him more enraged.   9110
He took one of the children, yanked him by the right arm.
Aiol, Elye's son, slyly took up the other one
And placed him under his knee, in his striped tunic.
Makaire went off, may God do him harm,
Carrying off the child, whom he had no intention of leaving.   9115
Just as he was climbing the marble steps,
He heard the other child crying in the depths of the prison.
He was tremendously astonished and almost went mad
And said that it wouldn't stay there. He'd have it with the
   other one.
He summoned his seneschal, Ginart, Ylaire's son: 9120
"You fool! Don't you hear that child? There's still another one!
May God confound me if I don't take it.
I'll never eat again as long as I know it's alive."
When Aiol heard this, he almost went insane with rage.

243.

"Mercy, Lord Makaire," said Aiol, the noble,   9125
"For the love of God, who is the Redeemer of all,
If you don't want to accept my friendship,
Take me and my wife and my sons, who were born here,

⚜ A Chanson de Geste ⚜

And put all four of us into the depth of a pit.
Let us go far away from this land, 9130
And I'll gladly and willingly swear to you
That I'll never remain in Christendom.
I don't intend to stop until I'm in pagan lands,
I'll stay there forever to raise my children."
When the traitor heard this, he began joking. 9135
He told his seneschal: "Go and bring the other one to me.
By that apostle whom pilgrims seek in Nero's Field,
I'll never eat again until I've dismembered them."
When Aiol heard this, he began to weep.
The seneschal went down into the prison, which wasn't wise, 9140
As he wasn't carrying any arms to protect his life.
Aiol, Elye's son, got to his feet:
"Whore's son," he said, "How dare you think you're going to do this!
I know I'm going to die — I can't escape it —
But by that holy apostle pilgrims seek in Nero's Field, 9145
No matter how this turns out, you're going to pay!"
He reached down and picked up a huge beam.
It was big, thick and heavy — just as much as he could lift.
In a ferocious rage, he lifted it high above him.
In the middle of the seneschal's chest, he dealt him such a blow 9150
That he rammed it through and crushed the heart in his chest.
Still, Aiol was not yet finished with that noble.
He strikes the seneschal upon his head, causing his eyes to fly out.
Makaire, who was upstairs, began to shout:
"You fool! Come on up! What's taking you so long?" 9155
The seneschal couldn't reply. He lay dead at the base of a wall.

244.

Makaire was at the top of the stairs. He called out to his man:
"You fool! Get up here in a hurry, God damn you!"
The seneschal lay dead beside a wall and couldn't reply.
When Makaire figured this out, he had never felt so much grief. 9160
Fiercely, he rushes down into the prison.
He became enraged when he saw his man dead
And was about to strike Aiol with his long sword
When he's stopped by his nephew, Lord Gerard of Gascony,
And Guy and Alerand take his sword away from him. 9165
They turn him around instantly and quickly;
"Lord Makaire, don't even think about doing it for an instant,

❧ Aiol ❧

Because the king outside there holds our nephews and uncles.
If you kill Aiol, we'll never see them again!"
"My lords," said Makaire, "this is causing me enormous shame.   9170
He killed my man in the depths of my own prison.
His sons will pay for it before noon.
I'll be damned if I'm going to become their nursemaid!"
He took the two children and went back up the stairs.
Full of anguish, Mirabel fell down in a faint on the marble floor.   9175
Aiol felt greater grief than he had ever felt before.
Then you would have seen the ladies come there in great anguish
And throw themselves at Makaire's feet, but he had no
   pity at all for them.
"Have mercy, Lord Makaire, don't commit such a shameful act!
Turn that lady over to us, and we will keep guard over her for you.   9180
Whenever she goes to Mass, we'll keep an eye on her for you."
When Makaire heard this, he bowed low towards the ground.
There occurred to him a great ruse to deceive his men:
He didn't want to lose their support and loyalty.
"Ladies, go ahead and take her, but I'll want her back.   9185
I'll bring up the children until they're adults."
The ladies thanked him, throwing themselves at his feet.

245.

The ladies thanked him. They thought they had secured
   their plea.
They quickly went straight to the prison
Where Mirabel lay anguished and distraught.   9190
Then they carried her on a bare mattress
Back as far as the main palace hall.
Anyone present would have seen the maidens weeping and
   lamenting over her.
"Oh! Noble lady," they said, "how horrible is your fate!
You were so noble when you first came here."   9195
Straight to the house they brought her without stopping.
They laid her in a bed whose mattress they'd freshened up.
Makaire, the traitor, was in a state of turmoil;
He went through all of Lausanne's main streets,
Came onto the bridge over the Rhône and threw the children
   into the water.   9200
That night God made his power known:
The swiftly flowing Rhône did not sweep away the children!
Thierry was under the bridge, fishing in the moonlight.

⚜ A Chanson de Geste ⚜

He was a noble man who would never do an evil deed.
He clearly heard Makaire going away down the street   9205
And saw the two children floating in the water.
With his two hands he took them and gently pulled them out.
He put them in his boat and brought them aid.
He stripped down, taking off his cape and all his clothing.
He puts the children in it and starts navigating straightaway.   9210
He didn't want any noise from them to be heard.
He left there right away, nothing made him feel safe.
He went away to his house, feeling very nervous and frightened.

246.

Now Thierry sailed on — he greatly loved God of glory —
He rapidly went to his house, carrying the two children.   9215
His wife came out to meet him, Lady Aie of Montoire,
Straight out through a door, down to the river bank.
In her hand she carried a lighted candle.

247.

Thierry, the worthy man, came to his dwelling.
He got out onto the river bank and moored his boat.   9220
His wife came to meet him, Lady Aie of the bright countenance.
In her hand, she's holding a lighted candle.
Politely and courteously, she began to speak to him:
"My lord, do you have some fish? Now hand it over!
You've never fished so long in your whole life!"   9225
"Dear sister," said Thierry, "we have lots of fish,
But they're the kind that we can't eat.
If you don't believe me, look here in my clothes."
Lady Aie ran to the boat and unfolded the clothing:
She sees the fists, the feet, the eyes, the noses   9230
And the handsome faces of the newborn infants.
The lady felt such fright she didn't dare touch them.
Her fear caused her to let out a loud cry:
"For the love of God, dear lord, what have you brought!"
"Dear sister, sweet friend, speak more quietly!   9235
I was below that bridge where God had sent me,
And I dared not refuse to go there to fish.
Makaire, the traitor, the foul cur,
Brought these infants you see here.
He intended to drown them, the evil oath-breaker!   9240
He threw them into the water, the foul cur!

⚜ Aiol ⚜

When I saw them in the water, I was very scared.
I didn't want to go off and just leave them there.
I took them in my two hands and put them in my boat.
I'm certain who they are. We should take good care of them. 9245
These children you see here belong to Aiol,
The good and noble knight who's being held prisoner.
Aiol is your rightful lord — he holds your lands;
This traitor, Makaire, has betrayed him so evilly!
We should be holding all of our inheritance from Aiol. 9250
Dear sister, sweet friend, what advice can you give me?
How can we save them from death?"
"My lord," said the lady, "you'll have some good advice.
Let's go to sweet France, to the city of Paris.
There we'll find a great many barons, 9255
Who are Aiol's liegemen, the valiant knight.
Out of loyalty to him, they'll show us charity."
"Dear sister, sweet friend, don't even mention it!
I have no use for sweet France. I don't even want to set foot there.
If noble Aiol were to die in prison, 9260
Makaire would quickly be reconciled with the king,
And he'd have us killed and our limbs cut off
By passing out money, which he has in vast quantities.
But I've heard about the king of Venice,
The courteous Grasien, who is courtly and noble. 9265
He lives in Tornebrie, that good city.
He's very faithful to God, the King of majesty.
If Jesus wants to guide us to safety,
With his help, we can save the children from death."
"Sire," said the lady, "as you command. 9270
Make haste. We can't delay too long."

248.

"Dear sister, sweet friend," said Count Thierry,
"It was God's pleasure that we have no child.
We had one recently; he's died already.
With the milk from your breasts you're certainly able to feed them. 9275
Let's get into the boat. There's no peril there —
I bought it recently for four and a half marks.
If we're able to get to Tornebrie,
To mighty King Grasien, who's worthy and noble,
Under his protection, we can surely keep them safe from death." 9280
"My lord," said the lady, "what are we waiting for here?

❧ A Chanson de Geste ❧

So help me God, soon it will be broad daylight.
If Makaire notices us, we're in deep trouble,
And you and the children will have to die."

249.

His wife's advice made Thierry very happy.   9285
He entered the bedroom where Lord Guy was lying —
He was a learned man, a church canon.
The very first thing, Thierry exposed his plans.
He needed to do it well, because he was Guy's nephew.
When the cleric had heard him out, he got to his feet   9290
And set a candle in front of him.
He took ink and parchment and wrote a letter for them,
Stating that these are the noble knight Aiol's sons.
They would never be so far away in foreign lands
That they couldn't recover the truth in the letter.   9295
Thierry came to his boat and began to load it:
He loaded his silver, his gold, his denier coins,
His rich, striped fabrics, his silks and his ermines.
Then he and his wife boarded the boat,
Carrying in their arms the little heirs.   9300
With them were a total of four well-equipped servants —
Expert mariners, they toiled at the oars.

250.

Now Thierry sailed away, distancing himself far from Makaire.
All the way downstream, he sails and makes his way.
They never stopped until they came to a seaport.   9305
There they found merchants in different marketplaces.
Thierry gave them so much gold, silver and expensive fabrics
They let him come on board their ship with them.
I don't know their story or how to relate it to you,
Or how long they were at sea or their voyage lasted.   9310
They came to Tornebrie and docked in the harbor.
Thierry left the ship with his wife, Lady Aie.
He unloaded his possessions from it — leaving nothing
   on board —
And takes the two children gently so as not to crush them.
He wrapped them up in an expensive cloth,   9315
Then he went through the streets, which are great and wide,
Not delaying until he arrived at the main palace.
There he found Grasien, the king of that region.

⚜ Aiol ⚜

Thierry, who was courteous and wise, greeted him:
"May God save you, your highness!" "And you, lord envoy!"   9320
Who are you and from what land? Tell me about your lineage."
"Sire, we are from Burgundy, from that wide land.
A great war has destroyed my life there and forced me to flee.
I come to you, good king, here in this your kingdom,
That you may receive me for the sake of God, holy and great."   9325
"My friend," said the king, "you're very courtly and well bred.
By my beard, I'll gladly accept you into my service.
I'll give you much wealth: gold, silver and expensive fabrics,
According to what I see to be your worth."

251.
"My friend," said the king, "do you know any trade?"   9330
"Yes, in faith I do, sire, but they don't pay very much:
I know how to catch fish, I really know how to lure them in,
And I know the trade of hawking and falconry.
Sire, I know well how to lead a pack of dogs,   9335
And how to expertly dress venison,
And how to kill a powerful wild boar with a pike,
And for my rightful lord how to act as an envoy,
Firmly advocating his needs and his rights.
I have a wide experience. There's no need to seek better."   9340
"My friend," said the king, "that's an impressive set of skills.
You should be prized for even the least of them.
I'll gladly and willingly accept you into my service."
"Sire," said Thierry, "a hundred thanks to you.
Sire, worthy and noble king, now hear me, for the love of God.
When I left my land of Burgundy recently,   9345
God gave me two heirs by my noble wife.
I have them here in my tunic. They haven't been baptized.
For the love of God, I beg you to hold them over the holy font."
And the king replied: "By my faith, gladly!"
He summoned the head of the priests at the church,   9350
Had the children magnificently clothed,
And had both of them raised above the font and baptized.
Their godparents were the king and his noble wife,
Orclare, the noble and comely queen.
They named one Thomas, the other Manesier.*   9355
The noble knight gave two cities to them.
If they live long enough, he intends to dub them knights
So that they can command twenty thousand men and more.

⚜ A Chanson de Geste ⚜

Makaire will yet be troubled and angry:
They'll want to avenge their mother's imprisonment! 9360
The king studied the little heirs closely.
He addressed Orclare, his wife:
"Sweet sister, sweet friend, so help me God,
I'd never believe anyone on earth who says
That these heirs came from that man. 9365
Either he stole them, or he wants to help them,
Or they're sons of a king, a count or a prince."
"My lord," said the lady, "by my head, you're telling the truth!"
The king loves the children deeply and cares for them intensely.
He has them raised and nursed in his chamber, 9370
And they have four nurses, knight's wives.
When they were two years old and were going on three,
You'd never see such well-developed children anywhere on earth.
Mirabel, their mother — who's noble and comely —
Will never leave prison on any day on earth, 9375
Up until they free her once they're knights.

252.

Now the two children are safe from death,
Thanks to the Lord God, their master Thierry,
King Grasien and Orclare with the bright visage.
Now let's leave the children — may God bless them — 9380
And we'll tell you about Aiol, the noble knight,
Who was in the great prison, anguished and distraught,
He often prays to God, the King of paradise —
And Makaire the evil one — may God never help him —
Every single day had a thousand paid knights, mercenaries.* 9385
They had been inside the city for five full years.
They were totally lacking in clothing and possessions
And had pawned everything, palfreys and nags.
One of them said to the others: "We're in a bad situation.
We're not earning anything here. Instead we're losing money
    every day. 9390
We've pawned our hauberks and helms.
Mighty King Louis out there has besieged us for five years.
He's used the entire French army to lay this siege.
He'll not leave until he's captured us.
They have slain our men very ruthlessly. 9395
Of the thirty thousand we were, we're now only ten thousand.
Makaire doesn't care for us at all,

239

❧ AIOL ❧

Because he has a large, vast and well-stocked treasury,
Which he's kept underground, just like one more prisoner.
He doesn't want to pay or distribute our wages to us. 9400
Instead, he takes away our capes, sends them off to pawn them
   for wine,
Beats our squires and vilely insults them.
When we mention it, he acts even more falsely.
Be it rightly or wrongly, we have served him well.
My lords, let's go ahead and leave this ill-begotten cur! 9405
Let's go out there to the king of St.-Denis;
He's our rightful lord. It was wrong of us to have deserted him."
And the others replied: "You're telling the truth!"

253.

It was on the feast day of noble St. Michael
That the Burgundians spoke to proud Makaire: 9410
"Listen to us," they said, "noble knight.
We've been inside here for five full years.
We've pawned all our hauberks and our helms,
And we're without palfreys and warhorses.
You have your great treasure, marvelous and abundant. 9415
You have it stored underground as do the other usurers,
And you don't want to give us our wages, not even a denier.
Instead, you take away our capes and beat our squires,
And when we speak about it, you become haughty and arrogant.
Either you change your ways or we will take leave of you. 9420
In the morning, we'll leave your honors and your fiefs.
We'll go out there to the king who holds France,
Because he is our rightful lord. We were wrong to have left him!"
When the traitor heard this, he thought he'd lose his mind.
"My lords," said Makaire, "I request a delay from you 9425
Until dawn tomorrow when I'll have sought advice."
And they replied: "Sire, as you desire, so it will be."
Right away, they had their beds set up and went to bed.
Makaire went down underground to a cellar.
There he found Boidin, Durant, Anscier 9430
And Hercenfroi of Lausanne, the old and white haired.
The first was his watchman, the second his gatekeeper,
The third his seneschal and the other his bottle-bearer.
To them he revealed what he had in mind:
"My lords," said the traitor, "cease your chatter and listen to me. 9435
All my men want to shame and dishonor me.

⚜ A Chanson de Geste ⚜

Tomorrow they intend to leave my honors and my fiefs
And go out there to the king who holds France.
But if you agree to follow my instructions,
I'll make each one of you rich with gold and deniers." 9440
"My lord," said Hercenfroi, "get yourself ready for action,
Because we'll do whatever you need to have done."
And the traitor replied: "That makes me very glad.
Now I'll tell you what I have in mind to do:
All of you dress up as merchants — 9445
Dressed in cloth coats with caps on your heads —
Then have Aiol shod in big boots.
Then we'll take my entire treasure that's there,
My gold, my silver and my denier coins.
We'll tie the trunks on the strongest packhorses, 9450
And we'll bring Aiol out of the prison
And Mirabel, his wife, the noble and comely.
We'll have them swear inside that church
They'll never say anything that causes us to be captured.
Then we'll leave here, away from the king who holds France. 9455
I know their language; we won't be captured.
We'll go to Pamplona, to mighty King Mibrien.
We'll deliver to him his daughter, the noble and comely.
King Mibrien hates Aiol more than any man alive.
He'll lavish us with wealth, cities and farms, 9460
And if you want to renounce God the Father,
As I will do, I'm advised that
King Mibrien will give you more wealth and deniers
Than any reward you'd ever have from Louis or Lothaire."*
"My lord," said Hercenfroi, "we're all set! 9465
We'll do everything that will be your pleasure.
I'd rather renounce Lord God the Father,
Than be killed and hacked to pieces inside this city."

254.

Now hear about the traitor — may he be harmed —
How he wants all his men to be burned and hanged. 9470
Oh, God! They will be indeed. Not a single one will escape!
He had his treasure taken with them, all of it which was there.
All five of them dressed as merchants,
Wearing cloth coats and caps on their heads.
They brought Aiol up out of the prison 9475
And Mirabel, his wife, who had lain there too long.

241

⚜ Aiol ⚜

They brought them both into a church
And made them swear on saints' relics, five times or more,
They wouldn't say anything that would give them away.
Aiol loved God so much that he would never break his oath. 9480
Then they tied the trunks on their thick-maned horses.
They mounted Aiol and Mirabel on a mule.
They went out through a gate and followed the wall.
Makaire drew from its scabbard his sword's naked blade.
He took off the heads of the guards and the gatekeepers. 9485
He turned out towards the besieging army and started through it.
He didn't stop until he'd arrived at Louis' tent.
Now hear about Aiol, how he lost his senses,
Because he didn't want to say a single word that might cause them
    to be discovered
And clearly saw and recognized Elye, his father, 9490
And Louis, his uncle — it was a wonder he could contain
    himself —
And he never said anything to reveal himself!
Makaire dismounted — he wasn't recognized —
And he spoke in hushed tones, still unrecognized.
"May God of holy glory in heaven above, 9495
Save King Louis to whom we've come.
We are merchants from Pinel and from Bu,
And we came from here through the gate of Lausanne.
We gave Makaire two gold marks or more,
So the duke would give us safe passage through his lands. 9500
We're bringing with us such great wealth as never has been seen.
Now we have arrived in your lands, mighty king,
Afford us safe passage until we have passed through them."
And the king replied: "May you be welcome.
Wherever you go, you will enjoy my truce." 9505
To escort them, Louis commands Gautier of Montagu,
Beardless Duke Bevon and white-haired Jofroi.
And they escorted them easily three leagues or more.
When they were safely outside of the army,
Then Makaire spoke, the treacherous oath-breaker: 9510
"My lords, good knights, you've come with us,
And because you've led me to safety,
I'll tell you something that should be believed:
We came out from Lausanne to safety.
We found the gatekeeper and the watchman lying there — 9515
See over there where those thick-maned mules are walking?

⚜ A Chanson de Geste ⚜

Have your men arm themselves, the great and the small,
And attack Lausanne, the palisades and the walls.
The gates are open, you won't have to strike a single blow.
The city folk don't know that. They aren't keeping watch. 9520
You can take the city without a lance or a shield.
May the Lord God of glory never help your king,
If he doesn't capture the Burgundians and they're not hanged quickly!"
Hear about the traitor, how evil he is:
Because he wants his men to be completely done away with — 9525
And indeed they will be, because their day has come.

255.

Makaire told his escorts much of what he was thinking,
But he didn't reveal to them his great betrayal.
They turned back and set off on their way.
They arrived at the army before the dawn was breaking. 9530
They repeated what he'd said to the king of St.-Denis,
And when the French found this out, the army was in an uproar.
They didn't stop until they arrived at Lausanne.
On horseback and on foot they entered the city,
Carrying sharp axes and great polished lances. 9535
They hacked up and killed the Burgundians they found
And went to get Aiol in the stone prison
And Mirabel, his wife, but they didn't find them.
Makaire was leading them away, the foul cur, the traitor.
The king felt great sorrow and the old man, Elye. 9540
But since then, he has had uncontested possession of his land
  of Burgundy,
And afterwards, he hasn't lost any of it, not even a garlic
  clove's worth.
They go around searching for Aiol, in the town and the city.
But what's the use? They're not going to find any trace of him!
Makaire has escaped the French, the foul cur, the traitor, 9545
Taking Aiol with him and Mirabel, his beloved.
"Alas!" said the king, "I don't have my nephew!"
"Sire, rightful emperor," said Duke Elye,
"Makaire has killed him, the foul cur, the traitor!
Oh, Mirabel! Most noble lady, 9550
It was a sad day when my son won you by his chivalry.
Your time together did not last long.
When my wife finds it out, Avisse, the noble lady,
It'll be a wonder if she goes on living."

Now we will speak of Makaire, may he be cursed of God. 9555
He's leading Aiol and Mirabel away, angry, distraught.
They came to the Rhône and found a fleet of boats.
Makaire buys a boat with his wealth,
Then he goes on board with his four disciples.
They brought Aiol on board and Mirabel as well. 9560
They navigate down the Rhône, with great energy and
   determination,
All the way downstream they travel as far as St.-Gilles.
They won't have anything to do with the saint; they leave
   right away.
Now they follow the river downstream, but on the river bank.
They leave the mountain passes of Aspe, they reach those of Sire.* 9565
I can't tell you about each one of their hostels —
I won't be telling you anything about their lodging either.
They don't cease travelling until they reach Pamplona.
There they find Mibrien, the mighty Persian king,
Where he reigns over a great empire and has assembled a great army: 9570
From Navarre and the Basque country there were fifty thousand.
They're preparing to go as an army to invade France the bountiful,
Because of his daughter, Mirabel, for whom his heart is grieving,
And he hates Aiol more than any living thing.
But soon he will have Aiol in his power. 9575
Makaire is bringing him, the foul cur, the traitor.
Soon he'll want to make use of all his flatteries.

256.

On the main street, which heads towards St.-James,
Makaire finds lodging along with all his four men.
He summons his host, Floquipasse — 9580
That was the pagan's name who was keeping his treasure —
"Guard this Frenchman for me. Make sure he doesn't escape.
He's stolen a great treasure from me and caused me great damage."
And the pagan replied: "It's a bad day for him when you chose me
   to guard him.
When he escapes from me, it will be never to steal from
   anyone else." 9585
He put both Aiol and Mirabel in the depths of a prison,
In a treasure house, but he had the riches removed.
They put them in stocks and left them chained up.
Makaire went off with all four of his favorites,
And they went through the great, wide streets. 9590

⚜ A Chanson de Geste ⚜

They didn't stop until they'd reached the main palace.
There they found Mibrien, who was hard of heart.
Makaire greets him, the misbegotten, foul cur:
"May Mohammed save you, good king, you and your entourage."
"And may Mohammed protect you, friend, brother envoy. 9595
Where do you come from? From which land? What brings
   you here?"
"Sire, I'm from France, that vast land.
I'm the powerful duke of Burgundy. I hold all of it.
A great war has destroyed me, caused me to flee and brought
   me here,
Because King Louis has seized my lands. 9600
In Burgundy, below Langres' walls, a battle raged.
There I did something for you for which I'm blamed by all!
There I conquered Aiol, son of Elye the wise,
And Mirabel, your daughter, the courtly and the astute.
I've brought her here to you, to this, your land. 9605
They're right here in my hostel, my host has guard over them.
But you'll not have them ever, that's my intention,
Until you've shown me your god and your image.*
I've never seen Mohammed. It's right that I pay him honor."
And the king replied: "You're very courtly and wise." 9610
When Mibrien had heard Makaire, he raised the statue on
   its pedestal.
More than seven times, Makaire kissed the statue on its neck
   and face.
"My friend," said the king, "you're very courtly and intelligent.
I'll give you many lands, honors and baronies."
Now listen to me what treacherous Makaire said: 9615
"I know very well all the mountain passes and passageways to France.
All Christendom will be under your dominion.
Just let me have a force of your people, armed and on horseback,
And the Christians are dead and condemned to shame.
Louis, Charles' son, will curse the day he ever saw me. 9620
I'll yet take his head off his shoulders!
You'll hold the great land, and I'll be its overseer.
From you, I'll want to hold Burgundy as my hereditary fief."
"My friend," said the king, "you are courtly and shrewd.
In addition, I grant you the land of Navarre. 9625
I command Saracens that as part of their duty to me,
They must all serve you and do your bidding."

☙ AIOL ☙

257.

Mibrien takes Makaire and all his four followers
And brought them up into his palace,
Into the Mohammedry* where Mohammed was. 9630
Then Makaire spoke, the traitor, the oath-breaker.
"Mohammed," said the felon, "I have come to you.
I beg your help, lord, in my quarrel against the king of St.-Denis,
And afterwards, in destroying the French, all of them, one by one.
I don't know how to name them, you know them better 9635
Than I do, dear lord; you've seen them all."
(The Saracens are not naïve or lacking in craftiness.
They've hidden a peasant in Mohammed's torso,
Who had gone inside, because it was all hollowed-out.)
"My friend," said the peasant inside, "I've heard you well. 9640
I'll make you the king of France, the admiral and the duke,
And the king and the others will all be destroyed.
If you hold to me, much good will come your way."
The pagans led up to Makaire a long-maned steed,
And he kisses it on the mouth, doesn't delay any longer, 9645
And spits towards the sky in spite, against Jesus!
"And next, you'll kiss my asshole.
This will mean that you've given yourself to me,
You'll have rejected God and his powers,
And that he cannot be and that he never was!" 9650
"This I'll do, good lord," said the wretched one.
"I admit that I'm guilty of having waited so long,
That I've not always followed and supported you."
Makaire and his four henchmen kissed the statue.
The peasant farted, Makaire stood up straight. 9655
"Sire," said the traitor, "how your god stinks!"
"Not true," said Mibrien, "rather such are his virtues."
They all rapidly left the synagogue
And came back to the main palace.

258.

Mibrien took Makaire by the fold of his ermine cloak. 9660
"My friend," said the king, "I won't lie to you.
From now on, I love your company.
Take me to your hostel. I want to see my daughter."
And Makaire replied: "Gladly, gentle lord."
He goes through the streets, the town and the city, 9665
As far as his hostel he didn't cease or stop.

❧ A Chanson de Geste ❧

He called to Floquipasse and Propisse
And had Aiol brought out of his stone prison
And Mirabel his wife, who very wrongly had been placed there.
Mibrien saw his daughter, who was very downcast and humiliated   9670
From her long imprisonment. Her color had darkened.
When Mibrien saw this, he seized her by the hand.
He addressed her and began to speak to her:
"Have you renounced Mohammed, dear daughter?"
"Yes," said the lady, "for the love of God, dear lord,   9675
For me, your god Mohammed isn't worth even a clove of garlic!
What Saracens believe, I hold to be extreme madness,
When they don't believe in God, St. Mary's Son."
When Mibrien heard this, he almost went mad with anger.

259.

Mibrien took his daughter by her white right hand: 9680
"Have you renounced Mohammed, dear daughter?"
"Yes," said the lady, "say no more of it!"
When the Saracens heard this, they nearly lost their minds!
"What Saracens believe isn't worth even a hawthorn berry,
When they don't believe in God the glorious, heavenly one,   9685
He who lay there within the Virgin."
When Mibrien heard this, he was close to going mad.
He looked over at Aiol and took him by the right wrist:
"Whore's son!" he said, "evil, arrogant lecher!
You have taken away from me the thing I loved most on this earth!" 9690
He said to his seneschal: "Go get my sword.
Before I eat, I'll cut off his head."
Then Estorgant spoke, who was born in Valterne:
"Dear Uncle Mibrien, for Mohammed's sake, what are you doing?
Why do you believe Makaire — may Mohammed bring
    him harm —   9695
When disloyally he's abandoned his own faith and his own people?
Your daughter couldn't belong to a better knight,
Because this is white-headed Elye's son,
And he's the nephew of the king who holds and guides France.
If he wants to believe in Mohammed, give him much of your land."   9700
And Aiol replied: "That could never be!
I would rather die than deny the Lord God."

247

260.

Mibrien addressed noble Mirabel:
"Have you renounced Mohammed, dear daughter?
Now go and worship him and say your psalms to him." 9705
Four pagans led her — they dragged her by force,
By her arms, angry and grieved.
"My lords," said the lady, "let me go freely.
Since I must worship him, my heart's full of anger."
The foul, hated people let go of her. 9710
Instead of worshiping Mohammed and his idols,
She seized its arms and toppled it over onto the ground,
Shattering its sides, its arms and its flanks.
One pagan said to another: "That lady has lost her mind!"
"It's true," said Mibrien, "she's dead and finished." 9715
"I am not!" said Mirabel, "evil, hated people!
How can that worthless object ever help you?*
Now its real virtues appear: there's nothing to be feared!"
When the pagans heard this, they almost went insane with anger.
They have her turned over to Floquipasse and Propisse. 9720
These were two very evil pagans, who were full of anger.
They governed the king's land and administered his justice.
But later, God turned them to his cause,
Then they believed in Jesus, St. Mary's Son.
They threw them into chains and put fetters on them. 9725
They took Aiol down into the stone prison
And Mirabel, his wife, angry and grieving.
The king swore to Mohammed and his idols
That tomorrow he would have them killed and cut to pieces
If they won't believe in Mohammed, who reigns over all. 9730
However, St. Mary's Son can furnish them effective help.

261.

The next day, they were due to be dismembered and burned up.
Now hear what good fortune Jesus gave them:
Four Spanish pagans, Saracens from overseas,
Had come to that land because they'd heard 9735
Of a very great treasure they intended to steal
From mighty King Mibrien who'd amassed it
All together inside that prison,
There where lay Aiol and his wife, with the bright visage.
But the treasure had been removed from the prison, 9740
And inside they had left not one denier.

❧ A Chanson de Geste ❧

The robbers were knowledgeable, trained in their trade.
With their sharp, filed, steel chisels
They pierced a large opening in the wall
Into the prison, furtively, in secret.   9745
They searched for the treasure, but found nothing.
Aiol was lying in another part of the prison against a great pillar,
Which separated him from his wife, grieved and angered.
He heard the thieves going through their tunnel.
Politely he called out to them, in great simplicity: 9750
"My lords, who are you, who are going through the prison?
Did you come in search of treasure? Be careful, don't hide it from me.
Certainly, I don't believe there are two deniers here,
Only a captive from France, who's been imprisoned,
Both him and his wife, who's dying of grief.   9755
Since you came here to gain wealth,
Truly, I'll give you four mules loaded with it,
If you can get me out of prison.
Afterwards, I'll swear to you that, upon my honor,
If you can conduct me straight to France,   9760
I'll give you all the treasure you could ever want."
The thieves heard him and were filled with joy.
They ran to unfasten the fetters and bolts
And gently took off the iron neck collars.
The four thieves led Aiol out of prison.   9765
Just as they were going back for Mirabel,
The guards who were guarding them sounded the alarm.
One of the guards said to the others: "We're in a bad fix
If the Frenchman has escaped from us and our prison!
Tomorrow, we'll all be lynched and hanged."   9770
They turned in flight, they didn't dare to stay.
And the four thieves led Aiol away.
What's it to them if Aiol escapes and Mirabel remains?
Now may he console them, he who can save all,
Because they won't see each other after that for two full years. 9775

262.

The four thieves lead Aiol, keeping their part of the bargain.
Whether he likes it or not, Aiol has sworn an oath
That he'll not say a word. That would be a crime and felony.
Aiol loves God so much he won't lie at all.
They passed through so many forests and peaceful lands,   9780
They came straight to the port of Esclavonie.*

There they found a ship fitted and equipped.
They found their companions who were waiting to sail,
And these went to greet those arriving, shouting loudly:
"Do you have the treasure we want so much?" 9785
And the thieves with Aiol answered them: "That's crazy talk!
We broke into Mibrien's prison,
But we didn't find a garlic clove's worth of wealth,
Only this captive from France who's wealthy and rich.
He's very loyally sworn to us 9790
That if we bring him to France the plentiful,
He'll give us much wealth and treasure.
However, the French are arrogant and full of deceit,
So that if this man has power and possessions in France,
Very rapidly he'll have us killed and hacked to pieces, 9795
Because the French have no love at all for our faith in Mohammed.
So let's take him to be sold in the port of Tornebrie,
To mighty King Grasien, who's wealthy and powerful.
He'll give us more wealth, riches and possessions
Than all of our relatives have ever had in their lives." 9800
When Aiol heard this, he sighed and wept bitterly.
He doesn't want to break the oath that he's sworn to them.
He doesn't know yet the great joy to which Jesus is guiding him:
He'll find his sons, safe, sound free men,
And Thierry the courtly and Aie the noble 9805
And King Grasien who's raising his children —
There were none so handsome as far as the ports of Hungary!
Seven years have passed since Aiol saw them.*

263.

The four thieves went on board their ship.
Aiol, the battle-hardened knight, they brought on board too. 9810
They raised their sail and lifted anchor.
The Lord God gave them good winds and breezes.
I don't know what I should relate to you about their story,
And how long they were on the high seas.
They came to Tornebrie and went straight to shore. 9815
When they came to the harbor, they lowered their sail
And dropped their anchor and got themselves ready,
Disembarked on the shore and left their ship.
They found that day that a great yearly festival was going on.
Christians and Turks were comingling in harmony, 9820
And there was a great quantity of foreign wealth present.

⚜ A Chanson de Geste ⚜

They placed Aiol on sale, just like the other goods.
The thieves had dressed and outfitted him well.
He had a linen shirt and breeches with a flowered pattern
And also stockings of striped cloth and gold-embroidered shoes   9825
And an ermine-lined cape with gold-embroidered collar.
And finally, they'd put a fine cloth on his back
And fastened it with red brocade.
From there to Durestant,* there's no knight more handsome,
Were it not for all the time he had spent in prison —   9830
But he had spent five years in an enemy prison.
The peers of the city stared at him in wonderment
And said to one another: "This knight has great goodness.
Never did God make such a land or great kingdom,
That this man could not hold it. He embodies such goodness."   9835
Aiol's renown spreads so far through the princely houses
That King Grasien hears of it.
With thirty knights he descends the stairs.
There even the queen goes willingly
And Thierry the courtly and Aie of the bright visage.   9840
Thomas and Manesier went with them.
They didn't stop until they arrived at the shore.
There they found the thieves and Aiol with them.
The good king of Venice looked at Aiol.
He saw that Aiol was handsome, noble, slender and well-formed.   9845
He immediately looked at his godsons.
They strikingly resembled their father in their mouths and noses.
Never did God make a man who looked so much like the boys!
Aiol, Elye's son, had in his heart a presentiment.
He doesn't know who they are, but he thinks about it a lot.   9850
Mighty King Grasien then addressed the four thieves:
"Tell me, my lords, since you have him for sale, how much do you want?"
And they replied: "You'll find out right away.
You'll have to give sixty pure gold marks,
As well as four hundred silver marks, weighed out on a scale,   9855
Thirty marten pelts and nine fur-lined mantels
And a large pack horse, laden with silks and expensive fabrics."
"Barons," said the king, "by holy charity!
You've greatly mistreated him, so temper your demands.
Take counsel among yourselves as to how much you'll give him for."   9860
And the thieves replied: "You've taken us by surprise.
If we had absolutely known for sure

⚜ Aiol ⚜

You were the king of this mighty reign,
He wouldn't have been given to you for four times that amount."
"By my head," said the king, "my lords, you're very wrong.   9865
I would have paid you that much and more
Before I'd let such a handsome captive escape me."
The king had all the riches paid out and delivered to the thieves.
Just as the thieves were taking leave
And were going back to board their ships,   9870
They got into an altercation with their steel knives,
Trying to divide up the immense treasure they possessed.
Not one of the four could leave alive,
Because with their sharp knives they've completely disemboweled each other.
A messenger came to inform mighty King Grasien of this,   9875
And when the king found it out, he was filled with great joy.
He had all the wealth brought back to his treasury.
"My lord," said Aiol, "now I've cost you less."
They went back to the good city.
Up into the palace, they climbed all of the steps,   9880
Now they sat down on a bench, side by side.
"My friend," said the king, "listen to what I have to say.
Where are you from? From what land? Be careful, don't hide anything from me."
"Sire," said Aiol, "now you'll hear the truth.
It's certain that I'm from France, from a great family,   9885
And I've been in prison five full years,
And these thieves from whom you've bought me, stole me.
If you treat me well, you'll perform a very charitable deed."
And the king replied: "You've no reason to be afraid,
Because I won't fail you as long as I can live."   9890
When Aiol heard the king, he was filled with great joy.
He instantly fell at the king's feet,
When King Grasien had him get up again.
"My friend," said the king, "listen to what I have to say:
I'm waging a great war, which is causing me immense fear.   9895
It's with the king of Thessalonica,* who seized my inheritance."
"Sire," said Aiol, "outfit me,
And I will help you through dutiful loyalty."
"Oh, God!" said the king, "may your praise be eternal,
For bringing me this standard bearer!   9900
This knight will carry my standard onto the battlefield!"
Mighty King Grasien was courtly and noble.

❦ A Chanson de Geste ❦

He was in Tornebrie, the capital of his kingdom.
Throughout all of his lands he called together his army,
Because he intended to go to Thessalonica with a full force.*   9905
Never had anyone ever heard of a greater army!
Aiol had arms brought into the square.
They are very expensive and handsome. No one should criticize them.
When the king commanded it, Aiol armed himself.
He put on his hauberk, laced on his helm   9910
And girded his sword on his left side.
They led a good horse onto the square:
This was the king's own horse, Passeavant it was called.
The horse was so good and of such great ferocity,
That no one could come within six feet of it   9915
Except for its very own special squire.
Aiol, Elye's son, went over to it
And quickly and rapidly mounted it by the stirrup,
And hung from his neck his strong, banded shield
And gripped in his right fist a stout, square lance.   9920
A standard was attached to it with three solid gold nails.
They came out of the city to behold the Frenchman.
The king told and commanded a foot soldier
To set up a quintain in the middle of the field.
Now he'll find out how the Frenchman will bear   9925
His costly arms and equipment on the battlefield.

264.

They had a quintain set up in the verdant meadow;
It consisted of four stakes holding up a shield.
Aiol spurs the warhorse they call Passeavant.
The warhorse took off, shooting forward with great strides —   9930
Outside of Marchegai, the world didn't have a faster horse.
Aiol struck the quintain with such savage fury
His blow pierced the shield on its silver boss
And instantly split all four of the posts.
The shield and the quintain collapsed immediately.   9935
"Marchegai," said Aiol, "I loved you so much.
A while back I lost you and it's left me with a heavy heart."
The spectators all together said:
"Here's a good knight, bold and combative."
"Oh, God!" said the king, "by your holy command,   9940
You've sent me good help for what I'm asking of you."
The emperor spurs his good, ambling mule,

❧ AIOL ❧

Came up to Aiol and jokingly said to him:
"Dear Lord Aiol of France, I declare myself vanquished and I
   surrender to you.
May all of my lands be at your command!   9945
Go ahead and anger anyone you want. Don't hold back.
My very first grievance is with the king of Thessalonica,
Who's laying waste to my land — my heart is heavy because of it."
"Sire," said Aiol, "Hear my idea.
Put three thousand valiant knights under my command."   9950
"I can't do it," said the king, "because I don't have nearly that many,
Until they are summoned from my outlying lands."
"Sire," said Aiol, "tell me what you have in mind.
How many good, swift horses do you have?"
"My friend," said the king, "there are at least seventeen hundred."   9955
"By my faith," said Aiol, "that's a good start!
Now let's leave our planning until the break of day."
And the king replied: "Let it all be as you command."
They all entered Tornebrie, the great and the small,
And Aiol was well served, it goes without saying.   9960
That night they left off making plans until break of day.
That night, when they were seated at table,
Aiol's two children came before him.
And he called to them and said: "Step forward!"
From the cup of pure gold, the Frenchman gave them to drink   9965
And murmured between his teeth, in a soft whisper:
"Oh, Makaire! Evil one! May God bring you harm!
You took from me that which I loved most in the world,
Because if my two children were still alive
They'd be as big as these two — I'm certain of it."   9970

265.

They have the beds made up and go off to rest
Until dawn the following day when day would break.
Aiol, Elye's son, got up in the morning.
The king of Tornebrie had his fighting men summoned.
He commanded Joferant and Fouré to lead them.   9975
In the morning they set out when they were ready
Out the gates of Tournebrie, through which they exited.
From Tournebrie to Thessalonica, where they were supposed
   to go,
There were not more than seven leagues on a rested mule.
Aiol knew much of war and addressed the king: 9980

❧ A Chanson de Geste ❧

"Sire, mighty emperor, listen to what I have to say.
Let's leave a reserve force in that dense woods.
Let thirty knights lie in wait back here.
If from Thessalonica, the noble city,
Saracens ride forth in their arrogant fury, 9985
We'll confront them with our steel blades.
And if the Lord God, in his great goodness, gives us our wish
That King Florien rides out here all armed,
We'll greet him with our newelled lances.
But I don't know what arms the king carries: 9990
I'd gladly meet him in a joust."
"My friend," said Grasien, "I'll tell you all you need to know."

266.

Mighty King Grasien was very worthy and bold.
He turned to Aiol and politely said to him:
"I'll tell you all about mighty King Florien. 9995
There's not a better knight from here to the port of Brindisi.
On the king's shield is written: 'Apolin'.
'Tervagant' and 'Mohammed' are placed on his standard.
Upon his helm there is a circle of pure gold.
The warhorse under him doesn't seem wretched: 10000
It's covered with an Alexandrian silk cloth."
"Sire," said Aiol, "I've heard more than enough."
The king places his reserve force in the dense woods.
With thirty knights they start out,
Then they don't stop at all until they reach the city. 10005
Just like the game that's flushed out by beaters,
The Saracens quickly raced to arm themselves.
When King Florien heard the din,
He called for his arms in the lordly palace.
He prepared himself with great ceremony. He was evil and bold. 10010
He mounts on Ploiegant. Never a better horse was seen.
He seized the huge shield where Apolin was painted.
More than five hundred rode out through the front gate.
Ours rode up to meet them all along the paved way.

267.

Mighty King Florien decides to take up the pursuit. 10015
He has captured fourteen of our knights.
He rides a full two hundred feet past the hidden reserve force,
And the reserve force shouts in front and in back.

❦ Aiol ❦

Aiol leaps out from his hiding place and with him, King Grasien.
The worthy and agile knight shouts: "Monjoie."   10020
He looks out in front of him and sees King Florien.*
He recognized him easily, since he was informed as to his insignia.
He pricks Passeavant with the spurs on his feet.
Florien looks at him and charges towards him.
Great blows they deal each other on their broad shields.   10025
They crack and pierce their golden bosses.
Their hauberks are so strong they cannot rip their chainmail.
The king, who was a skilled knight, breaks his lance,
But Aiol strikes him with a blow worthy of a warrior,
So that cinches or breastplate are of no use to Florien,   10030
And the king is struck down from his warhorse in front of Aiol.
Aiol completed his charge as a good knight should
And then turned about, heading back towards King Florien,
Holding his drawn sword while gripping his shield.
In a loud voice Florien shouted: "Tell me who you are.   10035
You're not accustomed to wielding arms
In the style of our country — I've tested it well on you —
Because I've never been knocked off my horse by any man.
You seem to me to be one of those bold French knights.
Leave the king of Venice. He can't help a worthy man.   10040
I'll give you more silver, pure gold and deniers
Than even Louis or Lothaire ever had in France."
"Silence, foolish king," said Aiol, "there's no use in preaching,
Because I'll not fail my rightful lord.
I don't intend to shame myself for gold or for silver."   10045
As he was talking and arguing so much,
The king was very treacherous, evil and an enemy of God.
He was holding his drawn sword as he approached Aiol.
Right in front of the saddle horn he struck Aiol's horse,
So that he cut its head off from its shoulders.   10050
The horse fell dead, and Aiol landed on his feet.
Aiol looked around at his horse as a good knight should:
"How unfortunate for you, Passeavant, good warhorse!
He who gave you to me held you in marvelous esteem.
I'll die of sorrow if I can't avenge you."   10055
Aiol drew his sword and gripped his shield
And went to strike the king on his jeweled helm,
Which caused the flowers and gemstones to shower down.
He slid his blade down towards the king's right shoulder,
And his hauberk's chainmail wasn't worth a denier.   10060

⚜ A Chanson de Geste ⚜

The king's flesh was sliced away from his bones,
And the king staggered and fell to his knees.
Aiol went to strike him when he saw him bent over.
He dealt the blow to the king's left shoulder,
And it sliced a half a foot into his flesh.   10065
The king fell to the ground — couldn't defend himself any longer.
Aiol went and grabbed him by his helm's golden straps,
Then ripped away from him his polished steel blade
And seized Ploiegant that he'd been coveting.
"Cowardly king," said Aiol, "now we've settled accounts.   10070
With the flesh off your back, I've avenged my lord."
Aiol mounted Ploiegant by the stirrup.
At his side, he leads the king, whom he holds prisoner
And the reserve force comes out from the woods from in front
   and behind.
Now here comes mighty King Grasien, spurring his mount.   10075
Aiol calls out to him in great friendship:
"Sire, rightful emperor, I'm much indebted to you,
Because you bought my freedom. Now I'll reimburse what you spent:
I'll give you the king of Thessalonica as a prisoner."
"Many thanks, good and gracious lord," said King Grasien.   10080
"Cowardly king of vile lineage, do you want to be baptized?"
"You're wasting your breath talking about it," said King Florien.
"I'll never believe in the God who was crucified,
Whom the Jews tortured and who couldn't save himself.*
But Mohammed is my lord; we should exalt his name!"   10085
"Foul cur," said Aiol, "may God give you harm!
It's true that the Lord God sent him to preach,
Sent Mohammed first to praise his faith on earth,
But he was so self-important, he twisted God's commandments,
Drank so much he became completely intoxicated and incapacitated,   10090
And went into some woods to lie down.
Wild pigs attacked and devoured
His nose, face and the eyes in his head.
Since then, he's had no power, as he was not loyal to God."
When the pagan heard this, he thought he'd lose his mind: 10095
"Silence, foul cur of a Frenchman, you captured and bound me,
But I'd rather have you kill me and hack me to pieces
Than to abandon Mohammed in order to embrace your faith.
My soul will be saved if I'm destroyed.
Tervagant and Jupin will have sheltered it."   10100
"By my head," said Aiol, "if I'm given permission,

❧ Aiol ❧

You won't live any longer to humiliate our faith."
"Good lord Aiol of France," said King Grasien,
"Don't hold back because of me. I grant you permission."
And Aiol replied: "Many thanks be to you! 10105
I want to take vengeance on one of the Lord God's enemies."
He drew his sword and took off his head.
Before King Grasien, Aiol slays Florien down under his green helm.
"My lords," said the king, "that's a blow worthy of a knight.
Here's a very worthy man when it comes to punishing evil felons." 10110
Then they attacked those who had been pursuing them so long.
Anyone there would have seen Aiol supporting everyone,
To the right and the left, seeking out powerful groups of warriors,
Charging at them, holding his naked steel blade.
Wherever he goes, he clears out the enemy ranks. 10115
Anyone whom his blow strikes has no need of a doctor.
The pagans turn to flee — the faithless foul curs.

268.

The pagans turn to flee, those vile, foolish people.
My lords, it's not a lie, but rather proven truth:
A poorly planned battle cannot last long! 10120
They pursued the pagans with their slashing steel blades.
They chased them rapidly for an entire league
Without striking a blow or engaging in a joust.
Aiol spurs Ploiegant with the golden saddle.
He found a lance with a fringed standard. 10125
He leans down from his horse and seizes the standard.
He slips his arm through the strong shield's double-mailed
  arm straps
And goes to strike Estorgant on his shining shield,
Breaking and smashing its golden boss
And ripping and tearing the hauberk on his back. 10130
The shaft passed clear through his body.
As long as the shaft would hold up, Aiol struck him down
  dead on the field.
Near them stopped the Venetian barons
Who had all entered together into Thessalonica.
Those whom they found inside had their heads cut off; 10135
Anyone who did not want to believe in God was paid bitter wages.
This is how Aiol conquered the city
And brought the war with King Florien to a close.
Mighty King Grasien goes out to take control of the countryside.

❧ A Chanson de Geste ❧

The army the emperor took with him was so great 10140
That no one opposed him without having his head cut off.
A great many of that nation were baptized and lifted over holy fonts;
The ladies of that land became Christianized,
And King Grasien of the noble demeanor
Gave them to the noble men of his land. 10145
Through these women, the land was populated with Christians.*
Florien's daughter was presented to Aiol:
There was no more beautiful maiden as far as the frozen sea.
"Good Lord Aiol of France," said the emperor,
"If this is appealing to you, by the faith I owe my father, 10150
I'll give her to you as a wife, along with this whole region
That we've won by force from the Turks."
"Sire," said Aiol, "may it not please God the Father
That I ever take a spouse as long as I live,
As long as I have not freed my wife from prison, 10155
That one, blessed lady, my wedded wife.
She's in Pamplona, in her father's prison.
There Makaire holds her prisoner, the traitor, the foul cur.
That's the man I hate more than any born of mother,
Because he drowned the two sons my wedded wife gave me 10160
Just before daybreak in the waters of the Rhône.
May God grant me the vengeance I've so desired."
When Thierry heard this, he raised his head.
He looked at the children and Aie the prudent,
But he didn't want to voice his thoughts at that moment. 10165
When they had truly seized and won the land,
The castles and the borderlands all fully conquered,
And Grasien had completely populated the land with his people,
From there to Tornebrie, they didn't rein in their mounts.
The king gave leave to his subjects, and they returned to their lands. 10170
The king's entire court turned towards Aiol:
Thanks to his goodness, all was secure.
Then he fought many a battle with his sharp sword:
I don't know if I'd ever be able to tell you about them all.
Now you can hear about how his sons proved themselves 10175
And by what manner they got to know their father.

269.

In the king's court, Aiol was greatly esteemed.
He sees his sons daily, but the noble knight doesn't know who
  they are.

🌸 Aiol 🌸

Thus they have lived with each other in the court some five years
Without one knowing what the others had in their minds
    and hearts. 10180
Whenever Aiol the courtly is able to encounter his sons,
More than seven times he kisses them on the mouth and
    the cheeks.
Every moment his heart and his thoughts go out to them.
Lady Aie, the courtly, was well aware of the truth,
Along with Thierry of Lausanne, the worthy and noble, 10185
That these are his children, but they don't want to talk about it,
Because they love these children so much who are in their care.

270.

It was at Pentecost — a high holy day —
Thierry came out of church with the good Lady Aie.
Aiol hastens to speak to him and addresses him. 10190
He calls Thierry to a meeting in a vacant grotto.
"Thierry," said Aiol, "you're very worthy and wise.
Now why don't you place your sons in my care, for God the
    heavenly Father?
If they can live long enough to be able to bear arms,
I'll have them bear handsome arms, as befits a knight. 10195
Never will you see a man who would do it more willingly!"

271.

"Thierry," said Aiol, "I often feel immense sorrow
When I think about the two sons my beautiful wife gave me.
Makaire drowned them, the foul cur, that evil being,
In the waters of the Rhône. I've heard all about it." 10200
When Thierry heard this, he dropped his head:
"Good Lord Aiol of France, that was a most tragic loss."
Lady Aie, the courtly, addressed her lord:
"My lord, for the sake of God the glorious of heaven,
Don't tell him yet that these must be his sons. 10205
I'd never have any joy in this earthly life
If I were to lose my children for whom I've left my homeland."

272.

"Aiol," said Thierry, "my children are very handsome.
At their baptism, King Grasien stood as godfather to both of them
And granted them, as his vassals, two mighty and valiant cities, 10210
If they can live long enough to bear arms as knights,

🕆 A Chanson de Geste 🕆

Which will allow them to command twenty thousand, one
  hundred men.
If you want any vengeance exacted on evil Makaire,
They'll be able to provide you with great assistance."
"Oh, God!" said Aiol, "If only I were to live so long!   10215
It wouldn't matter to me if, from that day on,
My soul were separated from my body, but God wouldn't lose."
Immediately they went up into the great palace.
Then Thierry spoke up loudly, so everyone would hear:
"Sire, rightful emperor, hear what I have to say.   10220
Both your godsons here are my children.
Here is Aiol of France, the bold warrior,
Who is asking me for them both, to take charge of them from
  now on.
He will raise them to be refined and courtly,
Until they'll be able to bear arms and put on armor.   10225
Then he'll have them given fine and costly equipment."
When Aiol heard this, he rose to his feet.
The noble knight spoke so that all could hear him:
"For God's sake, rightful emperor, don't deny me this!"
"Of course not, by my faith!" said Grasien the bold.   10230
"Starting right now, I command both my godsons
That they serve you faithfully from this day on."
And they both replied: "Just as you command."

273.

Now both Aiol's sons are squires.
Their love and caring for each other is wonderfully intense. 10235
Aiol still does not know they belong to him.
The two children were well outfitted
And served mighty King Grasien at table.
Aiol watched them and bowed his head.
The noble knight wept tenderly.   10240
When Thierry saw this, he was overcome by pity,
But he didn't dare willingly disclose the truth
That these were his children, because they were so dear to him,
And his wife, Lady Aie, had warned him against this.
Aiol sat at the table, bent over and sorrowful.   10245
Grasien addressed him in a very friendly way:
"Dear lord, Aiol of France, who has you so downcast?
There's never been a man so powerful that he would still be
  my friend."

⚜ Aiol ⚜

"I'll tell you about it now, emperor with the proud visage.
By the powers of heaven, you'll hear it all. 10250
I've never said this to any man here on earth.
My king, I was born in France to the bravest and most valiant,
And I'm the nephew of King Louis, the warrior.
I'm the son of his sister, Lady Avisse of the proud countenance.
Elye is my father, the old knight, 10255
Who is duke of Burgundy, its lord and governor.
Makaire of Lausanne, the foul renegade cur,
Captured me through treachery below Langres' walls.
He then kept me in prison for five full years.
My uncle and my father were not able to free me, 10260
Because Lausanne is so well-fortified they couldn't overcome
    its defenses.
God gave me two sons by my noble wife.
Makaire drowned them, the foul cur.
Then he made me swear and pledge on saints' relics
That I wouldn't say a word that could harm him, 10265
And I loved God so much, I didn't want to break my promise.
He tied me up and led me straight through my uncle's army
As far as Pamplona to mighty King Mibrien,
Both me and my wife with the proud visage.
He now holds my courtly spouse in prison. 10270
I'll never be truly happy if I don't get her out of there."
"My friend," said the king, "now don't be disconsolate,
Because I've brought many a war to an end
And won many realms with a polished steel blade.
My best and richest fiefs I'll gladly grant you. 10275
All of Thessalonica I want you hold to from me,
And all of the kingdom that must be ruled over,
And half of Venice I grant you gladly.
For your fine service you'll be richly rewarded.
We'll cross the sea during this high summer, 10280
And we'll go to Pamplona to confront King Mibrien.
He won't be able to seek refuge in his castles, cities or farms.
We'll drag him out by force, no matter the cost,
And we'll free your noble wife from prison.
Since you love her so much, you shouldn't leave her there." 10285
Aiol starts to kneel and kiss the cordovan leather of the
    king's shoes,
And the king, who holds him wondrously dear, raises him up.

A Chanson de Geste

274.

"Sire," said Aiol, "you're giving me a huge amount of land.
I'll go tomorrow to take possession of it, if you so command.
And we'll lead a force of twenty thousand armed men.　　　　10290
If there's anyone in that land who would voice any protest,
Watch out that, in exchange, he'll have his head cut off."
And the king replied: "Just as you command!"
In the morning, at dawn, they were completely armed
　　and dressed.
The king put twenty thousand men under Aiol's command.　　10295
Aiol set out to take possession of and consolidate his lands
Including all of Thessalonica, which was so praiseworthy.
He took a castle by force, which was stoutly defended.
Those who defended it all had their heads cut off.
There he conquered a war prize that was most praiseworthy:　10300
Two of the best horses that can be won,
Two luxurious swords, which possessed great dignity,
And four extremely costly spurs.
Afterwards Aiol gave these possessions to his two children.
He still has no idea that he sired them.　　　　　　　　　　10305
Nor did he know about the arms — how good they would be —
Because he wouldn't have given them up for the gold of ten cities.
It was at the feast of St. John in summer
That Aiol had established complete control over his lands,
And all Thessalonica and the whole kingdom.　　　　　　　10310
He goes to Tornebrie to thank King Grasien.
Now he wants to dub his two sons —
He still won't know how much he should love them,
Up until the moment he will be shown the letter
Thierry had caused to be written in order to save the children — 10315
With two hauberks and two helms of great nobility,
Two shields and two lances that they could put to good use
　　for jousting.
But that day great was the joy and nobility!

275.

On the feast of St. John, the holy day God made,
Aiol made both his sons knights.　　　　　　　　　　　　　10320
The equipment they're wearing is very expensive,
But the arms that are coming to them are even better.
The children are so handsome, courtly and well-raised!
God never made a man who wouldn't hold them dear;

❦ Aiol ❦

They resemble their father more than any man alive. 10325
The men of that country stared at them intently
And said to one another, quietly and discreetly,
"This is the most incredible thing that could ever happen,
If they did indeed belong to their father Thierry!"

276.

Aiol had the two hauberks brought in to the public square: 10330
Two very luxurious helms, worthy of praise,
Two very expensive blades of bright shining steel,
And two gleaming shields with golden bosses.
Then they brought out two well-planed lances,
And Aiol had led out two powerful horses, 10335
When they returned from the army where the mighty Grasien
Made him the confirmed lord of a great kingdom.
The expensive equipment that he was able to win there
He had given to his children on that day.

277.

The two valiant horses were led out onto the square. 10340
Their saddles were richly embroidered in topaz.
Both horses were covered with a very luxurious, thin cloth.
There were not two faster mounts known to be on earth.
The top of their saddle bows was made of gold and sapphire.
God never made a vavassor of such obscure lineage 10345
That if he were mounted on these horses and carrying these arms,
He wouldn't appear to be a prince, duke or admiral.
Aiol gives them to his sons, who are worthy and wise.

278.

Now, the warhorses were the best in the land.
The young knights mounted up, who were worthy and bold. 10350
They ride into the meadows around Tornebrie, which are green
  and in bloom.
Beside them ride Aiol and their master, Thierry,
And King Grasien and his closest companions.
The two noble barons strike the quintain
With two huge blows, greater had no one ever seen. 10355
When they returned, it was past noon,
And they climbed the steps of the lordly palace.
The tables were set up, and they sat down to dinner.
Beside King Grasien sat Aiol the bold,

⚜ A Chanson de Geste ⚜

Thomas and Manesier, the two noble knights.   10360
Aiol looked at them and began to sigh.
He wept tender tears from his eyes.
Thierry looked at Aiol and bowed his head,
Politely and courteously began to address him:
"Good lord, Aiol of France, for the sake of God who never lies,   10365
What's making you cry? Why are you so pensive?"
"Lord, Master Thierry, I have reason enough,
For the love of God, when I remember my little children
Makaire drowned, the foul cur of evil lineage.
Now they would have been like your sons.   10370
But I don't say it because of them; may God give you joy from them.
You'll never see anyone who loves them more than I do."
And when good Master Thierry heard this,
Even if he'd been given Paris, he wouldn't have held back.
From telling the truth he wouldn't have refrained.   10375
"Good has now come to you, Aiol," said Thierry.
"By the faith I owe you, these *are* your sons.
I was born in Lausanne and so were my closest companions.
I was living there when King Louis
And Elye, your father, laid siege to its walls.   10380
I was under the bridge, because God had sent me there,
And I was fishing by moonlight — I won't lie to you about it —
When evil Makaire, to whom God should do harm,
Threw the boys into the water, intending to have them perish.
The Lord God of holy glory wanted to protect them,   10385
And I pulled them both into my boat to save them.
I fled from that land with the children.
Aiol, for the sake of your children, I became a refugee
And left my homeland and went into exile.
Through the grace of God, who never lied,   10390
We've raised and brought up the children to the point
They are knights fully outfitted and equipped.
Take a good look at this letter, written and sealed."
He took the letter from his belt and handed it to the king,
And the king passed it to his chaplain, Henri.   10395
The chaplain broke the seal and studied the writing;
He turned to the king and, weeping, addressed him:
"Lord, rightful emperor, now you can hear something marvelous!
This man was born in France, King Louis' nephew,
And the son of Duke Elye, who is worthy and bold.   10400
Never from such exalted lineage did any knight ever descend.

❦ AIOL ❦

These are his two children, whom you have raised.
Thierry, through his goodness, saved them from death."
And when the king heard this, he was overcome with joy.
Great was the joy in the noble palace.   10405
You would have seen the father kiss his two sons
And King Grasien and Master Thierry
And Aie, the courtly, whose visage is so bright,
And the high-born queen of noble bearing,
And the noble knights who served him.   10410

279.

"Children," said Aiol, "your mother's still in captivity
And is in Pamplona in her father's prison.
Makaire holds her there, the traitor, the foul rogue.
I had to leave her there, suffering and distraught."
"My lord," said Thomas, "it's time for battles and jousting.   10415
Go ahead and assemble the people that God has given you,
And we'll have those who are in your region.
The Saracen land will be laid to waste."
"And I will go with you, my lord," said the emperor.
"I won't fail you as long as I live."   10420
Aiol and his two sons went to fall at his feet.

280.

"Good king," said Aiol, "listen to what I have to say.
I have some good advice for you if you want to help us.
Go ahead, take a messenger and send him
To good King Louis, who is to be greatly feared.   10425
Tell him how I escaped from death.
In early August, before they reap the wheat,
Let him be outside of Pamplona with his assembled force.
And Elye, my father, the old and white bearded,
Should, with his Burgundians, make all haste.   10430
If God wills it and St. Peter, he'll find me there —
Me and the two sons Jesus saved for me,
Whom Makaire intended to drown and kill.
You, good king, you'll want to honor yourself by coming."
"By my head!" said the king, "you can be certain of it!   10435
Anyone who refuses this advice should surely be shamed."
The noble and worthy Thierry got to his feet.
He spoke loudly so he would be sure to be heard:
"Good lord, Aiol of France, listen to what I have to say.

⚜ A Chanson de Geste ⚜

I'll be that messenger, gladly and willingly." 10440
"By my head!" said Aiol, "you have spoken nobly,
Because your service is highly gratifying to me.
If the Lord God allows me to bring my great war to a close,
I'll give you so much you won't be reproached for it.
The city of Lausanne I'll grant you as your fief. 10445
In doing this, I'm giving you the city where you were born."
When Thierry heard this, he went to fall at Aiol's feet.
Aiol raised him back up, the noble and worthy.
Good King Grasien had made ready for him
A very luxurious dromond* at the seaport. 10450
Fourteen knights, bold and battle hardened,
Are commanded, by the eyes in their heads, to mount guard.
They are given and provided with a great amount of wealth.
The mariners are well trained who are going to navigate
   their ship.
They left the port when they had lifted anchor 10455
And unfurled the sails and began their voyage.
The Lord God guided them, and they had good winds.
I don't know what I should tell you about their story:
They went straight to St.-Gilles and entered the harbor.
Once they had landed, they did not delay 10460
And came to St.-Gilles, to the holy saint's body.
When they had said their prayers, they then returned
And climbed into the saddles of well-rested mules.
They travelled through Provence. They spent very little time there.
They crossed through the Limousin region, skirting the
   Berry region, 10465
And came to Orleans, that marvelous city.
There they found Elye, the old white-bearded man,
And Duchesse Avisse, with the noble bearing.
Thierry, the envoy, entered the castle.
He will say words that they will find to their liking! 10470
Now don't even ask if they were well lodged,
Both Thierry and all those whom he brought with him.
Elye and his wife sit down side by side,
Beside the fire, on an embroidered rug.
"Dear sister," said Elye, "listen to what I have to say. 10475
To whom will we be able to leave our rich fiefs?
Aiol, our son, is dead and gone to his end.
Not a day goes by that I don't think about it.
Last night I had a dream, which has me very anxious.

⚜ Aiol ⚜

Coming towards Spain, making great haste, 10480
Was an army of people who were luxuriously equipped.
There was my son, Aiol, the noble and brave,
With him he had two sons, as fair as a bright day.
Now may he advise me, he who was hung upon the cross,
It seems to me that the dream was the truth." 10485
Now here's Thierry, who has come up into the palace,
Accompanied by fourteen or so stalwart knights.
He greeted Elye politely, because he'd received a good upbringing:
"The Lord God of glory who was hung on the cross,
May he save Duke Elye and his powerful court 10490
On behalf of his son, Aiol, who has been much forgotten."
When Elye heard this, he rose to his feet.
He was so overcome with joy when he heard Aiol's name
That he couldn't have said a word for all the gold in ten cities
During the time it would take a man to walk a full two
   hundred feet. 10495
And when he finally was able to speak, he cried out:
"My friend, lord messenger, it's certain that you're welcome here!
Is my son, for whom I've been longing, still alive?"
"Yes, by my faith, my lord, and full of good health,
With King Grasien, who's noble and worthy. 10500
Through me he sends you the message that you should get
   completely ready,
Together with all your lineage that you can assemble.
Be in Pamplona before they reap the wheat.
Makaire, the traitor, who escaped from you,
Is in Pamplona, the marvelous city. 10505
He has renounced God and turned towards Mohammed.
There the proven traitor holds Mirabel.
Aiol intends to free her from prison."
"Oh, God!" said Elye, "may you be adored,
If I still had my son, whom I've longed for so much, 10510
God never made a man who could stop me!"
And Avisse, his mother, began to pray to God:
"Holy Mary, Lady, give me back my child!"
Thierry addressed him very cordially:
"My lord, high-born duke, listen to what I have to say: 10515
I'll tell you about a joyous event of which you don't know
   a single word.
When evil Makaire, may God do him harm,
Held your son captive in his prison in Lausanne,

🜲 A Chanson de Geste 🜲

God gave him two sons by his wife of the bright countenance.
Makaire, that lowly scum, couldn't love them.   10520
Instead, the traitor took them shortly before daybreak.
This evil man came to the Rhône to throw them into its waters.
There he intended to drown them and deliver them to death.
I was under the bridge, because God had led me there,
And I was fishing by moonlight, secretly and discreetly,   10525
When I saw the children floating in the water.
With God's help, I was able to save them in my boat.
I took off all my clothes to wrap them up.
And Lady Aie, my wife with the bright visage,
Nursed them abundantly with the milk from her breasts.   10530
Then I left the city secretly and clandestinely.
We were in great fear of Makaire, the foul oath-breaker.
I sailed so far down the Rhône that I came to the sea.
God guided us very well, through his goodness,
Straight to Tornebrie, the marvelous city.   10535
There I found Grasien, the mighty crowned king,
And he had the children baptized and lifted over the holy font.
Then he had them raised in joy and goodness.
Afterwards, by chance, your son was brought there
By four thieves who had stolen him away from Pamplona   10540
Where he had been placed and imprisoned by Makaire,
Who had abandoned God and converted to Muhammed.
Never has anyone ever heard such an adventure told!
Then King Grasien bought Aiol,
And he spent five whole years in the king's court,   10545
Without the one knowing what the other had in his heart
   or mind.
Thanks to the grace of God, who was hung upon the cross,
We brought up and nourished the children to the point
That, at this Pentecost, we dubbed them,
Mighty King Grasien and Aiol the wise.   10550
There are not more handsome knights from here to Durestant.
They've never seen you, but they've sent me to enjoin you
To rescue their mother, if you love them at all."
"Lady St. Mary," said Elye, the noble,
"This is the one thing on earth that I've desired the most.   10555
Now I have to ask my lord, Louis,
That he help his nephew, if he wants to have his goodwill."
"Noble husband," said Avisse, "for God sake, go ahead and
   ask him!

❧ Aiol ❧

I'll never be happy until this expedition is a sure thing."
The noble, well-born duke has a letter sealed.   10560
He has a messenger go straight to Paris,
And he sends to Louis, whom he can trust so well,
Asking that he rescue his nephew for God of majesty:
If he ever held him dear, he shouldn't forget him.
Going straight to Paris, the messenger found Louis.   10565
First of all, he greeted the king on behalf of Duke Elye.
He gave him the paper and the sealed letter.
Louis gave them to his chaplain, who broke the wax seal.
The king found out the news and was filled with great joy.
"Oh, God!" said the king, "Praise be to you,   10570
Because he's the man on earth that I should love the most."
The king had the seals put on the letters and the charters.
From all his lands he summoned his nobles;
His army was so great that no one should be amazed
He didn't let any of the common foot soldiers go with them   10575
Because he wanted the rescue force to move very rapidly.
When the king had assembled all of his troops,
They quickly set out on the road towards Spain.
At this point, I'll leave good King Louis
And old Elye and his powerful entourage —   10580
The noble knight led his force and his people.
Now we'll speak of Grasien and wise Aiol,
Who, from all of Venice, had his nobles assembled,
And straight from Thessalonica, the marvelous city,
And all the lands under his governance,   10585
To the plains of Tornebrie, where their armies came together.
All along the seashore, the ships were outfitted
And loaded with food and clear fresh water,
Enough to supply the kingdom for five years.
The mariners are skilled in guiding their people.   10590
They raised the sails and set out to sea,
And there were fully a hundred thousand of them in ships
    and barges,
In dromonds, galleys and iron-nailed vessels.
Never had any man born of woman seen such an army!
They didn't stop until they had reached France's army.   10595
Makaire will make a huge error, the confirmed traitor,
If he waits so long that they're all assembled.
I don't know what I should tell you about their story,
Nor about how much they sailed out on the open sea

⚜ A Chanson de Geste ⚜

Straight to St. Nicholas, of whom you've heard, 10600
That one they pray to at Bari. There they arrived one morning.
Directly to Pamplona, they didn't stop traveling
As soon as they came into Spain, into infidel lands.
They galloped throughout the land, laying it to waste.
Mighty King Mibrien heard about it 10605
And also the evil Makaire — may God do him harm —
So they assembled their people from throughout the kingdom.
They intended to do battle on a designated day.

281.

Most great were the armies from throughout the land.
They ruined the countryside, destroyed it and laid it to waste. 10610
Makaire, the traitor, addressed Mibrien:
"By my faith, sire," said Makaire, "you've suffered a very great loss.
This is Aiol who's waging this war on you,
And all for his wife whom you hold prisoner.
She's so insane and corrupted, she refuses to believe in Mohammed. 10615
I'll consider you as very evil as long as you haven't cut off her head."
And Mibrien replied: "This really ought to be done."
He drew his sword with its sharp blade,
Quickly he goes down into the underground prison
And comes to Mirabel and would have instantly taken off her head, 10620
When the pagans shouted to him: "Hold it, sire. Don't do it!
Do you want to get rid of your daughter because of a foreigner?"
"Sire," said Mirabel, "this is a very unworthy war."
The enemy people spoke among themselves
And said to each other: "We've suffered great shame. 10625
May Makaire be cursed for having wanted to commit treason,
Because — may it please Mohammed, who rules the world —
If Aiol had Makaire out there in his encampment,
We know it very well to be true that he'd take off his head
And the troops out there would return to their own lands." 10630

282.

Most great are the armies from all the lands
That Aiol and his children had brought there.
And they ride throughout the land, and burned and laid everything
  to waste.
There remains no town or city that wasn't destroyed.
Makaire, the traitor, who was so foul and thieving, 10635
Addressed the king with the noble bearing:

❦ Aiol ❦

"Listen to me, sire, rightful emperor.
Will your land be devastated and laid to waste in this manner
Without even a long and well-fought battle?"
And the king replied: "It will be as you wish." 10640
They sound four trumpets. Their people arm themselves,
And they ride out through the gates, which they've unlocked.
The barons from Venice armed themselves richly;
Thus the battle will be severely contested.
When the first blows were struck there went up a great cry. 10645
There was many a lance shaft cracked and many a head cut off.
Thomas and Manesier greatly loved the melee
And ride among the ranks, each one with drawn sword.
Anyone whom their blows can reach has little time left.
Aiol, Elye's son, has a lance at the ready. 10650
You should have seen the two sons and the father together
Slashing through the ranks of the foul unbelievers.
Now Makaire makes sure that's he's not anywhere near them!
They are the people he hates the most on earth.
Aiol spurs Ploiegant with the golden saddle 10655
And goes to strike Hercenfroi on his golden shield.
He cracks and breaks it on its golden boss
And passes his lance clear through his body.
As long as the lance holds up, he strikes him down dead on
 the field.
These men have renounced God, now they're reaping their reward. 10660
Now the people of that region have one fewer traitor,
And Mibrien leads away his defeated people.
When they were back inside the city, they closed the gates again
And climbed up to the walls, because they were sorely afraid.
The barons assail them, making a tremendous effort, 10665
And Louis rides on, his standard held high.
With his great force, they pass through great mountains and lands,
And when they were beyond the mountains, they rested three days,
Because the army was worn out and exhausted.
Right straight to Pamplona they made their way. 10670
Elye, with the salt-and-pepper beard, led the force.

283.

Now the noble barons ride on together
And head towards Pamplona. They've passed through the mountains.
They ride so much together, night and day,
That they see the standards of Grasien's army, 10675

A Chanson de Geste

Its tents, awnings and capitals.
One Frenchman said to another: "My lord, what shall we do?
Look at Mibrien's army, the evil Saracen!
We've got to be aware he has a great advantage over us.
It's certain he has a much bigger army than we have.   10680
God! Father of the whole world, where is Aiol now?
We were supposed to find him here. I think we were lied to
By the envoys who came to France recently.
Go arm yourselves. We'll not seek another peace.
Instead, we'll charge them, the base and vile felons."   10685
And they did it right away, with strength and great vigor.
Oh, God! They didn't know, good and glorious Father,
How, against their will, they stir up discord among themselves.
Thomas and Manesier take up their arms again.
The barons from Venice arm themselves energetically.   10690
When they were armed, they mounted up, full of fury.
Thomas and Manesier were in the very first rank.
But had they joined with the enemy at that moment, their
   suffering would've been great,
Because they were convinced that they were facing a hostile army,
Until Aiol, the courtly, spotted the gonfalons   10695
And the familiar look of their rich embroidery
And recognized the oriflamme of the land of France.
He shouts out loudly in a strong voice:
"Barons, thanks be to God, our Creator!
These knights are from France, from that great land,   10700
Who are coming to help us with force and vigor!
It's Elye, my father, with the bright visage,
And Louis, my uncle, the son of King Charles.
Come on, let's go to meet them in joy and happiness,
And we'll bring them joy however we can."   10705
Now here comes Elye pricking with his spurs
Mounted on Marchegai who's galloping swiftly,
And he spots Manesier and Thomas, the barons,
Who were riding a bowshot's distance in front of the rest.
Elye addressed beardless Duke Bevon: 10710
"Tell me, noble knight, who are these two knights?
They're very good-looking knights, both in face and body.
They resemble my son, Aiol, more than any other man on earth.
That's what he looked like as a boy when I was raising him."
"My lord," said Thomas, "we certainly ought to look like him!   10715
The noble knight sired us while he was lying in prison

❧ Aiol ❧

In Lausanne, in Makaire's jail, the evil felon."
When Elye heard this, never did any man know such joy
Since God lodged St. Peter in Nero's fields.
You'll never hear of such great joy in song or story   10720
As is felt by these knights when they come together that day.
At their encounter they experience immense elation.
Anyone there would have seen Louis and Aiol kissing each other.
Thomas and Manesier, the noble barons,
Go to kiss Elye, their lord, their grandfather,   10725
And they do the same to King Louis, causing him great joy.
"My lords," said Louis, "hear what I'm thinking.
Let's go and assault the city from all sides."
And they all replied: "We'll do your pleasure!"
They ran to arm themselves and took up their equipment.   10730
No one since has ever heard of such a great war.
They attacked Pamplona that day from twenty-four directions.
Those inside the city defended themselves. They had great need of it!
Makaire of Lausanne was full of spite and venom.
When he saw the king, he addressed him: 10735
"Let's ride out against them, gonfalons unfurled!"
And the king replied: "We'll do as you command."
Within the city the evil felons armed themselves.
They rode out through the city gates, suffering and distraught,
And the French attacked them, the noble barons.   10740

284.

The battle was immense and fighting was everywhere.
Near the gate, the Saracens forced them into combat,
And the French attacked them, who had no love for them.
Thomas spurs his horse, who took off galloping swiftly,
And goes to strike Auchier, who rejected Jesus.   10745
He thrust his lance into Auchier's golden boss
And ripped and tore the hauberk on his back.
Clear through his body, Thomas thrust iron and wood.
As long as his shaft held up, he struck him down dead from his horse.
When Makaire saw this, he almost lost his mind.   10750
He spurs his horse and goes to strike Thomas.
Thomas' shield was so strong that no damage was done.
Thomas was such a strong warrior, he didn't leave his stirrups even for a moment.

A Chanson de Geste

Instead he struck back at Makaire with a blow worthy of a knight,
Which guided his lance clear through Makaire's body.   10755
The foul cur fainted, lying stretched out on the ground.
Thomas would have made him prisoner when immediately
King Mibrien came to his rescue with all the power at
   his command,
And his Saracens rushed there, angry as leopards.
With more than fifteen lances they struck at Thomas,   10760
And the noble knight drew his sword with its crystal hilt.
Anyone within reach of his blows will never again ask
For a physician to heal him, because he has no need of him.
Now here comes Manesier on a swift horse.
He sees his brother in the fray and became extremely angry.   10765
Immediately, he shouted to Aiol, his father:
"Come on, my lord, rescue your dear son, Thomas!
If you lose your child, you'll suffer great harm."
Louis and Aiol spur their mounts in that direction,
With King Grasien, who loved the children dearly,   10770
And Thierry, the good master, who protected them so well.
Beardless Duke Beuve, Engerant and Gerard
Along with fifty knights, rescue Thomas,
That noble youth who had caused such losses with his steel blade,
Like a wild boar who cuts down the dogs.   10775
It seems that any wise pagan knight would stop, when in
   this need,
And then Manesier rode up, angry as a leopard!
He pricks and spurs. His horse carries him rapidly.
He goes to strike Estorgant on his enameled shield.
This pagan knight was bearing the insignia of Mibrien,   10780
But he receives no protection whatsoever from all his arms.
Manesier thrust iron and wood clear through his body.
As long as his shaft held up, he knocked him down dead from
   his horse.
Then he drew his sword and slipped his arm through his
   shield's straps.
Anyone his blows reach has no protection from death.   10785
Anyone there would have seen the two brothers fight the
   disloyal people,
How they slash their sides and their arms!
Never did God ever make a man who didn't fear their blows.
"Oh, God!" said Louis, "What brave warriors we have here!
Blessed be the mother who bore these children!   10790

275

She should love the one who saved them from death."
Makaire turned to flee. He didn't dare stay there.

285.

The battle was great, violent and destructive.
The French are full of joy, and the Saracens are losing.
Manesier pricks and spurs all the way down a hillside 10795
And goes to strike Durant on his new shield.
He breaks and shatters its golden boss
And rips and tears the hauberk on his back.
Clean through the pagan's body, he thrusts his new shaft.
As long as it holds up, he strikes him down dead on the ground. 10800
This was one of Makaire's closest companions of that vile lineage.
Thomas gives his Castilian warhorse free rein
And goes to strike Mibrien on his new shield.
His polished lance pierces the king's golden boss,
And the hauberk on Mibrien's back wasn't worth a speck to him. 10805
Thomas guides his lance along the king's left side,
And as long as his lance holds up, knocks him down to the ground.
Then Thomas draws his sword with its sharp blade.
Full of great spite and anger he stops over the king.
In my opinion, Thomas would have taken off his head 10810
When the king cried out in his loud and clear voice:
"My friend, I beg you, by your God in heaven, to have mercy!
Child, you're my grandson, so I can't be completely evil.
Through me you'll get your mother out from the underground
  prison."
And Thomas replied: "That's what ought to happen." 10815
By the king's nosepiece Thomas leads him over next to his horse
And turned him over to Grasien, who rules Venice.
King Grasien doesn't hesitate for a moment.
Instead, he comes over to Louis and quietly speaks to him:
"Sire, rightful emperor, our war's over 10820
Because the king who rules this land is our prisoner.
Thomas, Aiol's son, defeated him in the melee.
Never did better children ever mount up into a saddle
Than the two noble knights who've demonstrated such prowess!"
"By God!" said Louis, "They must be my nephews!" 10825
And Makaire turns away, flees from the fray.
He's leading a thousand Saracens who willingly serve him.
They entered Pamplona through the gates, which were opened
  for them.

⚜ A Chanson de Geste ⚜

Anyone there would have seen the anguish of the enemy people.
They miss Mibrien who was worthy in the war.   10830
"Oh, this is a sad day for you, good sire!" said Makaire.
"You're certainly the model of an honest knight."
Sixty Saracens address the traitor:
"Oh, lord, stop this minute the great sorrow you're feeling.
We'll make you king and lord of the land.   10835
You'll have a golden crown on your head,
And you'll hold Pamplona, Toledo, Luiserne
And all the lands that Mibrien governed."
Makaire replied: "This you ought to do."
He had his physicians summoned to the most beautiful chamber   10840
To treat his wounds because he thought they were getting worse.
The physicians were skillful, the best in the land.
They heal him in three days. However, it won't last long —
Makaire's joy — because death is stalking him!

286.

Makaire was up there in the marbled chamber.   10845
Now hear about Floquipasse, who's worthy and noble.
He went to take counsel between him and Propisse,
Because God, St. Mary's Son, filled them with the Holy Spirit.
They believed in God and didn't forget him for a second,
And they had four priests from the Holy Land.   10850
They rescued Mirabel from the stone prison,
And made a subterranean, vaulted grotto.
They kept her there in lordly luxury.
Every day she could hear Mass and matins.
They're not worried about Makaire. He'll never find her.   10855
The next day, at first light, as dawn was breaking,
The armies from noble France put on their armor.
From twenty-four directions they assailed the city.
The sappers, who were undermining the walls, were skillful.
They caused the wall to crumble and got inside the city.   10860
A stretch of wall more than two hundred feet long fell all at once.
The French and Venetians shouted very loudly:
"Barons, strike hard in the name of St. Mary!"
The pagans turned in flight. They abandoned the battle.
They make their way as far as the citadel.   10865
This did them little good, for they were ruthlessly attacked.
Makaire, the foul scum — may God curse him —
Did not make it to the citadel in time, because the French
    overtook him.

❧ Aiol ❧

Manesier gave his warhorse free rein and let it gallop freely.
He goes to strike Boidin on his flowery shield.   10870
He breaks and cracks its golden boss.
The hauberk on Boidin's back isn't worth a garlic clove to him.
Manesier strikes him down dead from his warhorse. Noble
    Aiol shouts:
"May God protect my children, I so love their companionship!"
Now here comes worthy, old Elye through the fray.   10875
He spurs Marchegai, who gallops rapidly,
And goes to strike Makaire on his flowered shield.
Duke Makaire strikes back so well on the varnished shield
That he breaks and shatters its golden boss,
And rips and tears the hauberk on Elye's back   10880
And guides his iron and wood into Elye's left side.
Elye was wounded, but he didn't come close to falling.
Instead, he struck back at the foul cur in great anger,
So that he knocked Makaire down from his Hungarian warhorse.
Then Aiol cried out: "Monjoie, with God's help!"   10885
Thomas and Manesier heard their father shouting.
Each one spurs his warhorse with drawn sword.
They see the blood flowing from Elye's body.
You should not be amazed that this caused them anguish.
"Children," said Elye, "by the body of St. Denis,   10890
I'm just slightly injured. The wound will heal rapidly.
Right over there is the traitor. May God curse him!
If he escapes you now, I'll consider it as cowardliness."
"By my head," said Aiol, "his life will be very short!"

287.

Makaire, the traitor, stood on his feet before them,   10895
And held his drawn sword with its steel blade.
He defends himself stoutly, and he needs to.
And the French, who are good knights, attack him.
Thomas and Manesier assault him from every side,
And Aiol, their dear father, and Elye, the proud,   10900
And Louis of France and King Grasien
Seize Makaire from all sides and tie his wrists.
Out from the city they lead him on foot.
They disarm him rapidly; they don't want to delay.
Immediately, they have his arms and legs ripped out.   10905
Using four strong ropes to execute him,
Then quickly, attached to the tails of four powerful warhorses,

⚜ A Chanson de Geste ⚜

They had him torn apart: thus they exacted their vengeance.
Then they took Pamplona, the walls and all its earthen works.
Those inhabitants who consented to be baptized and raised
  above the holy font,   10910
Lost nothing of their possessions, not even three deniers' worth.
Those who refused to believe in God were rapidly executed.

288.

Shortly after the mighty city of Pamplona was taken,
Floquipasse and Propisse left the prison.
They led Mirabel out of the vaulted grotto.   10915
When they entered the streets, they shouted very loudly:
"Where are you, Aiol of France, the bountiful?
Look! Here is your wife, the noble Mirabel!
We've kept her as befits a high-ranking personage."
When Aiol heard this, he tugged on his rein: 10920
She was the one thing in this world that he most desired.
He dismounted and seized her by the hand:
"Lady, daughter of a king, you were so distraught when I left you."
Now here come Thomas and Manesier themselves.
When they spot their father, they call to him passionately: 10925
"Lord, who is that lady whom you've won?"
"Children, this is your mother, whom you've never seen."
When the young knights heard this, they were filled with great joy.
"My lord," said Mirabel, "what are you talking about?!
My sons were drowned, in suffering and pain."   10930
"My lady," said Aiol, "may God bless me,
A brave man, who was worthy and noble, rescued them.
There aren't such knights from here to the gates of Hungary.
My lady," said Aiol, "don't hide it from me.
Aren't those Floquipasse and Propisse your hosts here?   10935
These are the most evil men on earth!"
"My lord," said the lady, "may God bless me.
It truly is they, but they're the ones who preserved me from death.
Exact your justice upon them if that's you will,
However, two better converts your eyes will never see.   10940
Have them baptized. They want to be Christians."
"Gladly," said Aiol, "may God bless me."
He has them baptized with pomp and ceremony.
One they call Aiol, the other Elye.
They came to their lodging, to their tents of Sire.   10945
That night they ate a lordly feast.

⚜ Aiol ⚜

After the supper, the seneschal cried out:
"Go to your lodgings, brave noble knights!"
The barons repaired to their purple cloth tents.
In the middle of Aiol's tent, a luxurious bed was set up.　　　10950
There Aiol lay down beside his beloved Mirabel.
She addressed Aiol with great respect:
"My lord, when you were outside the stone prison,
God rescued you, St. Mary's Son.
You have, I suppose, taken another wife,　　　10955
Or you have, some time ago, met a new love?"
"Fair one," said Aiol, "what you're saying is madness!
I pledge to you in faith and swear by St. Mary,
That since I left you I've not had the company of women."
Now the worthy knight has pledged his faith to her,　　　10960
But she is so well instructed that she refuses the pledge.*
That night they enjoy themselves in pure delight
And don't be amazed if they played games behind the curtains
Until daylight the next day when dawn began to break,
When the barons were getting up and the army was awakening.　　　10965
I'll recount for you the life of mighty King Mibrien.
He had himself baptized in the name of St. Mary.
They kept his name; they didn't change it a bit.*
Then he believed in God and placed his entire trust in him.
Mibrien held all his land as fiefs from the king of St.-Denis.　　　10970
At this point, the army split up.
Mighty King Grasien goes off to Tornebrie
And King Louis to France the bountiful.
Thomas and Manesier return to Venice.
Powerful Duke Elye goes back to Burgundy.　　　10975
Together with him, Aiol the noble knight,
They bring Mirabel, with a great mounted troop.
They take leave of Mibrien, once they have conferred with him.
King Mibrien kisses Aiol and Mirabel, his beloved,
And commends them to God, St. Mary's Son:　　　10980
"May that Lord, who reigns over the whole world, protect you!"
Those who have listened to me, I pray that they do not forget!
The rhyme of this account of Aiol is now finished.
May God, who has all in his keeping, give us his support!
Amen! Amen! Now let each one of you repeat this!　　　10985

　　　　　　THIS HISTORY HAS ENDED.

APPENDIX

69.

Des ore chevauche Aiol, grains et iriés
Por chou qu'il s'ot gaber et laidengier.
Moult le gabent, serjant et escuier,
Meïsmes Loëys, qui Franche tient, 2620
Qui fu en son palais grant et plenier!
Al matin s'est levés de son mengier,
Et vit l'enfant Aiol ens el marchié,
Et les gent qui tant l'orent contralié.
Li rois en apela ses chevaliers, 2625
A haute vois s'escrie, «Baron voiés!
Chi vient un chevaliers aparelliés,
Qui vaura anqui estre as cos premiers!
S'aquitera ma tere et mon resnié;
Il vaura ma guerre bien traïre a chief. 2630
Riches hom l'a nori et ensengiés,
Si l'a por grant saudee cha envoiés:
Il les conquerra bien a son espiel!»
Quant Aiols ot le roi, moult fu iriés;
Un borgois en apele quenu et viel, 2635
Que devant lui estoit en cel marchié.
«Amis!» che dist Aiols, «Bien ait vos ciés! *[114v-a]*
Qui est chis qui me gabe en ces sollier?
«Sire, chou est li rois qui Franche tient,
Et si vous a gabé et laidengié». 2640
Quant l'entendi Aiols, moult fu iriés,
Et dist entre ses dens, c'on nel ot niet:
«Hé! Dieus, chou est mes oncles, je sui ses niés!
Si ne me deüst mie contralïer!»*
Sel seüst l'enperere qu'il fust ses niés, 2645
Ja n'i fust plus gabés ne laidengiés;
Ains i fust richemens aparelliés!
Por quel gabe, li rois ne fait pas bien:
Anqui en ert Aiol si bien vengiés,
Qu'il l'abatra a joste de son destrier, 2650
Si quel veront serjant et chevalier!

ILLUSTRATIONS

1. Here begins the accurate account of Aiol and Mirabel, his wife, as you will hear in the book. Fol. 96r.

2. This is how Aiol took leave of father and of mother and of holy hermit and goes to France.   Fol. 99v.

3. This is how Aiol came to Orleans and how the king of France and his people mocked him.   Fol. 114r.

4. This is how Aiol and his two companions go to Pamplona on diplomatic embassy.   Fol. 128v.

5. This is how Aiol won the maiden.   Fol. 133v.

6. This is how Aiol and Mirabel meet a thief and how he's going to lodge them. Fol. 142r.

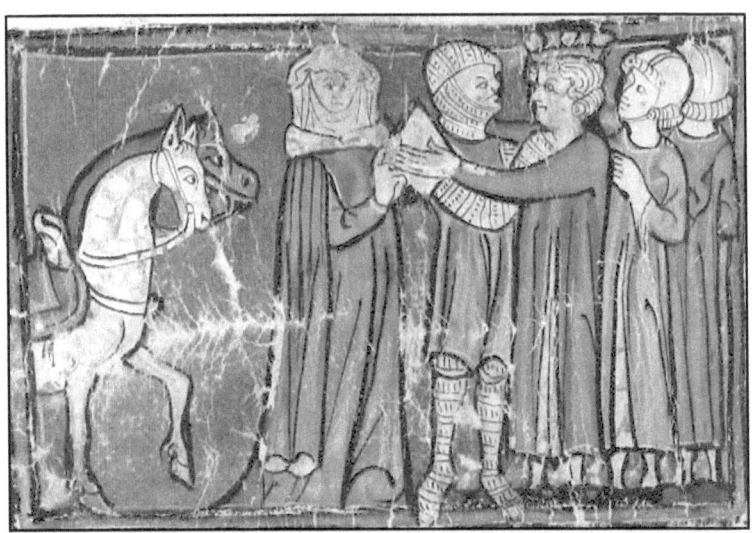

7. This is how Aiol comes back to France and how he brings Mirabel, Mibrien's daughter. Fol. 151v.

8. This is how Elye returned to France. Fol. 153v.

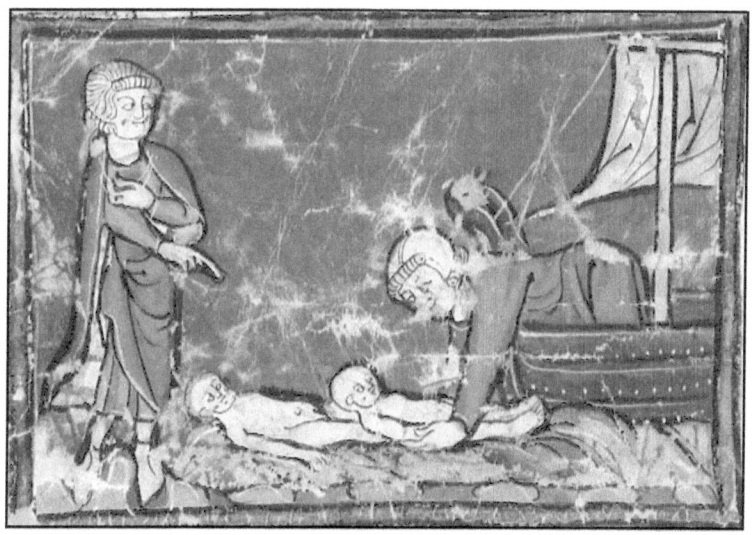

9. This is how Makaire the traitor wants to drown Aiol's children.
Fol. 160v.

10. This is how the thieves sold Aiol and kill each other.   Fol. 165r.

11. This is how justice is done with Makaire.   Fol. 172v.

NOTES

A = Aiol; NR = SATF edition of Normand & Raynaud; F = Foerster's edition; G = Greimas

12   The topos of disparagement of other minstrels was common in the epic, as was that of the "truth" of the tale. Both a literary figure and an actual fact, the poet here likely refers to the numerous northern noblemen and poets (Conon de Béthune and Villardouin, for example) who had returned from the Crusade in the early thirteenth century. See Malicote, "Cil novel," 372, n46, 373 and 384.

17   A scribal notation in another hand marks this word with a "+" and notes in the lower left margin "+ Louis le debonaire."

31   This story was told in *Elye of Saint Gille*. (See Hartman & Malicote.)

68   For the polyvalence of the word and proper name "aiol/Aiol," see Malicote, "Cil novel," 369 and n37, 371 and n44; and Malicote, "Visual and Verbal Allusion," 104 and n60.

333   "Hersent" is used for Elye's sister and for the butcher's wife as well; at 3225, the former becomes "Marsent."

463   For a discussion of this use of literary and Christian amulets, see Skemer's *Binding Words*, p. 147.

474   This verse possibly alludes to a similar passage in the romance *Eracle* produced by Gautier d'Arras for Baudouin VIII of Flanders. (See Gautier d'Arras' *Eracle*, introduction v–vi.)

546   This is a possible allusion to Chrétien de Troyes' *Perceval*, produced for Philip of Flanders, in which Perceval's mother swoons at his departure. Aiol later refers to his mother's fainting spell, while Perceval had forgotten his mother's grief (7903).

681   We have chosen to translate "Mohammed" rather than "Mahomet" in the interest of cultural accuracy. See Introduction.

954   The literary allusion, part of the so-called debate of the minstrels, is to the scabrous mock-epic *Audigier* and to the epic anti-hero "Fouré."

960   The allusions to the drunkards and their quarrel, as the town's own version of "monks," their drinking as "prayers" and the tavern as "monastery" is parodic and satiric at once. See Malicote, "Cil novel," 382ff.

994   Raiberghe is another mock-epic character in *Audiger*, where she is Audiger's mother.

1041   John W. Baldwin notes this type of humorous literary allusion to the scholastic *disputatio* (*Masters*, v. I, 29).

1083   The epic contains fictive names, those that allude to fictional characters in other poems and names of real people. Villehardouin speaks of Gautier de Saint Denis, a nephew of the Chatelain de Coucy; Gautier accompanied Baudouin IX on the 1204 Crusade. See Villehardouin (vol. I, vii).

1084   The seneschal was the steward or senior chief administrator of a noble medieval household.

1366   Saint Simon (as one of the twelve Apostles, not Peter) was the patron saint of tanners, so this may be a humorous reference.

AIOL

1391 Makaire of Lausanne is a "losengier," an instance of an untranslatable pun (paronomasia). See Malicote's "Visual," 97 n49.

1553 Palm Sunday occurred on 3 April in 1205, which Villehardouin identifies as the date of the famous battle between Baudouin IX and Johannis of Bulgaria, in which Baudouin was defeated, leading to his demise (Villehardouin I, vii). For the probable historical accuracy and allusions to the Fourth Crusade of these geographic and chronological specifics, see Malicote, "Cil novel," 367ff and n36.

1585 This proverbial saying is found in *Girart de Vienne*, which A amplifies. See Malicote, "Cil novel," 376.

1676 Scarlet, in this context, is not a color (although it was often red, which lead to the name of the color), but rather a high-quality woolen cloth. G traces its etymological origin from lat. "scarlatum," deriving from the Persian "saqirlat." The weaving technique was also of Middle Eastern origin and made the cloth elastic, so it was good for tights and hose.

1718 The literary topos of "the world in decline" was amply described by Curtius. What follows can be considered as a lengthy amplification and modernization of the topos.

1727 Godefroy notes that "forestier" was the title of the original rulers or governors of Flanders before it became a county. "Thierry of Flanders" was the father of Count Philip of Flanders and an important ancestor of Jeanne, for whom A was possibly written. The use of real titles and names lends depth to the fictive characters here.

1847 Since the sword is right at his side, he draws it, the lance being useless as the inexperienced young knight has gotten too close to use it.

1990 "Lusiane" ("Louisiane") is clearly named for her celebrated uncle, King Louis of France.

2087 King Yon of Gascony is a literary character in the OF epics *Renaud de Montauban*, *Girart de Vienne*, and refers once to Geoffrey of Anjou, an ancestor of the House of Flanders, according to Langlois' *Table* (360).

2089 Langlois lists this literary character as appearing in the epic of *Ogier le Danois* as well as in *Aiol* (270). See Pratt's *Shifts and Transpositions*, 28, for a discussion of the multiple interpretations open to this allusion. NR take it as a scribal error for the actual city of Pontarlier in eastern France. This kind of allusion was sometimes used by the poet to signal works from which episodic developments were drawn. See our *Elye*, 185 n18.

2090 The Christian holiday, celebrated three days before Ascension, included processions, fasting and prayers for a good harvest (Mershman, xii.110–11).

2288 This name appears in the *Roland*, *Renaud de Montauban*, *Ogier* and *Aiol*, among others, according to Langlois (452).

2352 NR interpret this locale as Sivny and Vauclaire in Champagne, although they are likely fictive or literary in origin.

2433 This apocalyptic image, found in Psalms 18:7–19, became an epic commonplace. See Malicote, "Cil Novel," 390 n75. Cf. 2734.

2583 These episodes are so significant that they are illuminated at the new laisse (2619). They call to mind the pelting of Odysseus with a cow's hoof upon his return and encounter with the suitors, but it is unlikely that our poet knew a school version of this text or episode. See Homer's *Odyssey*, XX, 285ff.

2668 For the rôle of money and usury in the poem and in northern civic and economic life, see Flori and also Malicote, "Cil novel," 387ff.

2685 For the role of this episode in the "Bataille des Jongleurs," see Malicote, "Cil Novel," 387ff.

2691 The first part of the line has been erased, possibly because of its obscenity.

⚜ Notes ⚜

2950 Isabel informed Aiol earlier (2280 and 2343) that the land is in chaos due to the invasion of the people of Berry (NR gloss) (including warriors and pillagers) and of the Saracens. Robbers and disorder abound.

3197 The poet implies that he doesn't know specific names of courtiers associated with the count's household who are in the fray.

3211 The poet speaks of the historical roots of the story and of dialectical argumentation in general. See Malicote, "Visual and Verbal Allusion," 101ff.

3224 In the left margin is a scribal notation impossible to interpret: two parallel back slashes (extending from approximately 3221–24), with a line and arrow (?) pointing to 3224, and two vertical parallel slashes from 3225–27. This note may highlight the dialectical argumentation and historical allusion.

3368 Aiol mistakenly identifies the king as part of the enemy army.

3659 This is obviously how Louis readily agreed with Makaire's wish to oust Elye and Avisse from the king's entourage. Aiol responds as a courtly and honorable man, showing the difference between himself and Makaire under similar circumstances and gently chides the king for his mockery. Cf. 3970–71.

3788 "Mercenaries," or paid soldiers, did not carry a pejorative connotation; they were noblemen. See *Elye*, 215 n1753.

3983 The name is fictional here; in 1213, a *jongleur* or *istrion* named Torneboeuf at the court of Prince Louis received a monetary gift from the prince (see Malicote, "Cil Novel," 368 n36).

4671 The implication here is that the granting of fiefs, if strongly advised by the king's curia, will be more solid than merely by the king's judgment alone.

5010 The manuscript lists the third knight as "Grenoart"; we alter the translation for consistency.

5891 The reference is not clear; the robbers are sinning against Christ first, by robbing, secondly, by disguising themselves as holy men of God.

6042 The observation is perhaps a double-entendre, referring to Aiol's comic saintly physical restraint, and also to Saint Ayoul.

6147 The episode now narrated is, according to Bancourt, adapted material from the Byzantine epic *Digenis Akritis*. One of the goals and results of the Fourth Crusade was, in fact, the importation of manuscripts and artefacts from the East. See Bancourt.

6152 The paranomasia, or wordplay (Aiol the character and the word for serpent), is evident: Aiol is sexually tempted by Mirabel in this metaphoric adaptation of *Digenis Akritis*. See 6147.

6189 We translate literally here, although the meaning is not clear. Longinus was the name given in the Apocrypha to the Roman sentry who pierced Jesus' side. It is not clear if this is a reference to Longinus' legendary blindness ("who could not see"), miraculously cured by the blood of Christ.

6255 "Dominus videt" is the name generally given to the place of sacrifice by Abraham after God provided a ram, sparing Isaac. The Vulgate gives this name, which means "and the Lord sees," meaning "God will provide." We have left the Latin original, as the poet did (Gen. 12.14).

6444 The poet foreshadows coming episodes here.

7484 Having ridden sidesaddle, Mirabel now straddles the horse to perform her duties as squire.

7526 The previous editors of the poem had trouble interpreting this difficult speech. F calls it "unclear," since Antiaume shouldn't be speaking here: Aiol is, after all, talking to Geraume. However, Antiaume is clarifying his difficult ethical position (which is clearly related to that of Geraume). Technically they both owe allegiance to Rainier as their liegelord. Antiaume has already denounced his treacherous father; but the technicality means little to him, since his father's behavior was unconscionably base and has caused so much pain and suffering.

AIOL

7589 Throughout the entire speech of Rainier, he uses the familiar form "tu," stressing Antiaume's social inferiority. Cf 7526 and 7595, where Rainier puns that he'll literally raise that social standing even higher by hanging the youth in punishment for his behavior. See Malicote, "Visual and Verbal Allusion" for the complete study of Antiaume's and Esmeraude's roles in the poem's careful development of dialectical argumentation.

7822 St. Archedeclin is the legendary name of the groom in Christ's first miracle of the wedding at Cana. Matt. 15: 22–28.

7880 It's interesting that the poet uses "Turkish" fire, instead of the usual "Greek" ("gregeois") fire. Exchanging the adjective of nationality was not forced by metrical considerations.

8107 Aiol takes Mirabel by the hand here; her presence is integral to his argumentation, since the purpose of revealing his identity is to clarify his relationship to Lusiane and to directly respond to her accusations. In so doing he fulfills his vow to his father as well.

8160 The king will not set a date; ideally it would be at Pentecost and at Aix, for the regal setting the wedding deserves. Instead, it will be immediately at Orleans. V. 8310 ff.

8238 Elye's ironic and terse blessing — that the king be blessed exactly as he has deserved, is countered by the king's own gentle remonstrance that a truly good friend should have helped to avoid the bad advice of the traitors.

8279 This episode echoes the mockery of Aiol when he first arrived in town.

8540 F notes this comment as a commonplace and a trite trope, but in reality, some of the material in the coming verses treats in a fictional manner historical matter, drawn from Orderic Vitalis, relating to Helias of Maine, one of the most illustrious ancestors of the House of Flanders. See Malicote's "Visual and Verbal Allusion," 101ff.

8721 NR and F mistakenly emend "Aiol" to "Makaire" here; but this scene is repeated and amplified at 8766, where the poet explains how Aiol came to overhear this debate and how he shouted his response and counteraccusation.

8817 The Breton messenger's name is first given here; in Orderic Vitalis' account referred to above (8540), the Breton standard-bearer and envoy is named "Herveum." See Malicote, "Verbal and Visual Allusion," 104 and n61.

8823 Guinehot haughtily and disrespectfully uses the familiar form of address to the king.

8839 The king's diatribe against the Lombards reflects a common epic topos in OF literature, also related in some histories, such as Orderic Vitalis' *Ecclesiastical History*. See Malicote, "Visual and Verbal Allusion," 104ff and n61.

8845 In the mock-epic *Audigier*, the Lombards eat refuse, as in the Old French epic *Girart de Vienne*. Their gastronomic habits, language and accent are all mocked. See 8839.

8858 The theme of aristocratic bastardry is frequently found in the OF epic, as in the old aristocratic families themselves. William the Conqueror, for example, was one of the most famous, but the theme and phenomenon were common to the Carolingian dynasty from the beginning. It's impossible to be certain of the other two allusions here.

8888 This scene echoes Aiol's kind treatment of the emissary Tornebeuf earlier in the poem.

8967 The allusion to Pinabel probably refers to the *Roland*, where Pinabel defended the traitor Ganelon; it's metonymic here for treachery in general.

8982 Sops were usually bread and meat and wine juices tossed to the dogs after the meals; the culinary slander of the Bretons reverses the custom, using milk. In the epics and learned texts, "bread and milk" are associated with infants but also with those who have not yet begun serious instruction and learning.

Notes

9052 NR and F identify a lacuna here, but the context makes it clear that this is the beginning of the long siege, where the Burgundians are camped within the city walls.

9062 The reference is to the Biblical Noah.

9355 Manesier was the name of a famous poet at the Court of Jeanne of Flanders; he composed a notable continuation of Chrétien de Troyes' *Perceval*, which had been written for Jeanne's uncle, Count Philip of Flanders. The name also appeared at 8379, for an enemy.

9385 The poet clarifies at 9396 that of the original thirty thousand knights inside the walls, only ten thousand now remain.

9464 May allude to "Lothaire," one of Charlemagne's three grandsons, supported by the Lombards in his rebellion against his brothers.

9565 Epic geography is partly fictional and partly accurate in general. The Aspe Valley is in the French Pyrenees; "Sire" is discussed by Léon Gautier's notes and variants to the *Roland* where he identifies the mountain passes of Roncesvals and "Sizre," which was still in the late nineteenth century called "Cize." (Gautier, *Les Epopées*, v.1, 101.) Cf. the mention of Navarre and the Basque region, 9571.

9608 The Islamic idols and images are literary topoi; see Introduction.

9630 In the epic world, this fictive structure is religious in nature, dedicated to Mohammed. We don't translate "mosque," in order to remain true to the literary, rather than realist, element of the fiction. The epic antecedent, as F points out, occurs in *Roland*, where "les sinagoges et les mahomeries" occur in v. 3662. Cf. 9658, where the edifice is termed a "synagogue."

9717 See *Elye*, 196 n926, for the concept that the Saracen gods are literarily depicted as hollow, inert objects, devoid of any generative or vivifying characteristics, thus "faillie," or lacking.

9781 "Esclavonie," given the Mediterannean geography of this section of the poem, would likely be "Slavonia."

9808 F comments on the chronological inaccuracy of this portion of the poem, cf. 9776, where the poet says that Aiol and Mirabel won't see each other for two years. If the boys were born at the start of Aiol's and Mirabel's five-year imprisonment, and he is to see them seven years from this point, they'll be twelve years old, that is, old enough to bear arms.

9829 NR identify this fictional town as a possible allusion to the fictional Spanish town in the *Roland* of this name, as does F, although noting a scholarly hypothesis of "Dorstadt." Cf. Jenkins, 315.

9896 Salonika refers to Thessalonica. This Greek city was well known in the West due to its appearance in Acts and in Paul's Epistles to the Thessalonians. See 9300.

9905 All critics and editors agree that this episode begins the allusion to the Fourth Crusade of 1204, when Count Baldwin of the House of Flanders and Hainaut became the emperor of the Latin Empire.

10021 The poet is practicing the technique of abbreviation here, eclipsing the battles synoptically in a series of succinct, single verses. The form and content match perfectly, as the poet points out in 10124 — a poorly-planned battle can't (and doesn't, narratologically speaking) last long.

10084 The allusion to "the Jews" who crucified Jesus is a common epic trope, much like the references to Muslims and to the Islamic religion. There was, however, expulsion and confiscation in Philip Augustus' reign and both literary and actual anti-Judaism in thirteenth-century Flanders as well. See Levy, 217–18.

10146 As in *Elye* (229 n2647), the allusion here is to "Sancho le Poplador," or "Sancho the Populator," king of Portugal, famous for his role in the Reconquest and for repopulating and rechristianizing the north of Portugal. Sancho was the brother of "Queen Mathilda," who arranged the marriage of Ferrand to Jeanne of Constantinople.

10450 The dromond was a medieval galley.

❦ AIOL ❦

10961   This little scene parallels the refusal of Aiol to touch Mirabel until after her conversion. Mirabel here shows her own scruples, as she will not touch Aiol until assured of his fidelity to his sacred wedding vows. The father of Jeanne of Flanders was praised in the chronicles for his marital fidelity, not the characteristic behavior of noblemen (or women) at this period.

10968   Mibrien, like his daughter, does not change his name when baptized, a detail found in epics such as *Le Couronnement de Louis*, at the baptism of Galafre, who retains his name (vv. 1291–92).

SELECTED BIBLIOGRAPHY

Albéric des Trois Fontaines. *Chronica, Monumenta Germaniae Historica Scriptores Series* 23. Hanover: Bibliopolii Hahniani,1874, 23: 716.

Allaire, Gloria. *Andrea da Barberino and the Language of Chivalry*. Gainesville, FL: University Press of Florida, 1997.

Aristotle. *The Categories: [and] On Interpretation*. Edited and translated by Harold P. Cook and Hugh Tredennick. Cambridge, MA: Harvard University Press, 1962.

Baker, A.T. "Le Futur des verbes *avoir* et *savoir*." *Romania* 63 (1937): 1–30.

Baldwin, J.W. "The Image of the *Jongleur* in Northern France Around 1200." *Speculum* 72 (1997), 635–63.

—. *Masters, Princes and Merchants: The Social Views of Peter the Chanter and His Circle*. 2 vols. Princeton: Princeton University Press, 1970.

Bancourt, Paul. "Etude de quelques motifs communs à l'épopée Byzantine de *Digénis Akritas* et à la chanson d'*Aiol*." *Romania* 95 (1974): 508–32.

Baumgartner, Emmanuèle, ed. *La Chanson de geste et le mythe carolingien: Mélanges René Louis*. 2 vols. Saint-Père-sous-Vézelay: Musée archéologique régional, 1982.

Bayless, Martha. *Parody in the Middle Ages: The Latin Tradition*. Ann Arbor: University of Michigan Press, 1996.

Bayot, A. "La chronique dite de Baudouin de Flandres." *Revue des Bibliothèques et Archives de Belgique* 2 (1904): 419–32.

—, ed. *Le Poème moral*. Paris: Palais des Académies, 1929.

Bédier, Joseph. *Les Légendes épiques: Recherches sur la formation des chansons de geste*. 4 vols. 3rd ed. Paris: Champion, 1926.

Berger, Roger. "Littérature et société arrageoises au XIIIe siècle: Les chansons et dits artésiens." Diss.: Arras: Commission départementale des monuments historiques du Pas-de-Calais, 1981.

Besamusca, Bart, *et. al.*, ed. *Cyclification: The Development of Narrative Cycles in the Chanson de geste and the Arthurian Romances*. Amsterdam: Royal Netherlands Academy of Arts and Sciences, 1994.

Biblia Sacra Vulgatae Editionis. Edited by Valentin Loch. Ratisbon: Manz, 1895.

Boethius. *De topicis differentiis*. Translated by Eleonore Stump. Ithaca: Cornell University Press, 1978.

Boutet, Dominique. *La Chanson de geste: Forme et signification d'une écriture épique du Moyen âge*. Paris: Presses universitaires de France, 1993.

Brown, Catherine. *Contrary Things: Exegesis, Dialectic, and the Poetics of Didacticism*. Stanford: Stanford University Press, 1998.

Busby, Keith. *Codex and Context: Reading Old French Narrative Verse in Manuscript*. 2 vols. Amsterdam: Rodopi, 2002.

❧ AIOL ❧

Camille, Michael. "Body, Soul and Surplus: The Kiss in Medieval Art." In *Yale French Studies Special Edition: Contexts, Style and Values in Medieval Art and Literature.* Edited by Daniel Poirion and Nancy Freeman Regalado (1991): 151–70.

Carlvant, Kerstin. *Thirteenth-Century Illumination in Bruges and Ghent.* Ph.D. diss., Columbia University, 1978.

Cingolani, Stefano M. "The *Sirventes-Ensenhamen* of Gureau de Cabrera: A Proposal for a New Interpretation." *Journal of Hispanic Research* 1 (1992–93): 191–201.

Crosland, Jessie. *The Old French Epic.* Oxford: Blackwell, 1951; rpt. New York: Haskell House Publishers, 1971, 201-8.

Curtius, Ernst Robert. *European Literature and the Latin Middle Ages.* Translated by Willard R. Trask New York: Bollingen Foundation, 1953.

Dane, Joseph A. "Parody and Satire in the Literature of the Thirteenth-Century Arras." *Studies in Philology* 81 (1984): 1-27, 119–44.

Daniel, Norman. *Heroes and Saracens: An Interpretation of the Chansons de Geste.* Edinburgh: Edinburgh University Press, 1984.

Dehaisnes, C.C.A., *Documents et extraits divers concernant l'histoire de l'art dans la Flandre, l'Artois et le Hainaut avant le XVe siècle.* Lille: impr. de L. Danel, 1886, 880–81.

Delbouille, Maurice. "*Aiol:* Problèmes d'attribution et de composition." *Revue belge de philologie et d'histoire* 11 (1932): 45–75.

—. "Problèmes d'attribution et de composition II: La Chanson d'*Elie* et la geste de Saint-Gilles." *Revue belge de philologie et d'histoire* 11 (1932): 577–97.

De Weever, Jacqueline. *Sheba's Daughters: Whitening and Demonizing the Saracen Woman in Medieval French Epic.* New York: Garland, 1998.

Edwards, Robert R. *Ratio and Invention: A Study of Medieval Lyric and Narrative.* Nashville, TN: Vanderbilt University Press, 1989.

Essor et fortune de la chanson de geste dans l'Europe et l'Orient latin. Actes du IXe Congrès international de la Société Rencesvals pour l'étude des épopées romanes, Padoue-Venise, 29 août–4 septembre 1982. 2 vols. Modena: Mucchi, 1984.

Finet-Van der Schaff, Baukje. "Etude comparée d'*Aiol,* chanson de geste du XIIe siècle et des fragments d'*Aiol* en moyen-néerlandais." Thesis, Paris, 1987.

—. "Quelques remarques sur les chansons d'*Elie* et d'*Aiol.*" In Besamusca, *Cyclification,* 151–52.

Flori, Jean. *L'essor de la chevalerie, XIe–XIIe siècles.* Genève: Droz, 1986.

—. "L'idéologie aristocratique dans *Aiol.*" *Cahiers de civilisation médiévale* 27 (1984): 205–21.

Foerster, Wendelin, ed. *Aiol et Mirabel und Elie de Saint Gille.* Heilbronn: Henninger, 1876–82.

Gallo, Ernest, ed. *Geoffroi de Vinsauf, The Poetria Nova and Its Sources in Early Rhetorical Doctrine.* The Hague: Mouton, 1971.

Garnier, François. *Le Langage de l'image au Moyen âge: Signification et Symbolique.* Paris: Le Léopard d'or, 1982.

❧ BIBLIOGRAPHY ❧

Gautier d'Arras. *Eracle*. Edited by Guy Raynaud de Lage. Paris: H. Champion, 1976.
Gautier, Léon, *Les épopeés françaises. Étude sur les origines et l'histoire de la littérature nationale*. Second ed. Paris, 1878–96, 1:106.
Gerritsen, W.P. "Les Relations littéraires entre la France et les Pays-Bas au Moyen Âge." In *Actes du septième congrès national de la Société Française de Littérature Comparée, Poitiers 17–19 Mai 1965*. Paris: Didier, 1967.
—, ed. *Van Aiol tot de Zwaanridder*. Nijmegen: SUN, 1993.
Godefroy, Frédéric. *Dictionnaire de l'ancien français et de tous ses dialects du IXe au XVe siècles*. 10 vols. Paris: Wieweg et Bouillon, 1881–1902; rpt. New York: Kraus Reprint Corp., 1961.
—. *Lexique de l'ancien français*. Paris: H. Welter, 1901; rpt. Paris: H. Champion, 1994.
Gossen, C.T. *Grammaire de l'ancien Picard*. Paris: Klincksieck, 1970.
Gravdal, K. *Vilain et Courtois: Transgressive Parody in French Literature of the Twelfth and Thirteenth Centuries*. Lincoln: University of Nebraska Press, 1989.
Greimas, A.J. *Dictionnaire de l'ancien français jusqu'au milieu du XIVe siècle*. Paris: Larousse, 1968.
Guesnon, A.H. *La Satire à Arras au XIIIe siècle*. Paris: E. Bouillon, 1900.
—. "Nouvelles recherches biographiques sur les trouvères artésiens." *Le Moyen âge* 15 (1902): 137–73.
Guidot, B., ed. *Burlesque et dérision dans les épopées de l'occident médiéval*. Actes du Colloque International de la Société Rencesvals, Strasbourg, 1993. Besançon: Annales littéraires de l'Université, 1995.
Hartman, A. Richard, "L'Enfance du chevalier: la première miniature dans l'unique ms. d'*Aiol*." In Luongo, *L'Epopée*, 1:71–78.
—. "Initials and *Laisse* Division in Two Later Epics: *Aiol* and *Parise la Duchesse*." *Olifant* 12 (1987): 5–27.
— and Sandra C. Malicote, eds. *Elye of Saint-Gilles*. New York: Italica Press, 2011.
Heintze, Michael. *König, Held und Sippe: Untersuchungen zur chanson de geste des 13. und 14. Jahrhunderts und ihrer Zyklenbildung*. Heidelberg: C. Winter, 1991.
—. "Les techniques de la formation de cycles dans les chansons de geste." In Besamusca, *Cyclification*, 21–58.
de Hemptinne, Thérèse, "Aspects des relations de Philippe Auguste avec la Flandre au temps de Philippe d'Alsace." In *La France de Philippe Auguste: Le temps des mutations*. Edited by Robert-Henri Bautier. Paris: Editions du Centre National de la Recherche Scientifique, 1982.
Holmes, Urban Tigner. *A History of Old French Literature*. New York: F.S. Crofts & Co., 1948, chapter 11.
Homer. *The Odyssey*. Translated by E.V. Rieu. Harmondsworth: Penguin, 1946.
Hughes, M.J. "The Library of Philip the Bold and Marguerite of Flanders, First Valois Duke and Duchess of Burgundy." *Journal of Medieval History* 4 (1978): 145–88.
Jenkins, T.A., ed. *La Chanson de Roland*. Boston: D.C. Heath and Company, 1924.
Jodogne, Omer. "*Audigier* et la chanson de geste, avec une edition nouvelle du poème." *Le Moyen Age* 66 (1960): 495–526.

❧ AIOL ❧

Johnston, Oliver. "The French Condition Contrary to Fact." *Modern Language Notes* 16 (1901): 129–37.

Kay, Sarah. *The Chanson de geste in the Age of Romance, Political Fictions*. Oxford: Clarendon Press, 1995.

—. "The Nature of Rhetoric in the *Chansons de geste*." *Zeitschrift für Romanische Philologie* 94 (1978): 305–20.

Kinoshita, Sharon. "'Pagans Are Wrong and Christians Are Right': Alterity, Gender, and Nation in the *Chanson de Roland*." *Journal of Medieval and Early Modern Studies* 31 (2001): 79–111.

Langlois, Ernest, ed. *Table des noms propres de toute nature compris dans les chansons de geste*. Paris: É. Bouillon, 1904.

Le Glay, Edouard. *Histoire de Jeanne de Constantinople, Comtesse de Flandre et de Hainaut*. Lille: Vanackere, 1841.

LeGros, H. "De *Vivien* à *Aiol*, ou, d'une sainteté archaïque à la sainteté moderne." In *Essor et fortune*, 2:931–48.

LeRider, Paule. *Le Chevalier dans Le Conte du Graal de Chrétien de Troyes*. Paris: Société d'édition d'enseignement supérieur, 1978, 111–41.

—. "Le Rire dans *Aiol*." *Pris-ma: Bulletin de liaison de l'équipe de recherché sur la littérature d'imagination du moyen âge* 12 (1996): 57–71.

Levy, Richard S., ed. *Antisemitism: A Historical Encyclopedia of Prejudice and Persecution*. Santa Barbara, CA: ABC-CLIO, 2005.

Luongo, Salvatore, ed. *L'Epopée romane au moyen âge et aux temps modernes: Actes du XIVe Congrès international de la Société Rencesvals pour l'étude des épopées romanes*. 2 vols. Naples: Fridericiana Editrice Universitaria, 2001.

Luykx, Theo. *Johanna van Constantinopel: Gravin van Vlaanderen en Henegouwen*. Antwerp: N.V. Standaard-Boekhandel, 1946.

Madelénat, Daniel. *L'Epopée*. Paris: Presses universitaires de France, 1986.

Malicote, Sandra O. "The Illuminated *Geste de Saint-Gille*." *Romanic Review* 90 (1999): 285–300.

—. "'Cil novel jougleor': Parody, Illumination and Genre Renewal in *Aiol*." *Romania* 120 (2002): 353–405.

—. "Visual and Verbal Allusion: *Disputatio* and the Poetics of *Elie de Saint Gille* and *Aiol*." *Romania* 124 (2006): 77–111.

Mancini, Mario. "*Aiol* et l'ombre du père." In *VIIIe Congrès de la Société Rencesvals*. Pamplona: Institución principe de Viana, Diputación foral de Navarra, 1981, 305–11.

Martin, Jean-Pierre. *Les Motifs dans la chanson de geste: Définition et utilisation*. Lille: Centre d'études médiévales et dialectales, Université de Lille III, 1992.

Melli, Elio. "Nouvelles recherches sur la composition et la rédaction d'*Aiol* et d'*Elie de Saint Gille*." In *Essor et fortune*, 1:131–49.

Ménard, Philippe. "Le Thème comique du 'nice' dans la chanson de geste et le roman arthurien." *Boletín de la Real Academia de buenas Letras de Barcelona* 21 (1965–66): 177–93.

❦ BIBLIOGRAPHY ❦

—. *Le Rire et le sourire dans le roman courtois.* Genève: Droz, 1969.

Mershman, Francis. "Rogation Days." In *Catholic Encyclopedia.* New York: Catholic Encyclopedia, 1912.

Moison, André. *Répertoire des noms propres de personnes et de lieux cités dans les chanson de geste françaises.* Genève: Droz, 1986.

Mussafia, A. "*Aiol* (vers 7644–5, 8186)." *Zeitschrift für romanische Philologie* 3 (1879): 257.

Norman, Jacques Clary Jean, and Gaston Raynaud, eds. *Aiol: Chanson de geste.* Paris: Firmin Didot, 1877.

Obergfell, Sandra C. Malicote. "The Problem of Didacticism in the Romance Epic: *Aiol.*" *Olifant* 6.1 (1978): 21–33.

—. "The Role of Manuscript Illumination in the Chanson de geste *Aiol.*" *Romania* 114 (1996): 316–34.

Orderic Vitalis. *The Ecclesiastical History.* Edited and translated by Marjorie Chibnall. Oxford: Clarendon Press, 1975.

Paris, Gaston. "Dioré." *Romania* 14 (1885): 274–75.

—. Review of Publications de la Société des Anciens Textes Français (1872–86). "Deuxième Article." *Le Journal des Savants* (août 1886): 469–80.

Paris, Paulin. *Histoire Littéraire de la France.* 22 vols. Paris: V. Palmé, 1842–52, 22: 416–25.

Parkes, M.B. *Pause and Effect: An Introduction to the History of Punctuation in the West.* Aldershot: Scolar, 1992.

Penon, D.G. "Les Chansons d'*Aiol* et d'*Elie de Saint-Gille.*" *Taalstudie* 4 (1883): 269.

Petit-Dutaillis, Charles. *Etude sur la vie et le règne de Louis VIII (1187–1226).* Paris: É. Bouillon, 1894.

Pratt, Karen, ed. *Shifts and Transpositions in Medieval Narrative.* Cambridge: D.S. Brewer, 1994.

Raynaud, Gaston, ed. *Elie de Saint Gille.* Paris: Didot, 1879.

Ribard, Jacques. "'Chausée' et 'chemin ferré'." *Romania* 92 (1971): 262–66.

Richardson, L.B. "The *Confrérie des Jongleurs et des Bourgeois* and the *Puy d'Arras* in Twelfth- and Thirteenth-Century Literature." In *Studies in Honor of Mario A. Pei.* Edited by John Fisher and Paul A. Gaeng. Chapel Hill: University of North Carolina Press, 1972, 161–71.

Rutebeuf. *Oeuvres complètes.* Edited by Michel Zink. Paris: Bordas, 1989–90.

Skemer, Don C. *Binding Words: Textual Amulets in the Middle Ages.* University Park: Pennsylvania State University Press, 2006.

Stanger, M.D. "Literary Patronage at the Medieval Court of Flanders." *French Studies* 11 (1957): 214–29.

Suard, François. *Chanson de geste et tradition épique en France au Moyen âge.* Caen: Paradigme, 1994.

—. *La Chanson de geste.* Paris: Centre des Sciences de la Littérature, Université Paris X-Nanterre, 1994.

—. "La description dans la chanson de geste." *Bien dire et bien aprandre* 11 (1993): 401–17.

❧ AIOL ❧

—. "Les Héros Chrétiens face au monde Sarrasin." In *Aspects de l'épopée romane: Mentalités, idéologies, intertextualités*. Edited by Hans van Dijk and Willem Noomen. Groningen: E. Forsten, 1995, 187–208.

— and Jean-Pierre Martin. *L'epopée: mythe, histoire, société*. Paris: Centre des sciences de la littérature, Université Paris X-Nanterre, 1996.

Tobler, A., and Erhard Lommatzsch. *Altfranzösisches Wörterbuch*. Stuttgart: F. Steiner, 1989.

Ungureanu, Marie. *La Bourgeoisie naissante: société et littérature bourgeoises d'Arras aux XIIe et XIIIe siècles*. Arras: Commission des monuments historiques du Pas-de-Calais, 1955.

van den Berg, Evert, and B. Besamusca. "Middle Dutch Charlemagne Romances and the Oral Tradition of the *Chansons de geste*." In *Medieval Dutch Literature in Its European Context*. Edited by Erik Kooper. Cambridge: Cambridge University Press, 1994, 81–95.

Villehardouin. *La Conquête de Constantinople*. Edited by Edmond Faral. 2 vols. Paris: Société d'édition "Les Belles lettres," 1938–39.

Walters, Lori J. "Jeanne and Marguerite de Flandre as Female Patrons." *Dalhousie French Studies* 28 (1994): 15–27.

Warlop, Ernest. *The Flemish Nobility Before 1300*. 2 vols. Kortrijk: G. Desmet-Huysman, 1975–76.

Warren, F.M. "The Enamoured Saracen Princess in Ordéric Vitalis and the French Epics." *Publications of the Modern Language Association* 29 (1914): 341–58.

Wartburg, Walther von. *Französisches etymologisches Wörterbuch*. Basel: Zbinden, 1922.

Wolff, Robert Lee. "Baldwin of Flanders and Hainaut, First Latin Emperor of Constantinople: His Life, Death, and Resurrection." *Speculum* 27 (1952): 281–322.

—."Romania: The Latin Empire of Constantinople." *Speculum* 23 (1948): 1–34.

Wright, L.M. "More on the Meanings and Uses of *Jongleur* and *Menestrel*." *Romance Studies* 17 (1990): 7–19.

Zumthor, Paul. *Histoire littéraire de la France médiévale*. Paris: Presses universitaires de France, 1954, 191–210.

This Book Was Completed on February 6, 2014
at Italica Press, New York, New York.
It was set in Adobe Garamond
and Charlemagne.

www.ingramcontent.com/pod-product-compliance
Lightning Source LLC
Chambersburg PA
CBHW022051160426
43198CB00008B/194